Sapphic Modernities

Sapphic Modernities

Sexuality, Women and National Culture

Edited by

Laura Doan and Jane Garrity

SAPPHIC MODERNITIES

First published in 2006 by
PALGRAVE MACMILLAN™
175 Fifth Avenue, New York, N.Y. 10010 and
Houndmills, Basingstoke, Hampshire, England RG21 6XS
Companies and representatives throughout the world.

PALGRAVE MACMILLAN is the global academic imprint of the Palgrave Macmillan division of St. Martin's Press, LLC and of Palgrave Macmillan Ltd. Macmillan® is a registered trademark in the United States, United Kingdom and other countries. Palgrave is a registered trademark in the European Union and other countries.

ISBN-13: 978–1–4039–6498–4

Library of Congress Cataloging-in-Publication Data is available from the Library of Congress.

A catalogue record for this book is available from the British Library.

Design by Newgen Imaging Systems (P) Ltd., Chennai, India.

First edition: June 2006

10 9 8 7 6 5 4 3 2 1

Transferred to Digital Printing in 2008

To Karen and Mar, partners and editors extraordinaire

Contents

Part 3 In and Out of Place: History, Displacement, and Revision

Part 4 Embracing Discursive Space: Re-Imagining Psychoanalysis and Spirituality

Illustrations

Introduction

Laura Doan and Jane Garrity

The significance of modernity is clearly not exhausted.

—*Rita Felski*

Modern Sappho

In late 1928 the artist Beresford Egan produced an astonishing Beardsleyesque illustration of a modern Sappho, in which the icon of sexual love between women floats with grace and elegance above two stolid and grotesque creatures of ambiguous gender (fig. I.1).[1] Sappho's hyperfeminine beauty, as marked by her lithe, slender yet curvaceous body and swirling, arabesque movements, stands in sharp contrast to the "she-male" monsters who lurk beneath her, gazing haplessly at this modern incarnation of the sapphic spirit. The occasion that inspired this drawing from a lampoon entitled *The Sink of Solitude* was the British government's successful prosecution of Radclyffe Hall's novel, *The Well of Loneliness* (1928), for obscene libel, an event that would drag the subject of lesbianism out into the open, where it would play on the lips of "millions of shop, office, and mill girls."[2] Egan's provocative drawing of a modern Sappho seems a good starting point to introduce a project that aims to show how the sapphic figure, in her multiple and contradictory guises, refigures the relation between public and private space within modernity. In much the same way, this essay collection seeks to explore the powerful allure of the sapphic in the cultural imaginary as well as in cultural production and to demonstrate evidence of the profound shifts—in terms of visibility, intelligibility, and accessibility—that occurred as a result of the growing public awareness of sapphism in modern Anglophone cultures between the two World Wars.

One of the first scholars to recognize the "multiple meanings" conveyed by the word "sapphic" was Diana Collecott, who observed that it embraces

Fig. I.1 Beresford Egan, "Sappho and the Latter-day Adolescents," *The Sink of Solitude,* 1928.

"aesthetics and intersubjectivity as well as sexual practice, with all that these involve for women in a patriarchal culture."[3] We contend that "sapphism" is a useful term in that it distances us from the more rigid contemporary categories of identity, such as "butch" or "femme," and reminds us that the claiming of a sexual identity—indeed, the exclusive connection of Sappho with same-sex desire—is relatively recent. The term "Sapphist," according to the *Oxford English Dictionary (OED)*, denotes women who have a "sexual interest in other women" or who engage in "homosexual relations between women."[4] The *OED* tracks the earliest entries for this term to 1890 (*National Medical Dictionary)* and the *Lancet* (in 1901), and we do know that the term "sapphist" did not enter the language until around that time in the writings of sexologists. Hence, our sense that the emergence of the sapphic within modernity is bound up with the circulation of medical and sexological knowledge in the late nineteenth and early twentieth centuries, with the publication of works such as Richard von Krafft-Ebing's *Psychopathia Sexualis* (1886) and Havelock Ellis's *Studies in the Psychology of Sex*, vol. II *Sexual Inversion* (1897), to name two studies that were most influential in identifying the category of "sexual inversion" in Britain and North America.[5]

One salient example of sapphism's engagement with the discourse of inversion that helps us to understand the ways it came to be associated with modernity occurs in the remarkable work of Olive Moore, a scandalously underread English modernist whose writings have been described as a cross between Virginia Woolf and Djuna Barnes, but with a more biting wit. In her second novel, *Spleen* (1930), an Englishwoman, Ruth Dalby, returns to London from Italy in 1929 where she encounters the postwar "new young woman" embodied by Joan Agnew.[6] Joan's "independence" and "self-expression" radiates a "certain glamour," but Ruth condemns this androgynous "look of today" as a transient cultural novelty. Ruth is "shocked" by her exposure to this "emancipated woman [who] wanted no children," even though she herself is guilty of this "monstrous" crime. Indeed, it is Ruth's guilt over her revulsion to maternity that leads her to believe that her son's deformities are the result of her own reluctance to reproduce. Ultimately, Moore borrows from the language of sexology to convey Ruth's predicament, describing her as "lonely as an invert." Throughout the novel Moore provides us with ample clues to mark Ruth as sexually deviant: she identifies with her father and values the intellect above all else; she detests her female corporeality; and she exhibits no heterosexual desire or impulses. Although Ruth does not identify with Joan, Moore's articulation of her sexual "difference" suggests that the invert is a kind of prototype for the new woman: "For surely (she thought) it was a form of mental inversion this loneliness of hers among her fellow-creatures." Here, "inversion" is not a physical malady, but a condition of being modern. Moore links lesbianism with modernity in order to break the stranglehold that heterosexist cultural standards have on women's lives, but in doing so she inevitably reproduces the pathologizing language of inversion, reminding us of sexologist and birth control reformer Stella Brown's denunciation of feminism as an example of what she termed "unconscious inversion."[7] What Moore fundamentally conveys is that to be modern is in effect to be a lesbian.

This medicalized visibility is, of course, highly problematic, but it does provide us with some historical parameters from which to speculate upon the uneasy relationship between sapphism and the modern. Yet we use the word "sapphism" advisedly; even though modernist women themselves deployed the term, it did not often appear in public discourse. In using "lesbian" interchangeably with "sapphist" in this collection, our goal is to avoid the clinical tinge of "invert" and to signal the discursive fluidity of female same-sex desire as an emergent cultural category. This is not to deny that the term "lesbian" was used as both an adjective and a noun to describe women who "desired and pleasured each other more than a century and a half before the *OED*'s first entry for that meaning."[8] Certainly, a spate of groundbreaking historical work tracking same-sex desire between women at various points in Western culture (e.g., Greek and Roman antiquity, the Renaissance, the seventeenth and eighteenth centuries) invites us to rethink the implications of the very different sort of lesbian visibility that emerges in modern and modernist discourse.[9] Such groundbreaking scholarship demonstrates that, in one form or another, the woman who sexually desires another woman has existed all along, even if she has been unnamed, variously named, or, indeed, clinically defamed. The word "lesbian" may be a neologism, as Terry Castle reminds us, but there "have always been *other* words" for the woman who loved women: "*tribade, fricatrice, sapphist, roaring girl, amazon, freak, romp, dyke, bull dagger, tommy.*"[10] Castle and other critics such as Emma Donoghue, Lisa Moore, and Valerie Traub all supply striking evidence of incipient lesbian cultural and self-awareness long before the so-called invention of the lesbian around 1900. Yet while such scholars confine themselves to dispelling the myth that pre-twentieth-century lesbians had no words to describe themselves, we contend that as an identity category that developed from the turn of the century onward, "sapphism" played a constitutive role in the construction of a specifically modern understanding of female sexuality.

One hurdle in attempting to account for the phrase "sapphic modernity" is that scholars in lesbian studies have been inordinately preoccupied with the question of "who counts" or "what is it that we count" in assigning modern categories of sexuality (lesbian, bisexual, straight, etc.); such questions are, in fact, at the crux of lesbian historiography. One objective of this project is to demonstrate that during the interwar period such discrete categorizations and boundaries were far more fluid than has previously been acknowledged. Annamarie Jagose's observations of an upper-class Englishwoman, Anne Lister (1791–1840), speak directly to this concern even though Lister lived in an earlier historical era than the one that preoccupies our volume:

> Lister's many sexual partners do not understand themselves, any more than she understands them, as sharing with Lister a sexual preference, let alone anything like asexuality. Without exception, Lister's sexual relations with women are not defined as transacted between subjects of the same gender; they are not even orchestrated under the rubric of a shared sexual subjectivity . . . sex between women does not itself necessarily constitute identity.[11]

That lesbianism is a problematic and contested category has been amply documented by scholars who have attempted to track female sexuality as an effect of historical change. Historians such as Judith Bennett and Martha Vicinus have tackled head on this problem of what constitutes "lesbianism" (whether it be acts, behaviors, claimed identities, or labels), reminding us of the importance of avoiding ahistoricism by differentiating between questions that concern us now (the urge and desire to know for sure) and what the historical record allows us to conclude (what might never be known).[12] Castle approaches the predicament in another way, with an inimitable exposition of the dictionary definition of "lesbian":

> What precisely does it mean . . . to "direct sexual desire toward another of the same sex?" To write another woman a romantic poem? To fantasize about making love to her? To share the same bed with her? To live with her for fifty years? To bring her to orgasm? . . . What about authors of whose intimate lives we know little or nothing? Where to put the great Sappho herself, for example, who lives on in literary history largely as a threadbare assemblage of textual fragments, scholarly guesswork, and titillating rumors? . . . [What about] female authors who take up lesbian themes but declare themselves asexual or bisexual or heterosexual or in some other fashion *not*-lesbian? How much weight should we give to a writer's self-description?[13]

Some of the women we consider in *Sapphic Modernities*, such as Alice Anderson, Phyllis Barron, Elizabeth Bowen, Mary Butts, Edith Ellis, or Dorothy Larcher, easily fall within these kinds of cracks, and thus we should be wary about assigning them to *fixed* categories.

Yet while we cannot reach firm conclusions without evidence, it might be productive to speculate on the cultural effects of sapphism's "suggestibility," to borrow a concept from Jodie Medd, who, in this volume, argues that inconclusiveness may enrich our understanding of sapphic modernity: "instead of charting lesbianism's 'visibility' or lamenting its invisibility, we might consider hermeneutic, epistemological, and functional questions about lesbianism's (mis)interpretability and cultural deployment." This might preclude conclusions beyond the idea that certain relationships seem to have been important (and creatively productive) to women. But it may not be necessary to *know for sure*. We need only to clarify that there seems to be a possibility (a suggestibility) of sapphism—and to speculate on what that might mean. In this sense, we build on Castle's solution by interrogating the "category itself," that is, by focusing less on "lesbianism-as-lived-experience" than on "lesbianism-as-theme"—or the " 'idea' of lesbianism."[14] As our title *Sapphic Modernities* indicates, the *idea* that concerns us ultimately is that of the sapphic specifically in modern interwar culture. We thus propose a fixed time in which to examine a figure in flux within particular national cultures (e.g., Britain, France, and Australia), that of the lesbian undergoing profound cultural change. Of course, as we have already argued, the lesbian is not uniquely modern, but our scrutiny of her crucially redefines the modern. Whether as an object of fascination or idealization, the figure of Sappho has captivated the literary avant-garde for over a hundred years, and thus she is bound up with both modernism and modernity, terms discussed at length throughout the volume, but requiring some further explanation here.

Sapphic Modernity

It was only in the late nineteenth century that the linkage of the sapphic with the modern began to emerge in the work of such avant-garde writers as the French poet Charles Baudelaire, who regarded the lesbian as "an evocative symbol of a feminized modernity . . . an avatar of perversity and decadence, exemplifying the mobility and ambiguity of modern forms of desire."[15] Over the past two decades, feminist scholars of literary modernism have extended Baudelaire's effort to link the sapphic and the modern by deploying the phrases "sapphic modernism" or "lesbian modernism" as part of a wider strategy to expand the high modernist canon, including a more diverse group of writers, and perhaps even constituting a literary subgenre.[16] In a lucid analysis of the evolution of "lesbian modernism," Joanne Winning argues that such a process of recovery of female writing from the "canonical wilderness" shows the "fundamentally complex yet crucial relations between lesbian sexuality and textuality in the modernist period."[17] These no longer forgotten literary works, such as Woolf's *Orlando*, Bryher's *Development*, Barnes's *Ladies Almanack*, or Gertrude Stein's *Q.E.D.*, to cite only a handful, represent the quintessence of "sapphic modernism," a movement that, as Shari Benstock explains, "constitutes itself through moments of rupture in the social and cultural fabric."[18]

We take a somewhat different approach, however, as our tracking of the shifts from "modernism" to "modernity" points, toward an understanding of the social forces and cultural conditions that made the connection between sexuality and modernity imaginable and representable. The phrase "sapphic modernism" is indicative of the convergence of both esthetic and political objectives at work in the creation of this "modernism of the margins," yet—and here our thinking is informed by Rita Felski's delineation of the meanings of "modernism" and "modernity"—we argue that the view of modernity via an exclusive engagement with literary modernism is "partial,"[19] since it limits our ability to change the conceptual framework of existing narratives of the modern itself. While the discursive formations of esthetic modernism have helped enormously in allowing us to make sense of the modern world, we must remain wary of regarding modernist art and literature as inherently "the most important or representative works of the modern period."[20] Thus we propose that "sapphic modernities" may prove to be the more useful phrase for our purposes since it encompasses not only the esthetic and political but much more. Through such an approach we hope to establish "a crucial link between the turn to cultural theories of modernity and the desire to write the histories of those traditionally absent from history."[21]

Sapphic Modernities

What forms of cultural production enabled the lesbian's emergence and self-definition during the interwar period? We consider, from several theoretical frameworks, the lesbian in relation to a wide range of cultural materials endemic to the period, including: the symbolic significance of the urban landscape; the role of art deco, home design, and portraiture; the utility of social taboos, such as smoking; the popularization of spiritualism, séances, and psychoanalysis; and the emergence of new technologies, such as motoring and mass-market periodicals. We make no attempt at a comprehensive cultural history here, despite our feminist and queer engagement with diverse aspects and styles of modern life, but we do lavish particular attention on what we see as the formative moment of lesbian visibility in early twentieth-century national formations—most extensively in Britain, but also ranging further afield to France (the Paris salons of 1910–1940) and Australia (the Melbourne of the 1920s)—to determine what range of "sapphisms" were circulating between the wars. Yet, while lesbianism was regarded by some as a menace to the nation (it was often conflated, in Britain, for instance, with the problem of "surplus" single women), it nonetheless functioned, we contend, as a kind of cultural stimulus that reinvigorated many domains of national life.[22] Despite the widespread perception in national cultures such as Britain, France, and the USA that the lesbian was a race apart, an unnatural being whose unreproductive masculinized body did not conform to the dominant ideal of women's procreation and inverted sexual norms, the diverse essays in this collection demonstrate incontrovertibly the existence of other, competing models of lesbian identity and desire. The cultural reinvigoration that we trace throughout this volume is at odds with the perception, articulated by both pro- and antifeminists, that lesbianism was a direct threat to national stability or that there was an official, state-sanctioned reticence about lesbianism. The contributors to *Sapphic Modernities* also revise or subvert the stereotype of the mannish female invert, extricating the lesbian body from its associations with degeneracy and perversion and offering a new perspective on the erotic interplay between women.

Our contributors regard the lesbian as an exemplary subject of modernity, a key figure in the period's articulation of itself as "newly modern," consciously breaking from constraining historical definitions regarding gender, identity, and sexuality.[23] While our volume seeks to understand the sapphic in modernity and modernity's relationship to the sapphic, clearly the limited scope of this volume cannot respond adequately to the plethora of distinctive features or social characteristics of British modernity and its cousins, nor can it give a full accounting of lesbian experience during this period. For example, none of the essays in this volume addresses issues such as the relationship between empire and female homosexuality or investigates the role of British lesbians of color during this interwar period; early twentieth-century lesbian histories of women of color or the working class in Britain are notoriously difficult to reconstruct because few documents exist.[24] Consequently, most of the essays here focus upon privileged white middle- or upper-middle-class lesbians precisely because they are the best documented. We also acknowledge the implicit class bias associated with the word sapphism, a term which, together with "romantic friendship," Lisa Moore argues, was "fundamental to the establishment of both the bourgeois private and the bourgeois public spheres" in the eighteenth century, and which persisted into the decades immediately following World War I.[25] When, for example, Woolf describes the beginning of her love affair in 1925 with the affluent Vita Sackville West by calling her "My aristocrat . . . [who] is violently Sapphic," we associate the lesbian with high culture, the English aristocracy, and glamorous excess.[26] Often, as is the case with Woolf, the terms "sapphism" and "sapphist" are shorthand for a lesbian of a certain class, pedigree, and social standing. When we refer to sapphists, therefore, we mean—in general—to signal a select group of British, Anglophone, and European lesbians who hobnobbed with the cultural and social elites. This shorthand is meant to streamline discussion, and not to homogenize the many differences among real lesbians living at this time.

Our collection begins with three essays that explore some of the transnational dimensions of emergent sapphic cultures. In Sexual Geographies: Circulation and Mobility, Joanne Winning and Tirza True Latimer interrogate the terms of our project—sapphic modernity—by focusing on the possibilities of modern urban life in Paris and London for lesbian writers and artists such as Bryher and Romaine Brooks. The section concludes with Georgine Clarsen's analysis of the motor garage "as a site in which young Australian women sought meaningful work within a new technological domain and an emerging nexus of private consumption." Chapters in the second part of the volume—The Sapphic Body in Space: Leisure, Commodity Culture, Domesticity—investigate sapphic negotiations with consumer cultures. While Penny Tinkler looks at the gendering of lesbian smoking practices as a marker of modernity, Laura Doan reads the pronouncements of conservative women such as Radclyffe Hall and Vita Sackville-West on domesticity and marriage as political interventions meant to reserve the privileges of modernity for an elect few. Bridget Elliott also scrutinizes some of the collaborative, modernist, aesthetic practices of women at the cutting edge of interior design. In part 3, In and Out of Place: History, Displacement, and Revision, Heather Love, Colleen Lamos, and Alison Oram all track the influence of the past on modernist and modern discourses of same-sex desire. Love examines Sylvia Townsend Warner's preoccupation with the "ghostly, backward-looking aspect of history" in her 1936 novel, *Summer Will Show*. For Warner, Love argues: "History is, more than anything else, a way of dreaming about alternative pasts and possible futures. The gap that opens between potential and reality is a space for speculation, fantasy, and desire." Lamos similarly probes "alternative pasts and possible futures" in her assessment of the influence of Greek language and culture on Woolf's understanding of female friendship and homoeroticism. The act of looking back is a central concern of Alison Oram also, as she detects the influence of 1890s decadence on accounts of women's relationships with other women in the print media of interwar London. Finally, in Embracing Discursive Space: Re-imagining Psychoanalysis and Spirituality, contributors offer us fresh evidence of the extent to which the specter of the lesbian was a preoccupying the fixture of the modern imagination. Jo-Ann Wallace and Jodie Medd both examine the passionate sapphic attachments beyond the grave. Wallace locates Edith Ellis's 1912 anthology of love poetry, *The Lover's Calendar*, within a continuing tradition of "sapphic idealism," inspired by the spiritual utopianism of Edward Carpenter, while Medd turns her attention to a curious confluence of spiritualism, slander, and sapphism, focused around Radclyffe Hall's 1920 court case. Like Medd, Petra Rau explores the limits and possibilities of lesbian representability in her reading of Elizabeth Bowen's *The Hotel* (1927) against Sigmund Freud's last case study *Psychogenesis*. Rau observes how "lesbian desire . . . makes all the more visible the rhetorics and strategies of conversion the texts strain to employ to obfuscate lesbian desire as a sign of the real." The final essay, by Jane Garrity, seeks to deepen our understanding of the period's extraordinary investment in what we might call the queer genealogy of modernist narrative, by examining Mary Butts's representation of the links between mystical experience, male homosexuality, and urban space.

These thirteen essays show how our collection brings together a diverse group of scholars from four countries who work in history, visual culture, literary theory, cultural studies, and queer/gender studies. Such interdisciplinarity is this project's distinctive feature, as *Sapphic Modernities* marks the first attempt to examine the representation of the lesbian in modernity from the multiple perspectives of literary, historical, visual, and cultural studies. It is our contention that despite the groundbreaking recovery work that has been done in lesbian and gay studies during the last two decades, the relationship between same-sex desire and women's experience of early twentieth-century modernity is still undertheorized and unexamined.[27] We hope that this collection will stimulate debate and encourage others to pursue new ways of understanding and investigating the meaning of the "sapphic" within modern culture. *Sapphic Modernities* is, we believe, poised to make an important contribution to modernity studies as well as to the ongoing cultural and historical mapping of lesbian identity, producing a more definitive account of the interwar period and explaining the particular stigmatization of, and fascination with, the prohibitive nature of female same-sex desire.

Notes

1. "Sappho and the Latter Day Adolescents" was the final drawing of six in a brilliantly scathing lampoon entitled *The Sink of Solitude* (London: Hermes Press, 1928) by Beresford Egan with a preface and lampoon by P. R. Stephensen. An extended analysis of this lampoon and others can be found in Laura Doan, "Sappho's Apotheosis? Radclyffe Hall's Queer Kinship with the Watchdogs of the Lord," *Sexuality and Culture*, 8, no. 2 (Spring 2004): 82–108.
2. Radclyffe Hall, *The Well of Loneliness*. 1928. (Reprint, New York: Anchor Books, 1990); Stephensen, *The Sink of Solitude*, no page numbers. For more background on the banning of Hall's novel, see Laura Doan, *Fashioning Sapphism: The Origins of a Modern English Lesbian Culture* (New York: Columbia University Press, 2001).
3. Diana Collecott, *H. D. and Sapphic Modernity 1910–1950* (Cambridge: Cambridge University Press, 1999), p. 2.
4. See the *Oxford English Dictionary Online* (Oxford: Oxford University Press, 2004). http://athens.oed.com
5. Richard von Krafft-Ebing, *Psychopathia Sexualis With Especial Reference to the Antipathic Sexual Instinct: A Medico-Forensic Study* (1886; reprint, New York: Stein and Day, 1965) and Havelock Ellis, *Studies in the Psychology of Sex*, vol. II *Sexual Inversion* (1897; reprint, Philadelphia: F. A. Davis, 3d ed., 1921).
6. Olive Moore, *Collected Writings* (Elmwood Park, IL: Dalkey Archive Press, 1992); all cited passages from the novel appear on pp. 125–26. For further analysis of Moore's work, see Jane Garrity, *Step-daughters of England: British Women Modernists and the National Imaginary* (Manchester: Manchester University Press, 2003).
7. See Stella Brown's 1923 "Studies in Feminine Inversion," in Lucy Bland and Laura Doan, eds., *Sexology Uncensored: The Documents of Sexual Science* (Chicago: University of Chicago Press, 1998), pp. 61–66.
8. Emma Donoghue, *Passions between Women: British Lesbian Culture, 1668–1801* (New York: Harper Collins, 1995), pp. 3–4.
9. See, for example: Harriette Andreadis, *Sappho in Early Modern England: Female Same-Sex Literary Erotics, 1550–1714* (Chicago: University of Chicago Press, 2002); Bernadette J. Brooten, *Love Between Women: Early Christian Responses to Female Homoeroticism* (Chicago and London: University of Chicago Press, 1996); Donoghue, *Passions Between Women*; Lisa L. Moore, *Dangerous Intimacies: Toward a Sapphic History of the British Novel* (Durham and London: Duke University Press, 1997); Valerie Traub, *The Renaissance of Lesbianism in Early Modern England* (Cambridge: Cambridge University Press, 2002); and Martha Vicinus, *Intimate Friends: Women Who Loved Women, 1778–1928* (Chicago and London: University of Chicago Press, 2004).
10. Terry Castle, *The Apparitional Lesbian: Female Homosexuality and Modern Culture* (New York: Columbia University Press, 1993) p. 9.

11. Annamarie Jagose, *Inconsequence: Lesbian Representation and the Logic of Sexual Sequence* (Ithaca and London: Cornell University Press, 2002), p. 21.
12. Judith Bennett, " 'Lesbian-Like' and the Social History of Lesbianisms," *Journal of the History of Sexuality* 9, nos. 1–2 (January/April 2000): 1–24 and Martha Vicinus, " 'They Wonder to Which Sex I Belong': The Historical Roots of the Modern Lesbian Identity," *Feminist Studies* 18, no. 3 (Fall 1992): 467–97.
13. Terry Castle, *The Literature of Lesbianism* (New York: Columbia University Press, 2003), p. 3.
14. Castle, *The Literature of Lesbianism*, pp. 5, 6.
15. Rita Felski, *The Gender of Modernity* (Cambridge: Harvard University Press, 1995), p. 20.
16. Makiko Minow is credited with coining the expression "lesbian modernism" in her 1989 review "Versions of Female Modernism: Review Article," *News from Nowhere* 7 (1989): 64–69. For further discussion of the terms "sapphic modernism" or "lesbian modernism," see: Shari Benstock, "Expatriate Sapphic Modernism: Entering Literary History," in Karla Jay and Joanne Glasgow, eds., *Lesbian Texts and Contexts: Radical Revisions* (NY: New York University Press, 1990), pp. 183–203; Susan Gubar, "Sapphistries," *Signs: Journal of Women in Culture and Society* 10 (1984): 43–62; Robin Hackett, *Sapphic Primitivism: Productions of Race, Class and Sexuality in Key Works of Modern Fiction* New Brunswick, NJ: Rutgers University Press, 2004; Karla Jay, "Lesbian Modernism: (Trans)forming the (C)Anon," in George Haggerty and Bonnie Zimmerman, eds., *Professions of Desire: Lesbian and Gay Studies in Literature* (New York: MLA, 1995), pp. 73–77; Cassandra Laity, "H. D. and A. C. Swinburne: Decadence and Sapphic Modernism," in Karla Jay and Joanne Glasgow, eds., *Lesbian Texts and Contexts: Radical Revisions* (New York: New York University Press, 1990), pp. 217–40; and Jane Marcus, *Virginia Woolf and the Languages of Patriarchy* (Bloomington: Indiana University Press, 1987); and Bonnie Kime Scott, *Refiguring Modernism: The Women of 1928* (Bloomington: Indiana University Press, 1995).
17. Joanne Winning, *The Pilgrimage of Dorothy Richardson* (Madison: University of Wisconsin Press, 2000), p. 5. Defining the contours of a "canon of female modernism," Winning draws up an impressive list of texts that "articulate some kind of narrative of lesbian desire and identity," p. 4.
18. Benstock, "Expatriate Sapphic Modernism," p. 198. Ironically, this often-quoted passage is tucked into a footnote of this important essay.
19. Erin Carlston, *Thinking Fascism: Sapphic Modernism and Fascist Modernity* (Stanford, CA: Stanford University Press, 1998), p. 4 and Rita Felski, *Doing Time, Feminist Theory and Postmodern Culture* (New York: New York University Press, 2000), p. 59. For another concise discussion of the distinctions between "modernism" and "modernity" vis-à-vis feminism and women's experience, see Katy Deepwell's "Introduction" to her edited collection, *Women Artists and Modernism* (Manchester: Manchester University Press, 1998) and Janet Wolff's *AngloModern: Painting and Modernity in Britain and the United States* (Ithaca and London: Cornell University Press, 2003), especially chapter three, pp. 68–85.

20. Felski, *The Gender of Modernity*, p. 25.
21. Felski, *Doing Time*, p. 57.
22. For example, Arabella Kenealy warned that the dangerously "masculinized" women who were biologically "incapable of parenthood" would precipitate a national crisis of "Race-suicide." Kenealy, *Feminism and Sex Extinction* (London: T. Fisher Unwin, 1920), pp. 246, 263.
23. As Felski explains, "the lesbian's status as heroine of the modern derived from her perceived defiance of traditional gender roles through a subversion of 'natural' heterosexuality and the imperatives of biological reproduction." See *The Gender of Modernity*, p. 20. Some critics have recently begun to express unease about the critical tendency to view the heightened visibility of "dissident sexualities" in the late nineteenth and early twentieth centuries as "an index of modernization." See Suzanne Raitt, "Lesbian Modernism?" *GLQ: A Journal of Lesbian and Gay Studies* 10, no. 1 (2003): 112.
24. As British historian Barbara Caine reminds us, "the whole interwar period [has] only recently come to be recognized."See Caine, *English Feminism 1780–1980* (Oxford and New York: Oxford University Press, 1997), p. 173. Given this historical occlusion, it is not surprising that scholars would be inattentive to the importance of the British imperial context for the development of lesbian identity, or unaware of the cultural and social consequences of the British working-class, or nonwhite women's engagement with lesbianism. In general we know more about American lesbians of color and working-class lesbians than we do about the British context. See, for example, Lillian Faderman, *Odd Girls and Twilight Lovers: A History of Lesbian Life in Twentieth Century America* (New York: Columbia University Press, 1991); and Elizabeth Lapovsky and Madeline D. Davis, *Boots of Leather, Slippers of Gold: The History of a Lesbian Community* (New York: Routledge, 1993). Where, for example, is the British equivalent of Karen V. Hansen's important work on the love letters between two late nineteenth-century African American women? See Hansen, " 'No *Kisses* is Like Youres': An Erotic Friendship between Two African American Women during the Mid-Nineteenth Century," *Gender and History* 7, no. 2 (1995): 153–82. We need, following Jean Walton, to expose and address "the whiteness of lesbian sexuality as it has been constructed thus far," particularly how racial difference was central to the constitution of modern British lesbianism. See Walton, *Fair Sex, Savage Dreams: Race, Psychoanalysis, Sexual Difference* (Durham and London: Duke University Press, 2001), p. 40. Such omissions speak to the lack of historical resources and the great need for more archival research on this understudied group of lesbians. *The Lesbian History Sourcebook: Love and Sex between Women in Britain from 1780–1970*, Alison Oram and Annmarie Turnbull (London and New York: Routledge, 2001), is a step in this direction.
25. Moore, *Dangerous Intimacies*, p. 11.
26. Nigel Nicolson, ed., *A Change of Perspective: The Letters of Virginia Woolf, 1923–1928* (London: The Hogarth Press, 1977), p. 155.
27. A notable exception is Hugh Stevens and Caroline Howlett, eds. *Modernist Sexualities* (Manchester: Manchester University Press, 2000).

Part 1

Sexual Geographies: Circulation and Mobility

Chapter 1

The Sapphist in the City: Lesbian Modernist Paris and Sapphic Modernity

Joanne Winning

Toward Definition

This collection of essays on sapphic modernity is produced during the emergence of what is now coming to be called the new modernist critical studies, in which the parameters of modernism and modernity are being redrawn. Writing in this context, Susan Stanford Friedman considers the nature of the definition: "Definitions mean to fence in, to fix, and to stabilize. But they often end up being fluid, in a de-stabilized state of on-going formation, deformation, and reformation that serves the changing needs of the moment. They reflect the standpoint of their makers. They emerge out of the spatio/temporal context of their production. [. . .] They change dramatically over time and through space."[1] Certainly we require definitions. Yet, as Friedman rightly identifies, the definition continues to fail to be a static, satisfactory thing and that which it excludes is at least as important as that which it contains. What might we mean by "sapphic modernity"? Undoubtedly, in posing this question, we are attempting to articulate an identifiable cultural phenomenon—the ways in which women who are, in their own moment, identified as sapphist, or whom we might now, in our contemporary context, identify as sapphist lived within exhibited and contributed to the definition of being modern and living within the amorphous temporal period cultural theorists have coined "modernity." Yet, even as we articulate it, we are immediately confounded by the resistance of these terms to the process of definition. What *is* a sapphist? And how might we form both adjective and noun out of that primary definition to produce the term "sapphic"? As I have argued elsewhere, mapping the practices, desires, and identifications that constitute the terms of same-sex desire and identity formations that emerge in and through them relies upon a post-queer understanding of the contradictions, fragmentations, and disavowals that go to make up any sexual identity, including heterosexuality. Taking into account the complexities of lived and psychic experience, it is evident that the term "sapphic" must function on different levels, drawing in issues of desire, identification, community, and dissidence. In this chapter, I want to mobilize the term "sapphic" across these different planes, examining the ways in which the sapphic is constituted by intimate relationships of love and friendship, functions as an identity and identificatory practice that structures notions of community and network, and is deployed as a positionality that, in its repudiation of existing dominant cultural traditions (in this case literary and esthetic) and thus, in all these ways, articulates a *modernity*. Importantly, too, I want to move outside the spatial boundaries of English sapphic culture and look to other cultural contexts that inform and, in a more transnational sense, tell us something about the ways in which sapphists of the early twentieth century *experience* and *utilise* the modernity that is both around them and *of* them.

But what might we mean by "modernity"? Undoubtedly, the second term of that pairing is just as troubling as the first. Cultural theorists continue to contest the parameters, dates, and forms of modernity, as Andrew Barry, Thomas Osborne, and Nikolas Rose ask: "Where are the limits—geographical, social, temporal—of modernity? Is modernity a type of society, or an attitude or a mode of experience? Is modernity a functionalist, a realist, or an idealist concept? Where is modernity heading?"[2] Wherever its final destination, it remains the case that the relationship between dissident sexuality and the experience of early twentieth-century modernity is still undertheorised. In his famous formulation of modernity, constructed via Marx, Marshall Berman defines the lived *experience* of becoming modern. This description has so influenced our understandings of the internalized, psychic processes of living within and through modernity that it seems important to quote it at length:

> There is a mode of vital experience—experience of space and time, of the self and others, of life's possibilities and perils—that is shared by men and women all over the world today. I will call this body of experience "modernity." To be modern is to find ourselves in an environment that promises us adventure,

> power, joy, growth, transformation of ourselves and the world—and, at the same time, that threatens to destroy everything we have, everything we know, everything we are. [. . .] a unity of disunity: it pours us all into a maelstrom of perpetual disintegration and renewal, of struggle and contradiction, of ambiguity and anguish. To be modern is to be part of a universe in which, as Marx said, "all that is solid melts into air."[3]

Here the processes of becoming modern are always already structured on a binary; a mixture of possibility and closure, dissolution and formation, excitement and terror. Nevertheless, there is something beyond this binary, another dimension to our understanding and experience of modernity that may well be useful in our collective endeavor here to define *sapphic modernity*. Where dissident identities are to be inaugurated, is it not just this slippage, this tending toward dissolution, that exactly creates the space in which *new* formations of identity and experience may be wrested and lived out. Considering the slippery nature of modernity from a similarly Othered perspective, the Caribbean theorist Eduoard Glissant argues that *our* experience of *our* modernity is unusual only in the intense degree of awareness and lived self-consciousness that we have of it:

> *On the notion of modernity*. It is a vexed question. Is not every era "modern" in relation to the preceding one? It seems that at least one of the components of "our" modernity is the spread of the awareness we have of it. The awareness of our awareness (the double, the second degree) is our source of strength and our torment.[4]

As such, then, what is both peculiar and distinctive about our period of modernity is the sense that it is not a condition or landscape that materializes around the unwitting subject but rather a state and process in which the subject is a knowing and active participant. The inherent doubleness suggested in Glissant's definition of modernity gives the Black British theorist Paul Gilroy sufficient conceptual space to think about black subjectivity and the ways in which it represents a "counterculture" of modernity.[5] Yet, as Gilroy notes, for all the theoretical and cultural debate about modernity, there has been little examination of the correlation between difference and modernity. If our modernity might be characterized by its *known-ness* and, simultaneously, our *knowing-ness* of it, I want to suggest that, in fact, the sapphist might see her opportunity for expression and sustenance in the active delineation of the modern. And more than this, that to be sapphist is *indelibly* to be modern; I want to suggest, through the following test-case, that there is a synonymous and deeply imbricated relationship between the expression of dissident sexual identity and the embracing and creation of the modern.

The aim of this chapter is to evidence sapphic modernity by turning to a specific historical and geographical site—Paris between 1916 and 1936—in order to tease out these relations between the sapphic and the modern. If David Harvey is right that Paris is indeed the "capital of modernity," this seems an important site of investigation.[6] In what ways does this site of burgeoning modernity function as a generative context in which the sapphic—as a set of desires, identifications and dissident ideas—articulates itself and comes into being? In her book *Paris Was a Woman*, Andrea Weiss notes:

> Women with creative energy and varying degrees of talent, women with a passion for art and literature, women without the obligations that come with husbands and children, were especially drawn to the Left Bank, and never with more urgency and excitement than in the first quarter of this century [. . .] They came because Paris offered them, as women, a unique and extraordinary world.[7]

Weiss rightly identifies the "freer" spaces of the early twentieth-century city as a social and cultural context in which women were able to substantially partake in cultural production in new ways. She notes too that one of the defining characteristics of this group—the women of the Left Bank—was their freedom from traditional heterosexual roles and constraints. In her retrospective *Souvenirs Indiscrets*, written in 1960, Natalie Barney argues for the singular freedoms of the city in which she creates sapphic space: "Paris m' a toujours semblé la seule ville où l'on puisse s'exprimer et vivre à sa guise"[8]

As has been clear since the biographical surveys of the women involved in both Anglo-American modernism and the Avant-Garde, there is a complex nexus between cultural production, lesbian sexuality, and the experience of the modern metropolis.[9] The city, we might say, functions as the spatial context of modernity. In its speed, its energy, and its sheer size, it epitomizes Baudelaire's famous definition of modernity as "the fleeting, the transient, the ephermeral." It functions too as the site of *the flâneur*—the stroller who observes and creates art out of the very stuff of the street. As the early twentieth-century sociologist Georg Simmel notes, in his influential formulation, the city and urban life change the boundaries of human experience, transforming understandings of the mind, the body, and the texture of the social.[10] Not least, of course, the modernity of the city turns us inward, intensifying our emotional and intellectual worlds to such an pitch that we *produce* both culturally and behaviorally in new ways. Raymond Williams, launching the critical conceptualization of the inherent links between the modernity of the city and its environs and modernism, argues "within the new kind of open, complex and mobile society, small groups in any form of divergence or dissent could find some kind of foothold, in ways that would not have been possible if the artists and thinkers composing them had been scattered in more traditional, closed societies."[11] This context is rich with potential for the sapphist since within the milieu of the modern city the terms of sexual identity and desire might also be negotiated. The modern city becomes a space in which the sapphist may articulate her desire and her identity, her sense of "becoming modern." In diverse forums across the urban spaces of Paris, for example, the salons of Natalie Barney and Gertrude Stein/Alice B. Toklas or the bookshops of Sylvia Beach and Adrienne Monnier, we witness the possession of cultural space by sapphists engaged in the creation of art and literature. Here, we witness one of the first substantial instances of sapphic cultural production and a definitive historical "moment" in which the sapphic begins to imagine itself and, most importantly, partake in the *generation* of modernity.

The Sapphist in the City

I begin with an instructive proleptic leap. In examining the Castro district of San Francisco, Manuel Castells makes the following assertions about lesbians and urban space: "Lesbians, unlike gay men, tend not to concentrate in a given territory, but establish social and interpersonal networks."[12] Castells draws this conclusion in his analysis of what he calls the "San Francisco Experience," in which gay men exhibit "territorial aspirations" in their endeavor to create a gay community within the spaces of the city. In order "to liberate themselves from cultural and sexual oppression," Castells argues, "they need a physical space from which to strike out." By contrast, lesbians are "placeless" and "tend not to require a geographical basis for their political organization." As a consequence of this unrooted, disenfranchised mode of existence, "there is little influence by lesbians on the space of the city."[13] Whilst Castells is writing within and about a late twentieth-century context, his argument is indicative of the masculinist paradigms through which lesbian participation in the formation of the city and its spaces is consistently read. Not least, such a position would seem very much at odds with the historical example of sapphic modernist appropriation of urban space in the early decades of the twentieth century in Paris. Using the example of one small street in Paris, the rue de l'Odéon in Paris' *sixth arrondissment*, it is clear that the street's most famous inhabitants and booksellers—Adrienne Monnier and Sylvia Beach, running their respective bookshops, La Maison des Amis des Livres and Shakespeare and Company—had a very different sense of what lesbians can do in the city.

In her account of the careers of Monnier and Beach, Shari Benstock argues that their sexuality cannot be disassociated from their intellectual endeavors: "These women made no distinction between their professional and private lives; their public and private interests were integrated to such a degree that it was difficult even for them to say how their professional alliance was different from their personal and intimate relationship."[14] To read the example of Monnier and Beach productively turns on understanding and theorizing *how* the sapphic modernists conceived and lived out the spaces of the modern city. Bemused in particular by Beach's own autobiographical account of the genesis and experiences of her modernist career, Benstock argues: "*Shakespeare and Company* does not make Sylvia Beach the heroine of her own story. Indeed, the memoir is not of her, but of the bookshop."[15] Yet, we might argue in response, of course, *the bookshop* occupies the very *center* of Beach's narrative because what "Shakespeare and Company, 12 rue de l'Odéon" represents is the very *core* of Beach's sense of her own intellectual contribution: the appropriation of city space in the service of modernism, sapphism and modernity itself. With its walls lined with Man Ray and Berenice Abbott portraits of "the Crowd" and its shelves and windows displaying the avant-garde and experimental literatures of modernism, Beach's bookshop might well be read as a definitive spatial signifier of sapphic modernity.

In the early summer of 1923, as a favor to the enthusiastic and awkward young Bryher, Sylvia Beach wrote a letter of introduction to Dorothy Richardson, the modernist writer engaged in the lengthy production of *Pilgrimage.*[16] Beach in Paris, notable by this time for her successful bookshop and publication of James Joyce's *Ulysses*, serves as conduit for a meeting between the two women in London. Beach's letter to the reclusive Richardson was a success and the result, as Richardson's biographer's Gloria Fromm notes, was: "an invitation to tea at Queen's Terrace."[17] One of the most compelling things about this literary introduction is the triangulation by which it comes about, and the way in which modernist and sapphic networks overwrite national boundaries. Indeed, cultural space is created beyond national boundaries, structured rather on literary, identificatory, and urban connections. The introduction of Bryher to Richardson by Beach was to prove decisive and influential for all concerned. Later that year, Bryher was to fund for Richardson a European trip, which culminated in a ten-day stay in Paris. Not only did this cement the important and life-long friendship between Richardson and Bryher, a friendship overwritten in its own way with questions of sexual identity, but it also allowed Richardson to enter the modernist scene in Paris and brought her to Beach's bookshop and its côterie. This trip to Paris was to be the only one Richardson ever made, yet its significance is evidenced both within the text of *Pilgrimage* and in later correspondence with Bryher; ten years later Richardson writes: "Stein is a delight and gave me a frightful nostalgia for Paris. I know one should be shocked but up to a point she is right with her meaning is a meaning is a meaning is a meaning is a meaning is a meaning is a meaning."[18] Here, as this vignette makes clear, Paris functions as a site of importance in the English sapphic modernist imaginary.

"We Founded Our House in November 1915"[19]: The Psychodynamics of the Bookshop

In his analysis of the body in the city, Steve Pile argues for either a "psychoanalysis of space" or a "psychodynamics of place."[20] Looking at the work of the behavioral geographers such as Roger M. Downs and David Stea (1973) and D. J. Warmsley and G. J. Lewis (1984), Pile rehearses the concept of cognitive mapping, arguing: "people after all need to know where the things they need are, what the area is like and how to get there."[21] As Pile notes, the concept of cognitive mapping, in its inception within the discipline of behavioral geography, fails to "grasp people's emotional dynamism." Nevertheless, a more nuanced analysis of the psychic processes by which people "map" their own space within the city—a *psychodynamics*—allows crucial elements of the use of space to emerge. What then are the psychodynamics of the bookshop? And, further, are there ways in which such a psychodynamics is, in part at least, defined by the identificatory practices of sapphism and sapphists?

It transpires that one of the most influential of the sapphic modernists hated city spaces and the texture and speed of the modern life lived within them. As Beach herself notes, "Bryher disliked cities—those 'rows of shops' as she called them. She shunned crowds, was no frequenter of cafes, and was very retiring."[22] Bryher's repudiation of the city suggests that one of the definitive experiences of modern urban life is alienation; as such the ability to create an internal map of our modern urban environment is one way of "controlling" this overwhelming space. In addition, such a map is a way of actively appropriating city space to make it one's own. As Pile argues "the cognitive map is not a replica of the external world, it is a means of taking control of the world and making the world anew."[23] It is thus important to note that Bryher's Paris had one focal point:

> There was only one street in Paris for me, the rue de l'Odeon. It is association, I suppose, but I have always considered it one of the most beautiful streets in

> the world. It meant naturally Sylvia and Adrienne and the happy hours that I spent in their libraries. Has there ever been another bookshop like Shakespeare and Company? [. . .] Number seven, on the opposite side of the rue de l'Odeon, was also a cave of treasures.[24]

Writing after Beach's death, with a degree of sensitivity to the nuances of space and spatiality, Bryher too ponders the importance of the physical location of the bookshop as a place of shelter for the artifacts of modernism and modernity that Beach amassed during her career: "What will their future be now? However well librarians or friends may care for them, what will they be but wood, canvas or paper, away from *these three rooms?*"[25] In the case of Bryher's "map" of Paris, the rue de l'Odéon functions as center because it is a space of sapphic modernity; a space in which she will find sameness of intellectual endeavor *and* sexuality, rather than difference.

In her memoir of modernist Paris another sapphic modernist, Janet Flanner, writes: "The *heart and home* of the Left Bank American literary colony after 1920 turned out to be Shakespeare and Company, the extraordinary rue de l'Odéon bookstore founded by the American Sylvia Beach."[26] Like Bryher, Flanner notes that Beach's bookshop cannot be defined without its counterpart on the other side of the street. The placing of these two institutions turns the street space itself into something that *belongs* to the two booksellers and, moreover, something that they transform from physical space to intellectual space, creating a "Franco-English language stream" that "[flows] down *their street*, visibly adding to the picturesque quality."[27] Here again Flanner constructs a map that locates the bookshops at the heart of the communities to which she belongs. Adding to these accounts in a typically hyperbolic (and spatially expansive) way, Gertrude Stein's record of Beach's bookshop in the poem "Rich and Poor in English" states: "I have almost a country there."[28] Thus the little street turns into a nation-state and its visitors into citizens. To be sure, one way of conceptualizing sapphic modernity here is to recognize the importance of a sapphic "cognitive map." In the minds of many of the sapphic modernists, a map could be drawn in which lines of connection ran from rue de l'Odéon to rue de Fleurus (Stein/Toklas' salon) to rue Jacob (Barney's salon). Walking the route of such a map was clearly a common occurrence, as Beach herself notes: "I saw Gertrude and Alice often. Either they dropped in to observe my bookselling business or I went around to their *pavillion* in the rue de Fleurus near the Luxembourg Gardens. It was at the back of the court. [. . .] The *pavillon* was as fascinating as its occupants. On its walls were all those wonderful Picassos of the 'Blue Period.' "[29]

Yet we might supplement this analysis by asking questions about the processes by which these two sapphic modernists claim and construct this space. How does the street become *theirs*? It is clear from Monnier's account of her bookshop that she felt as if the city space in which she located her adult self, sexuality, and career claimed her as its own before her own desires were concretized: "The Left Bank called me and even now it does not cease to call me and to keep me. I cannot imagine that I could ever leave it, *any more than an organ can leave the place that is assigned to it in the body*."[30] The corporeal metaphor suggests the embodied and embedded nature of Monnier's psychic investment in this space. Monnier's sense of city space was deeply influenced by the avant-garde discourses of the Unanimist Jules Romains, as she notes: "I was plunged into the unanimist experience."[31] Building his intellectual framework on key notions of community, space, and creativity within the city, Romains pronounces: "Space does not belong to anyone in particular. And no one has succeeded in appropriating for themselves a bit of space, in order to saturate it with their unique existence. Everything interpenetrates, coincides, cohabits."[32] This generative proximity is one of the central tenets of the Unanimist belief system; everything done within urban space impacts upon every other thing. For Romains, both urban space and the human subjectivity within it are plastic and mutable:

> At the present time, the life of the civilised man has assumed a new character. Essential changes have given different meaning to our existence . . . The actual tendency of the people to mass together in the cities; the uninterrupted development of social relationships; ties stronger and more binding established between men by their duties, their occupations, their common pleasures; an encroachment, even greater, of the public on the private, the collective on the individual: here are the facts that certain people deplore but that no one contends.[33]

As a sapphist and modernist, these ideas about the porosity and possibility of the city were productive for Monnier; as she makes clear in her account of the formation of her bookshop. With the avowed intention of promoting, selling, and *lending* modern literature, Monnier opened La Maison des Amis des Livres on November 15, 1915, with her then partner Suzanne Bonnierre. The bookshop was to epitomize a new attitude toward books and their readers: "We founded La Maison des Amis des Livres with faith; each one of its details seems to us to correspond *to a feeling, to a thought*. Business, for us, has a moving and profound meaning."[34] Later, after Beach's Shakespeare and Company left its first location in rue Dupuytren to take up residence opposite Monnier's establishment, Monnier and Beach were to accomplish their aim to reformulate the street and create a new and modern state of being—what Monnier herself called "Odéonia." In their "bookselling," both intended to partake fully in the avant-garde literary and esthetic movements they were disseminating. Monnier's active engagement in the cultural production of modernism is evident: "for every intelligent bookshop based upon the principle of lending and selling there is a public *whose taste it is easy to form.*"[35]

Throughout her essay on its inception, Monnier arrestingly describes the bookshop as a *house*: "we founded our house in November 1915."[36] In his *The Poetics of Space*, Gaston Bachelard argues for a technique of spatial analysis that he calls "topoanalysis" and describes it as "the systematic psychological study of the sites of our intimate lives."[37] Topoanalysis attends to the psychic investments we make in the primary spaces of our lives. Notably Bachelard analyses the need for shelter as a primal human drive, reading the importance of the house in the formulation of our psyches and imaginations:

> Of course, thanks to the house, a great many of our memories are housed, and if the house is a bit elaborate, if it has a cellar and a garret, nooks and corridors, our memories have refuges that are all the more clearly delineated. All our lives we come back to them in our daydreams.[38]

As the multitude of memories recorded in the memoirs under discussion in this essay prove, both bookshops function in this way, providing physical, psychic, and intellectual loci for the modernists who frequent them. In true Bachelardian style, Monnier describes her bookshop: "a place of transition between street and house."[39] Thus the bookshop is a liminal space. One of the first places upon which a topoanalytical study of Odéonia might fix is the recurrent signifier of the open door that features in both Monnier and Beach's narratives:

> At that instant when the passer-by crosses the threshold of the door that *everyone can open*, when he penetrates into that apparently impersonal place, nothing disguises the look on his face, the tone of his words; he accomplishes with a feeling of *complete freedom* an act that he believes to be without unforeseen consequences; there is a perfect correspondence between his external attitude and his profound self, and if we know how to observe him at that instant when he is only a stranger, we are able, now and forever, to know him in his truth.[40]

By creating her bookshop in a definitive way (housed with modern literature, functioning as a lending library as well as a place to buy books), Monnier invents a space with a modern "attitude." It is a space that transgresses and reformulates ordinary spatial boundaries; it is both house and street, inside and outside. The passerby who wanders in, invited to do so by the easily opened door achieves liberation and transcendence. Importantly,

Monnier's description of this space speaks of her committed and autonomous intervention in terms of modernity. Monnier imbibes the avant-garde ideas of Unanimism, Surrealism, and Futurism and then modifies these through her own conceptual framework. The ideas of her male peers, developing in and out of the experience of modernity, undergo a further modulation, reflecting Monnier's own specific worldview. Such a modulation demonstrates her intellectual autonomy and a certain confidence in the reshaping of avant-garde rhetoric. In this sense her intellectual and spatial acts articulate a sapphic modernity that is borne out of both cultural and sexual dissidence.

"There should have been a tunnel under the Rue de l'Odéon": The bookshop as "lived space" in Beach's narrative of her Left-Bank career opens with another open door; a door through which there is a space for sexual desire, companionship, and intellectual adventure—Monnier's bookshop in the "unfamiliar Odéon quarter": "As I stood near the open door, a high wind suddenly blew my Spanish hat off my head and into the middle of the street, and away it went bowling. A. Monnier rushed after it, going very fast for a person in such a long skirt. She pounced on it just as it was about to be run over, and, after brushing it off carefully, handed it to me."[41] The return of the Spanish hat represents both transaction and promise between Monnier and Beach. As Flanner notes, it will be Monnier who teaches Beach how to run a bookshop and locates the second larger premises for Shakespeare and Company in 1921.[42]

What happens to space in these interactions? In what ways might we argue that sapphists are putting space to use in order to participate in modernity? One of the most productive theoretical frameworks through which to understand these articulations of space is that of Henri Lefebvre's notions of "lived space." In *The Production of Space*, Lefebvre writes the following:

> Not so many years ago, the word "space" had a strictly geometrical meaning: the idea it evoked was simply that of an empty area. In scholarly use it was generally accompanied by some epithet as "Euclidean," "isotropic," or "infinite," and the general feeling was that the concept of space was ultimately a mathematical one. To speak of "social space," therefore, would have sounded strange.[43]

Lefebvre's endeavor is to map just this, the reality that space is in fact deeply "social." Lefebvre's analysis of space locates the effects of modernity upon our spatial practices and conceptualizations of space. For Lefebvre, the torsions and pressures of capitalism and consumerism have cut us forever adrift from what he calls "absolute space"—natural, emotionally and materially connected living within our environment. As a result, space within modernity is "flattened."

To define this effect, Lefebvre delineates his "perceived-conceived-lived triad"[44] in the following way: "perceived space" (*le perçu*) constitutes the space of the everyday and common sense, the space in which we *think* we live, "conceived space" (*le conçu*), the space of architects, urban planners, and property developers and then, most importantly, "lived space" (*le vecu*)—the conceptualization of space within the human imagination and an experience of space that not only incorporates the other two but also transcends them. Within the sociocultural context of a capitalist economy, space becomes "abstract space," that is to say, it is defined and articulated only through its exchange-value; by contrast, Lefebvre defines and celebrates the possibilities of "lived space," space that is constructed and understood through its use-value. Lefebvre's radical agenda is to foreground "lived space"—to return to thinking of space in terms of its use-value rather than the exchange-value imposed upon it within capitalist structures. The Monnier/Beach model of the bookshop would seem to be a compelling test-case for Lefebvre's notion of lived space since ostensibly, as a business enterprise, it would seem to articulate space through its exchange-value—as commercial enterprise constructed to entice consumers and their capital. Yet, as their own explications demonstrate below, the value of the space of the bookshop is far more precisely defined by its use-value. As sapphists striving to participate in cultural creation and, by extension, the terms and experience of modernity, Monnier and Beach go a considerable distance toward a Lefebvrean ideal. If "lived space" envelops and modulates both the "perceived space" of common sense and the "conceived space" enforced upon the modern subject through urban planning and architecture, what sense might we make of Beach's description of Odéonia?

> The cafés at Saint Germain des Prés in pre-Sartre-Beauvoir days were patronized by quiet literary people, though you might see Ezra Pound at the Deux Magots or Léon-Paul Fargue across the street at Lipp's. Except for our two bookshops, *where things were always happening*, our rue de l'Odéon, a few steps down from the Boulevard Saint Germain, was as restful as a little street in a provincial town. The only time there was any traffic was when the audiences on their way to or from the Odéon Theatre at the upper end of the street streamed past. [. . .] The Théâtre de l'Odéon fulfilled Adrienne's dream of living in a street "with a public building at one end."[45]

Notably, this quarter of Paris is relatively quiet, at times resembling a "provincial town"; it is their space within the microcosm of the street that most resembles the typical urban space of modernity, "things" are "always happening," there is speed, stimulation, and commercial and intellectual endeavor. The real example of Lefebvrean "lived space" is articulated here in Monnier's desire, defined by Beach, as a dream of having a "public building at one end." Here the "perceived space" of the everyday street and the "conceived space" represented by the architectural icon of culture—the theatre—amalgamate in Monnier's imagination. As Lefebvre argues, "lived space" is that which both has use-value and is imbued with lived meaning. If we extract the psychic resonances of the desire in the dream here, we might argue that Monnier seeks to utilize the signifier of theater to validate her own cultural enterprise and, perhaps more importantly, to create her own cultural "center" by undermining the hierarchies of traditional urban space.

If we attend to the question of use-value in relation to the fabricated space of Odéonia, "sapphic modernity" must undergo another modulation. How does this space function in such a way that Beach and Monnier begin to control cultural production? Something important emerges in the following statement by Beach: "Adrienne was as interested as I was in the American writers who were in and out of my bookshop, and we shared them all. *There should have been a tunnel under the rue de l'Odéon.*"[46] The metaphor of the connecting tunnel is instructive; it indicates Beach's sense of possession of both the street and the modernists frequenting it. This space certainly has use-value. Through their intervention, the rue de l' Odéon becomes the site of intense intellectual and literary endeavor and debate. It also allows both the opportunity to take part, act, generate, create. In this space, Monnier and Beach become keyplayers in the making of modernism; this is an intrinsic part of their modernity. Much has been written about the Joyce–Beach connection and the publication of one of modernism's most iconic texts, *Ulysses*, but what is compelling about Beach's account of it is the inherent spatialization at work in her narrative. In her record of their first meeting, the metaphor of the open door returns:

> It was in the summer of 1920, when my bookshop was in its first year, that I met James Joyce. One sultry afternoon, Adrienne was going to a party at André Spire's. [. . .] They had an apartment on the second floor of a house at 34 rue du Bois de Boulogne; I remember the shady trees around it. [. . .] I worshipped James Joyce, and on hearing the unexpected news that he was present, I was so frightened I wanted to run away, but Spire told me it was the Pounds who had brought the Joyces—we could see Ezra through *the open door*. I knew the Pounds, so I went in.[47]

Pound functions as the conduit that allows Beach to pass through the open door to the fateful encounter. Joyce then situates Beach in literary terms via her bookshop and agrees to visit her: "The very next day, Joyce came walking up *my steep little street* wearing a dark blue serge suit."[48] Symbolically, Beach locates and defines Joyce, in this first independent encounter, in terms of urban space: "James Joyce, 5, rue de l'Assomption, Paris; subscription for one month; seven francs."[49] As he becomes a regular patron, Beach writes: "I loved to see Joyce *walking up the street* twirling his ashplant stick, his hat on the back of his head. 'Melancholy Jesus,' Adrienne and I used to call him."[50] Importantly, Joyce in *her* street becomes "Joyce," a signifier of modernism that she (and Monnier) can empty of meaning and recalibrate—"Melancholy Jesus." The story of how *Ulysses* would not have been published without Sylvia Beach and her financial backing is a commonplace, yet it is important to see how the bookshop functions as a site in which the complex lines of connection that lead to production are drawn. Beach describes her bookshop as Joyce's "headquarters,"[51] and it is certainly through the bookshop that the question of the translation of *Ulysses* is resolved:

> The date set for the Joyce reading at Adrienne's bookshop was December 7, 1921—a little less than two months before *Ulysses* appeared.
>
> Larbaud, fearing his translations of extracts from Penelope wouldn't be ready in time, asked Adrienne to look around for someone to help him. Among those who *frequented the rue de l'Odéon* was a young composer of music, Jacques Benoist-Méchin. He and George Antheil had struck up a friendship *after meeting in my bookshop.*[52]

Notably, the bookshop is metonymically recorded by the street, but importantly too, Beach constructs her part of this space not just as a focal point for incoming connections but also as a focal point for outgoing dissemination. In an otherwise hostile literary and cultural environment, Shakespeare and Company becomes the only place from which the little magazines, those crucial organs of modernist publication, could be distributed. At its height, Shakespeare and Company was the only distribution point for all the major titles, including Eliot's *The Criterion*, Monroe's *Poetry*, Weaver's *Egoist*, Thayer's *Dial*, and Anderson's *Little Review*. Beach saw her space too as intrinsically *social*. For the many exiled modernists, Beach's space functioned as a kind of community "center":

> Shakespeare and Company was the American Express of the artists of the Left bank. We did banking, too, sometimes, and I used to call the shop "The Left Bank." Bryher thought our important postal service should have its box, and thenceforth a fine, large sort of case, with pigeonholes marked with the letters of the alphabet, made distribution of all that mail a pleasure.[53]

This image seems fittingly Lefebvrean: the "bookshop," deracinated from its traditional cultural place within commodity culture, becomes a space that serves an eclectic community of avant-garde experimentalists. Most importantly for the discussion of what sapphic modernity might be, this modern/modernist space is created and run by two women—sapphists and modernists—who were deeply committed to the processes of becoming modern and intent on playing their part within it.

In 1936, writing in *La Nouvelle Revue Française*, Adrienne Monnier records a conversation that had taken place between Sylvia Beach and André Gide eighteen months previously. The financial crisis that faced the French bookselling industry during the 1930s had hit Beach particularly hard and she was contemplating closing Shakespeare and Company. Gide reacted to this news with horror and, in his reply to Beach, articulates the central importance of this created space: " 'But that is impossible,' he said sharply. '*You play a role among us that we could not do without now. You give us invaluable help.*' "[54] The continuing project of modernism and its production is here inconceivable without the space created by the sapphic modernists and their intervention—their "role"—within the processes of becoming modern. What I have argued for Beach/Monnier's *sapphic modernity*—their careful, deliberate, and successful use of urban space in the service of modernist cultural production—is here revealed as inseparable from *all* modernity. In this sense, it stands not alone or separate but as a fundamental constituent of the landscape of the modernity of the early twentieth-century city.

Notes

1. Susan Stanford Friedman, "Definitional Excursions: The Meanings of Modern/Modernity/Modernism," *Modernism/Modernity* 8, no. 3 (September 2001): 497.
2. Andrew Barry, Thomas Osborne and Nikolas Rose, eds., *Foucault and Political Reason: Liberalism, Neo-Liberalism and Rationalities of Government* (London: UCL Press, 1996), p. 3.
3. Marshall Berman, *All That Is Solid Melts Into Air: The Experience of Modernity* (London: Verso, 1991), p. 15.
4. Edouard Glissant, *Caribbean Discourse: Selected Essays*, trans. and intro. J. Michael Dash (Charlottesville: University Press of Virginia, 1989), p. 151.
5. See Paul Gilroy, *The Black Atlantic: Modernity and Double Consciousness* (London: Verso, 1993).
6. See David Harvey, *Paris: The Capital of Modernity* (London: Routledge, 2003).
7. Andrea Weiss, *Paris Was a Woman* (London: Pandora, 1995), p. 17.
8. Natalie Barney, *Souvenirs Indiscrets* (Paris: Flammarion, 1960), p. 21.
9. See Shari Benstock, *Women of the Left Bank: Paris, 1900–1940* (London: Virago, 1987) and Gillian Hanscombe and Virginia Smyers, *Writing for their Lives: The Modernist Women, 1910–1930* (London: The Women's Press, 1987).

10. See "The Metropolis and Mental Life," in Georg Simmel, *The Sociology of Georg Simmel*, ed. and trans. Kurt H. Wolff (New York: Free Press, 1964).
11. Raymond Williams, "Metropolitan Perceptions and the Emergence of Modernism," in *The Politics of Modernism* (1989; reprint, London: Verso, 1996), p. 45.
12. Manuel Castells, *The City and the Grassroots: A Cross-Cultural Theory of Urban Social Movements* (Berkeley: University of California Press, 1983), p. 140.
13. Ibid.
14. Shari Benstock, *Women of the Left Bank: Paris, 1900–1940* (London: Virago, 1987), p. 198.
15. Ibid., p. 221.
16. See Dorothy Richardson, *Pilgrimage* (1913–56; reprint in 4 vols., London: Virago, 1979).
17. Gloria Fromm, *Dorothy Richardson: A Biography* (1977; reprint, Athens, Georgia: University of Georgia Press, 1994), p. 155.
18. Dorothy Richardson, letter to Bryher dated November 1933 (Dorothy Richardson Collection, Beinecke Rare Book and Manuscript Library, Yale University).
19. Ibid., p. 71.
20. See Steve Pile, *The Body and the City: Psychoanalysis, Space and Subjectivity* (London: Routledge, 1997), p. 15 etc.
21. See Roger M. Downs and David Stea, eds., *Image and Environment: Cognitive Mapping and Spatial Behaviour* (Chicago: Aldine, 1973) and D. J. Warmsley and G. J. Lewis, *Human Geography: Behavioural Approaches* (London: Longman, 1984). Pile *The Body and the City*, p. 27.
22. Sylvia Beach, *Shakespeare and Company* (1956; reprint, Lincoln: University of Nebraska Press, 1991), p. 99.
23. Ibid., p. 247.
24. Bryher, *The Heart to Artemis* (London: Collins, 1963), p. 211. Notably, Bryher's other coordinate in Paris was also a Sapphic space, Stein and Toklas' salon: "Apart from Shakespeare and Company, it is the long room in the rue de Fleurus that I remember most from my Paris visits," *Heart*, pp. 213–14.
25. Bryher, "For Sylvia," *Mercure de France*, 349 (August–September 1963), p. 17. Emphasis.
26. Janet Flanner, *Paris Was Yesterday*, ed. Irving Drutman, (New York: Harcourt Brace Jovanovich, 1988), pp. viii–ix. Emphasis mine.
27. Ibid., p. ix. Emphasis.
28. Gertrude Stein, "Rich and Poor in English," in *Painted Lace, and Other Writings (1914–1937)*, The Yale Edition of the Unpublished Writings of Gertrude Stein, vol. 5 (New Haven: Yale University Press, 1955), p. 95.
29. Beach, *Shakespeare and Company*, p. 28. This recurring motif of the *pavillon* is important and though there is not space to analyse it fully here, it is interesting to note that Henri Lefebvre, building on Bachelard's analysis of the house, examines the space of the *pavillon*—the detached house. Leonore et al summarise his analysis of this space thus: "The *pavillon* involves different levels, namely the appropriation of space and a utopia, which is both fiction and reality. [. . .] what

people want is to be able to hold onto and combine oppositions, such as inside/outside, intimacy and environment, and thereby reinvent a symbolic dimension." See Eleonore Kofman and Elizabeth Lebas, "Lost in Transposition," in Henri Lefebvre, *Writings on Cities*, trans. Kofman and Lebas (Oxford: Blackwell, 2000), p. 18.

30. Quoted in Introduction, Adrienne Monnier, *The Very Rich Hours of Adrienne Monnier*, trans. Richard McDougall (New York: Charles Scribner's Sons, 1976), p. 11.
31. Ibid., p. 87.
32. Quoted in translation in Christopher Butler, *Early Modernism: Literature, Music and Painting in Europe 1900–1916* (Oxford: Oxford University Press, 1994), p. 140.
33. Quoted in translation in Marjorie Perloff, *The Futurist Moment: Avant-Garde, Avant-Guerre, and the Language of Rupture* (Chicago: University of Chicago Press, 1986), p. 84.
34. Ibid., p. 69.
35. Ibid., p. 75. Emphasis mine.
36. Ibid., p. 71.
37. Gaston Bachelard, *The Poetics of Space*, trans. Maria Jolas (1958; reprint, Boston, MA: Beacon, 1994), p. 8.
38. Ibid.
39. Ibid., p. 69.
40. Ibid., Emphasis mine.
41. Ibid., p. 12.
42. See Flanner, *Paris Was Yesterday*, p. ix.
43. Henri Lefebvre, *The Production of Space*, trans. Donald Nicholson-Smith (1991; reprint, Oxford: Blackwell, 1995), p. 1.
44. Ibid., p. 40.
45. Ibid., p. 61.
46. Ibid., p. 117. Emphasis mine. This "sharing" spans out into a larger sapphic network. Noel Riley Fitch writes: "The writers who accompanied Sylvia to meet Gertrude, most of them Americans, enriched the life of the rue de Fleurus." See Noel Riley Fitch, *Sylvia Beach and the Lost Generation: a History of Literary Paris in the Twenties and Thirties* (New York and London: W. W. Norton and Company, 1983), p. 57.
47. Ibid., p. 34.
48. Ibid., p. 37. Emphasis mine.
49. Ibid., p. 40.
50. Ibid. Emphasis mine.
51. Ibid., p. 92.
52. Ibid., p. 73. Emphasis mine.
53. Ibid., p. 102.
54. Monnier, *The Very Rich Hours*, p. 135. Emphasis mine.

Chapter 2

Romaine Brooks and the Future of Sapphic Modernity

Tirza True Latimer

Remember, or failing that, invent.

—Monique Wittig, *Les Guérillières*

Consider the contradictions that the theme "sapphic modernity" articulates. The qualifier "sapphic" founds the genealogy of subjects whom we now identify as "lesbian" upon the terrain of classical antiquity. "Modernity," on the other hand, summons up the forces of expansion (colonial, urban, industrial, scientific, and technological) that have transformed Western societies over the past two centuries. The coupled term sapphic modernity holds these competing impulses—the mythical and the imminent—in tension; it harks back to the foundations of Western civilization to characterize one of the modern era's defining trends: the reclamation of cultural, social, and sexual alternatives by women.[1]

The early twentieth-century lesbian society painter Romaine Brooks harnessed such tensions—between past and present, mainstream and margin, actuality and myth, visibility and invisibility—to animate her most powerful works, including the iconic self-image that she produced in 1923 (fig. 2.1). The painter-subject's whole performance—the defiant torque of her shoulders, the sober costume with its rakishly turned collar, the unyielding set of the chin, those eyes ablaze from the shade of an outsized top hat—convinces the viewer of Brooks's social entitlement and professional stature. This near life-scale self-portrait inaugurated an artistic project that Brooks's

Fig. 2.1 Romaine Brooks, *Self-Portrait*, 1923. Credit: Smithsonian American Art Museum, gift of the artist.

lover Natalie Barney described as a "series of modern women."[2] The series provided a repertoire of countermodels to the caricatures of modern womanhood that proliferated within Parisian print culture between the two World Wars.

Popular psychologists, novelists, the authors of advice books, exposés, and gossip columns reveled in the *femme moderne* polemic. They described women demonstrating independence, strength, ambition, or accomplishment as "amazons" or "viragos"—words laced with sexual implications.[3] By 1930, thanks in part to the cumulative authority of these inflammatory terms, few women who exercised power in any walk of Parisian public life could avoid the indictment of deviance, and the concept of lesbianism doggedly shadowed that of feminism. Journalists such as Maryse Choisy routinely collapsed the economic and sexual autonomy of women into a single, global cliché:

> In Athens, as in Paris, as in New York, this "lesbisme" [*sic*] . . . is born of the woman who works, the woman who is no longer a madonna, but not yet the comrade whose independence men of breeding will respect.[4]

Sappho, represented in nineteenth-century French literature as the archetypal lesbian, was reclaimed by Choisy and her 1920s readers as "the Eve of liberated women."[5]

For Brooks too the lesbian appears to be a personification of women's liberation. By marking her portraits of modern women in ways that an initiated viewer would see as lesbian, Brooks engaged in the projection of emancipatory social, cultural, professional, and relational possibilities for all women. The artist participated, at the same time, in both the definition of the neologism "lesbian" and the elaboration of the visual codes and strategies that enabled women-loving-women of her class and generation to recognize each other and communicate across national and cultural frontiers. Choisy might have had Brooks in mind when she wrote, "There is no point in looking for Sappho in Mytilene. She is an artist. Therefore she moved to Paris."[6] By Choisy's lights, Sappho had migrated from a remote (if symbolically significant) island to the cosmopolitan capital of Western visual culture.

There, in Paris of the 1920s, Brooks labored to modify received conventions of portraiture, bringing herself and her illustrious sitters into alignment with historical and contemporary narratives of artistic genius.[7] The modern woman series amounted to a pan-European pantheon of culturally productive lesbians. The series—produced at a time when Brooks shuttled to and fro between her *pied-à-terre* in London's Tite Street and her Paris atelier—included works with titles that traversed the bounds of gender as well as nationality, titles such as *L'Amazone, Miss Natalie Barney* and *Peter, A Young Englishwoman*. This project performs the ideological work associated with portraiture from its inception: to affirm the portrait sitter's historical legitimacy, to recognize the sitter's status in the present, and to secure both the sitter's and the painter's place in posterity.

What concerns me most at present is the third dimension of the portraitist's challenge: that is, the afterlife of the portrait, the painter, and the portrait sitter. What initiatives did Brooks take, in the mature phases of her career, to assure the survival of her oeuvre, and thus the survival of this new "species" of portrait subject (the modern Sappho), which she undertook to represent? What traces did these initiatives leave?

Among the diverse framing devices conceived by Brooks to influence the conditions of reception for her work in the present as well as in the future, she produced (with Barney) a monograph, *Romaine Brooks: Portraits, tableaux, dessins,* containing portraits from the modern women series and selected critical excerpts.[8] The booklet's soft gray cover, which recalls the painter's palette and with it her reputation as a "peintre des gris harmonieux," features a photogravure of the artist's most widely recognized work, her 1923 self-portrait (fig. 2.2).

The self-portrait projects the artist's image into the future while presiding over the past achievements documented between the catalogue's covers. The simplification of form here, the effects of contrast, in addition to the portrait subject's iconic bearing, invest the cover image with a kind of graphic legibility, iconographic potency, and artistic self-assurance. The critic Claude Roger-Marx, who reviewed Brooks's work at its apogee during the 1910s and 1920s, used the word "effigy" rather than "portrait image" or "likeness" to describe the picture on the cover of the monograph.[9] The term, in French usage as in English, denotes a likeness representing a despised person or type. This choice of words undoubtedly appealed to Brooks, who, while seeking the limelight, paradoxically identified herself—in the tradition of aesthetes such as the martyred Oscar Wilde and the irascible James Abbott McNeill Whistler—as a "lapidé," a misfit, an outcast (literally, a victim of stoning).[10]

"Effigy" can also be taken more loosely to mean a symbol or logo. Brooks's self-portrait, reproduced in reviews of the work that she exhibited internationally in the 1920s, circulated in the pages of widely read publications such as *Le Figaro, Bulletin des Arts, Sketch, Revue de l'art, L'Art et les artistes, Vogue,* and *International Studio.*[11] The portrait image assumed the status of a trademark representing, in addition to the painter and her portrait oeuvre, a new class of self-identified lesbian cultural producers and underwriters, many of whom we find commemorated in the monograph. The members of this elite and highly mobile society included the French author Elisabeth de Gramont, the English painter Gluck, the Russian dancer Ida Rubinstein, the American decorator Elsie de Wolfe, Radclyffe Hall's English

Fig. 2.2 Front Cover, *Romaine Brooks: Portraits, tableaux, dessins*, featuring the artist's 1923 self-portrait.

lover and biographer Una Troubridge, the Italian pianist Renata Borgatti, and, of course, Parisian expatriate par excellence Natalie Barney—all figures of prominence in cosmopolitan lesbian society of the interwar period.

The critical observations that Brooks chose to reprint in the monograph characterize her work in terms more typically invoked by contemporary reviewers to extol the achievements of male artists, as opposed to the descriptive vocabulary associated with the so-called *femme-peintre*. These excerpts describe Brooks's painting as "original," "innovative," "vigorous," "penetrating," "cerebral," "precise," "affirmed," "sober," "rigorous," and "masterful."[12] In contrast, the esthetic of the stereotypical woman painter, as described by period reviewers, married "good taste . . . with delicacy." Her approach was "light-hearted," rather than sober, "intuitive" rather than cerebral.[13]

The critic Louis Vauxcelles, cited in the monograph, suggests that Brooks's "singular" nature (her lesbianism? her genius?) exempted her from the category of femme—and by extension from the category of *femme-peintre*. "The nature of the artist is singular," he alerts the reader, "marked by a cold perversity, a bit literary. Her drawing is firm, muscular, the composition always willful, leaving nothing to chance."[14] Roger-Marx viewed Brooks's work through a similar lens, comparing her portraits of Barney's lesbian salon society to the contemporaneous enterprise of Marcel Proust—at once thoroughly decadent and radically new.[15] Regarding Brooks's self-portrait, Roger-Marx exclaimed, "This top hat that overshadows a feminine face, these gloved hands, this virile costume recalls the most daring descriptions in *À la Recherche du temps perdu*."[16] Brooks's pictorial representations, as described by Roger-Marx, operate according the same "open-secret" logic that characterized Parisian cultures of same-sex desire in the Proustian era.[17] Similarly, the evocations of homosexual celebrities from Proust to Wilde that punctuate the period literature on Brooks catch the eye of the knowing reader/viewer while preserving a decorous margin of ambiguity.

While Brooks vied with her portraits of modern women to personify a sort of lesbian decadent aristocracy (analogous to the *haute homosexualité* of Robert de Montesquiou and Proust), she and Barney plotted to make a place in history for the portrait oeuvre and deliver it whole to posterity. Barney, in her literary portrait "Romaine Brooks: The Case of a Great Painter of the Human Face," made the immortalizing claim that her lover "belongs to no time, to no country, to no milieu, to no school to no tradition . . . .She is the epitome . . . of a civilization in decline, whose character she was able to capture."[18] For Barney, Brooks—as a modern woman, as a privileged member of Paris's expatriate society, as a lesbian artist-genius—represented a new species, the most refined and attenuated product of

Western civilization. The past and present converge in Barney's literary portrait of Brooks, a portrait (like the monograph) created for the benefit of both present and future "viewers."

Turning to the back cover of Brooks's monograph (fig. 2.3), we find a visual resumé of the Great Painter's portrait career. Eighteen faces, thumbnail details of paintings reproduced in the volume, frame the roster of Brooks's prestigious sitters, many of whom attended the weekly salon that Barney hosted from the first decade of the twentieth century until the 1960s. The subject of the monograph herself, "*L'Artiste Romaine Brooks*," tops the roll of honor, under the heading "Personnages d'une Époque." The painter, who was never obliged by financial imperatives to sell her work, conserved almost all of these portraits in her studio. She and Barney used the monograph as a promotional device in a protracted campaign to lodge the entire collection in the Smithsonian Museum, the Fort Knox of the American cultural economy. Having, like Whistler, made her name abroad, she meant to reclaim her birthright as an American phenomenon.

The Smithsonian's director approved the acquisition of several portraits but warned his head curator, "We should go easy on getting too many R. Brooks paintings; she will push hard for a whole gallery of her own!"[19] That was precisely what Brooks and Barney had in mind—and their agenda was even more ambitious. They also brought pressure to bear upon the director to publish Brooks's memoirs, "No Pleasant Memories," a hyperbolic account of the artist's evolution as an esthete and genius. The 1923 self-portrait could serve, they advanced, as the book's cover image.[20]

The first letters preserved in American Art Museum accession files concerning this master plan date from June 1933. Brooks had by then virtually stopped painting. In her sixties, she was looking back (polishing off her memoirs) and looking forward (exploring options for their publication). In New York, where she lived off and on from 1933 until America declared war on Germany (when she, bucking the trend, returned to Europe), Brooks hired a literary agent. In 1934, she reported to Barney that the agent had proposed the manuscript to a number of publishers but that it had not been well received. An editor at Knopf, for instance, had balked at the title "No Pleasant Memories," which the editor believed set the reader on "a downward trend" right from page one. According to Brooks, it was this editor's professional opinion "that at this present moment people want what uplifts them." "This is comprehensible," she admitted, given the tumultuous state of both domestic and international affairs, "but I think it better not to have the work published rather than change the character of the title."[21] She remained intransigent.

Fig. 2.3 Back Cover, *Romaine Brooks: Portraits, tableaux, dessins.*

The writer Carl Van Vechten, who sat for one of Brooks's last oil portraits in New York in 1936, was even less enthusiastic about the manuscript. Brooks confided to Barney,

> He remains intensely wary because of my, perhaps, future name as a painter and [the fact that the writing was] expressly done in a very simple way. No, he does not like the treatment which he says shows that I don't know how to write: 'you are a good painter Romaine but not a good writer.' Curiously enough, this verdict has spurred me on to finish the book.[22]

Most of Brooks's activities during her years in New York relate in some way to her "future name as a painter." However, her exhibitions during this period do not feature her paintings, but rather her small-scale line drawings. The catalogue essay for a show of fifty drawings held at the Arts Club of Chicago in 1935 announced, "Romaine Brooks has now turned from portrait painting . . . to enter a domain of fantasy all her own. For some time in the past, in the intervals of writing her memoirs, she has been doing line drawings."[23] In fact, she created several of these drawings as illustrations for her memoirs.

Her letters to Barney from New York are full of ambivalence about painting. She was not satisfied with the way Van Vechten's portrait looked. She was too exhausted, too uninspired, to finish the portrait she had begun of Muriel Draper, whose Wednesday afternoon salon in Manhattan provided an American counterpart to Barney's Friday gatherings in Paris. The unfinished Draper canvas reproached Brooks from the easel where it stood week in and week out, until one day she declared the portrait—whose curvilinear outlines relate this work to the drawings—done. "I'm tired of keeping my portraits around," she exclaimed, uncharacteristically. "I can't hang them in studio as they do not go with [my] drawings."[24]

The reference here is to a half a dozen line drawings that Brooks had projected and traced on the white walls of her studio apartment over Carnegie Hall. The enlarged tracings—symbolic of the painful relational configurations that titles such as "Double Bondage," "Breaking Apart," and "Dreams Reclaimed by Day" suggest—set the tone for the apartment's unsettling decor. "I was . . . trying to make my surroundings coincide with some disturbing significance within my artist's brain," she explained with respect to her interior decorative initiatives, of which this New York apartment would be the last.[25] Brooks described these line drawings, traced in the manner of automatic writing without lifting the pencil from the page (or, again, the crayon from the wall), as "inevitable."[26] "They evolve from the sub-conscious. Without premeditation, they aspire to a maximum of expression with a minimum of means."[27] Magnified, the deft line drawings created a mural program that Brooks believed adapted to "New York's atmosphere of modernity."[28]

Yet, with her European boarding-school education and her Grand-Tour training as an artist, Brooks could not have helped but recall a legend about the origin of Western painting as she outlined the figures projected on her apartment walls. Wittingly or unwittingly, she rehearsed the gesture of Dibutade, a Corinthian maiden who (according to Pliny the Elder) preserved the trace of a departing lover by outlining the shadow that he cast upon her wall.[29]

Here in Manhattan, during a period of estrangement from Barney, the artist made no attempt to replicate the atmosphere of her Paris apartment, where life-scale portraits locked eyes across chambers furnished in black lacquer, white porcelain, and "grey rugs, bordered in black like funeral announcements."[30] Robert de Montesquiou applauded the dramatic effects created by Brooks's use of black, white, and grey "not only in her paintings, but in her apartments and studios."[31] Ferdinand Bac too recalled the artist's residence in Paris. In his memoir *La Fin des "temps délicieux"* he wrote, "Mme Brooks has created a decor in harmony with her paintings. Everything is in black and white, from the concierge up to the attic. The apartment is a mournful symphony."[32]

Photographs of the New York apartment reveal a quite different black and white environment. There are no paintings in sight, only enlargements of Brooks's drawings. We see, for instance, a drawing titled "Time Divides" centered on the wall above a modern-style couch (fig. 2.4). The drawing, exhibited at Paris's Galerie Briant in 1931 and again at the Arts Club of Chicago in 1935, was one of the few selected by the artist for reproduction in the self-celebratory monograph. It represents a threesome—two women, arms encircling each other's shoulders, foreheads touching, wedged apart from below by a winged personification of time, an androgynous sprite who issues from the very center of the couple as if by monstrous birth. Time's widening limbs cleave the lovers' embrace, holding their bodies apart in isometric tension, while at the same time bridging the distance between them. Like Brooks's eternal black wardrobe and her dark painter's palette, the drawing seems to formalize some unresolved (and unresolvable) grief. On one level, the composition—with its motifs of separation and enclosure, temporality and stasis—could be viewed as emblematic of the couple that the artist formed with Barney, who remained in Paris writing melancholic letters to Brooks almost daily during this period. More broadly, both the iconography and line trace a continuum between *l'amour impossible* and *le deuil impossible*, melancholia for a passion that cannot abide in time, or in history—that is to say, in the space of representation.

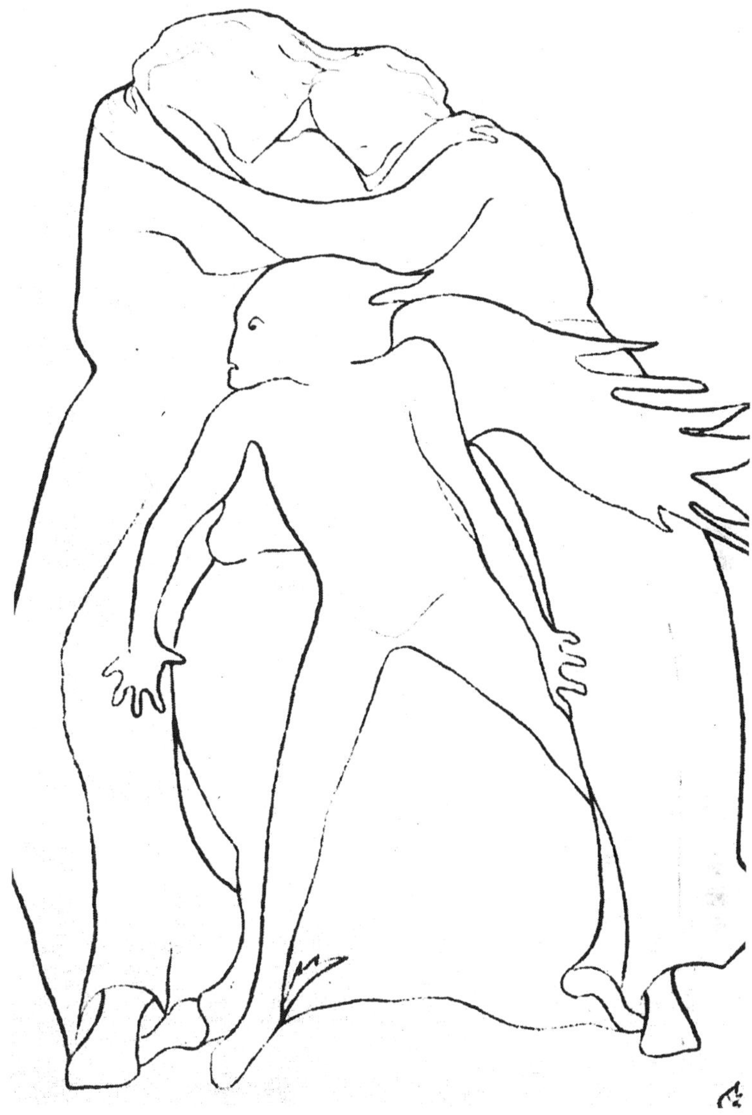

Fig. 2.4 Romaine Brooks, *Le Temps sépare* (Time Divides), c. 1930, reproduced in *Romaine Brooks: Portraits, tableaux, dessins.*

"These drawings should be *read*," Brooks claimed relating the project, with its cursive character, to her self-representational efforts as a memoir writer.[33] Indeed the drawings seem intimately attached, via the pencil that never leaves the page, to the gesturing hand of artist, as if to reiterate visions embedded in her psyche. Perhaps the shift in creative emphasis that takes place during Brooks's stay in New York—the changes of style, subject, and medium—parallels shifts in her self-image as a lover of women and an artist. Correspondence from this period repeatedly evokes her obsession with the drawings, her failed attempts to paint, her failure to publish "No Pleasant Memories," her failing health, her frustrated efforts to interest a major museum in her work, and her alienation from Barney's circle of Paris lesbians—intuitively linking these circumstances, as I do here.

One of the artist's letters, written in the late 1930s to Bryher (another prominent lesbian cultural activist), contained a copy of what may be the last self-portrait ever produced by Brooks: a snapshot catching the artist's long shadow, stretched across the grid-like pavement separating two wings of the retreat, Trait d'union [hyphen: mark of both separation and union], where Brooks and Barney reunited periodically during the early 1930s (fig. 2.5). The camera, poised on a tripod, frames the view from somewhere near the heart of the photographer's body. Her trousered legs, stance braced, feet spread, give Brooks's shadowy silhouette a triangular shape akin to that of the tripod itself and that of Time as pictured in the drawing. The signature "Romaine!" penned in the lower right-hand corner of the print marks the point where the shadow and its maker would meet were it not for the cropping of the camera's frame.

This shadow conjures up the artist's unseen body just as the continuous line drawings evoke the moving hand from which they issued. However, if the line drawings make manifest the artist's "disturbed" psyche (as she herself suggests), the attendant shadow here represents something different—perhaps, as per established iconographic conventions, the subject's troubled spirit or soul. Otto Rank, in his pathbreaking 1914 study *Don Juan et le Double*, considers representational devices such as the shadow, a form of body double, evidence of the psyche's "energetic refutation of the rule of death."[34] The same can be said of portraiture, mistrusted in some cultures for its ability to usurp the subject's spirit. Indeed, Brooks's portraits were specifically described (by Montesquiou and others) as "cambrioleurs d'âmes," theives of souls, for their uncanniness—the way that the portrait subjects seemed to stare back at (or even stare down) the viewer.[35] Photography too originally provoked awe and suspicion as a stealer of images—thus, a thief of souls. References to the soul (afterlife of the body),

Fig. 2.5 Romaine Brooks, untitled self-portrait, c.1938. Credit: The Beinecke Rare Book and Manuscript Library, Yale University.

and to the lost or stolen soul, accumulate in this image of Brooks: portrait, photograph, shadow, attenuation.

When Brooks slipped this portrait into a note of thanks to Bryher for contacting several prospective publishers on her behalf,[36] she knew that her friend would fully appreciate the implications of her choice of mediums: photography, which Baudelaire had famously described as the "last refuge of the failed painter."[37] The term *skiagraphia* (shadow writing) had been used by Henry Fox Talbot in the 1830s to describe the process that he innovated to capture a negative image on a paper.[38] The negative, a "drawing" made by what Fox Talbot described as the "pencil of light," served "to produce a second drawing, in which the light and shadows would be reversed."[39] The black and white photograph of Brooks's shadow seems to play with these notions of drawing, of projection, and of photographic reversal, as if her shadow were a negative that could be used to infinitely reproduce a durable image of the absent original.

A shadow of her former self, Brooks appears to muse here upon a declining moment in her portrait career, upon her legacy as an important painter (one who contrived to cast a long shadow). Via this identification with the shadowy trace, she glosses the art historical record, evoking portraiture's mythical originator, the maiden Dibutade, not to mention Plato's cave. She may have been thinking of another legendary female portraitist too: Elisabeth Vigée-Lebrun, one of the first women admitted to the French Royal Academy and a favorite of Marie-Antoinette. Vigée-Lebrun's remarkable self-portrait of 1790, which Brooks would have studied in Florence's Uffizi Gallery, draws the viewer's eyes to the point at which the tip of the artist's brush joins its own shadow cast upon the plane of representation, poised as if to perform an impossible act of self-mimesis by tracing its own contour.

Perhaps, with her own shadow play, Brooks reflects upon the feints and limitations of representation—and, more specifically, the paradoxes of *self*-representation by women of her generation, who remained socially and politically disenfranchised. The shadow offers an adequate metaphor, in any case, for the dusky zones between visibility and invisibility, absence and presence, that she and other lesbians of her milieu explored in both their private scenarios of seduction and their negotiations with the wider world. Scholars from Terry Castle to Annamarie Jagose have described the lesbian, historically, as "a presence that can't be seen."[40] Lesbian presence *can* be seen, of course, but often—and this certainly pertains to Brooks, her portraiture, and her art-historical profile—only by those who know how (and where) to look.

If invisibility has played a strategic role in the survival of lesbian relationships and cultures under fundamentally hostile circumstances, it has also played a significant role in the maintenance of heterosexual hierarchies.[41] Yet visibility creates its own (nearly identical) set of dilemmas, as a cartoon published in the trendy 1920s magazine *Fantasio* suggests (fig. 2.6). A couple of women—smoking, sporting the latest fashions, sharing an *apèritif* at a sidewalk café—are approached by an alluring third party (another woman). The cartoon's heading, "L'Eternel ménage à trois," identifies the theme, while its caption, ". . . Mais les éléments ne sont plus les mêmes," comments upon the variation. "But what does it matter," the satirist seems to ask, "who plays the parts, as long as the roles themselves don't change?" On the one hand, as Martha Gever has shown in a recent study of lesbian celebrity, "visibility may disrupt or contradict received ideas and accepted beliefs. It may propose new kinds of social categories or inject new meanings into old ones. On the other hand, such contests often extend the reach of dominant forces"—in that the theater of the visible is where dominance premiers, and where it casts its subjects.[42]

Does Brooks's photographic memento recapitulate or finesse the double binds of visibility? She presents us with a shadowy double that projects itself, between the converging orthogonals of the pavement at her feet, into a single vanishing point. That point marks the artist's head, site of her failing creative vision and her failing eyesight—and thus, the site of what the artist had yet to see upon her historical horizon: the "future society" of Sapphos and Amazons that she and Barney had envisioned.[43] The vertex of Brooks's triangular trace barely penetrates the horizon marked by the joint between the pavement and the wall. Is her figure breaking the horizon line or sinking beneath it? Is the light, low behind her, cast by the rising or the setting sun? She leaves these questions hanging. This intimate self-representational statement articulates the artist's ambivalent mode of operation (courting the light of public recognition while retreating into the shadows) as well as her stance as a standard-bearer for what might be described, oxymoronically, as a class of singular women: Modern Sapphos.

Twenty-three paintings representing this population and forty-one of Brooks's drawings were ultimately acquired by the American Art Museum. They typically hang—not in a gallery of their own—but rather in storage racks or curatorial quarters, as if to respect the conditions of visible invisibility that shaped their production. Yet the very fact of the work's institutional accession brings this oeuvre to fruition by making a past for the future society that Brooks and Barney envisioned. "Making a past for the future," what is more, describes the strategic logic of the collective project that we identify as sapphic modernity.

Fig. 2.6 Gerda Wegner, "L'Etérnel ménage à trois," published in *Fantasio*, 1926.

Notes

1. Laura Doan begins to map out the territory that this formulation takes into its sweep. In defining the concept "sapphic modernity," Doan builds on and modifies a term coined by Shari Benstock: "sapphic modernism." See Doan, "Introduction," *Fashioning Sapphism: The Origins of a Modern English Lesbian Culture* (New York: Columbia University Press, 2001), pp. xi–xxiii; Benstock, "Expatriate Sapphic Modernism: Entering Literary History," in Karla Jay and Joanne Glasgow, eds., *Lesbian Texts and Contexts: Radical Revisions* (New York: New York University Press, 1990), pp. 183–203.
2. Undated letter from Natalie Barney to Romaine Brooks, Fonds Natalie Clifford Barney, Bibliothèque Littéraire Jacques Doucet, Paris [hereafter FNCB, BLJD], NCB.C2.2996.38–39.
3. Pierre Vachet, *L'Inquiétude sexuelle* (Paris: Grasset, 1927) and Henri Drouin, *Femmes damnées* (Paris: NRF/Gallimard, 1929) participate in the explosive development of a popular genre of "expert-opinion" books on sexuality arising in response, Vachet explained, to the influx of "ménages de femmes" evident in postwar Paris. Vachet, p. 156. At the same time, journalists like Maryse Choisy (in "Femmes seules," *Le Rire*, May 21, 1932) went "under cover" to report on these emerging sexual subsultures while others, such as Marise Querlin, commented upon homosexual practices that transpired, with increasing frequency, in plain sight. *Il est de toute évidence que ces pratiques sont devenues courantes depuis la dernière guerre et que ceux qui s'y livrent le font ouvertement.* Marise Querlin, *Femmes sans hommes: Choses vues* (Paris: Editions de France, 1931), p. 48.
4. Maryse Choisy, *Un Mois chez les hommes* (Paris: Editions de France, 1929), p. 222. *À Ahtènes, comme à Paris, comme à New York, ce 'lesbisme' (qu'on ne connaît plus à Lesbos) naît chez la femme qui travaille, la femme qui n'est plus une madone, et pas encore la camarade dont l'homme bien élevé respecte l'indépendance.*
5. Maryse Choisy, "Dames seules," *Le Rire*, numéro spécial, May 21, 1932, p. 3.
6. Ibid.
7. See Whitney Chadwick, "Amazons and Heroes: Romaine Brooks and Her World," *Amazons in the Drawing Room: The Art of Romaine Brooks* (Berkeley and Los Angeles: University of California Press, 2000), pp. 10–39; Bridget Elliott, "Performing the Picture or Painting the Other: Romaine Brooks, Gluck and the Question of Decadence in 1923," in Katy Deepwell, ed., *Women Artists and Modernism* (Manchester and New York: Manchester University Press, 1998), pp. 70–82; Tirza True Latimer, "Looking Like a Lesbian: Portraiture and Sexual Identity in 1920s Paris," in Whitney Chadwick and Tirza True Latimer, eds., *The Modern Woman Revisited: Paris between the Wars* (New Brunswick, NJ: Rutgers University Press, 2003), pp. 129–43.
8. *Romaine Brooks: Portraits, tableaux, dessins* (Paris: Braun et Cie., 1952). Barney's sister Laura Dreyfus Barney and Laura Barney's brother-in-law, Carle Dreyfus (a curator of the Louvre) also had a hand in the production of Brooks's monographic booklet.

9. Claude Roger-Marx, "Personnages d'une époque," unreferenced, undated, clipping conserved in Brooks's press book, Archives of American Art [hereafter AAA], Smithsonian, reel # 5134, "Research Material on Romaine Brooks: Scrapbook, c.1910–35. *Marcel Proust et Colette n'eussent-ils pas désiré, pour un de leurs livres, l'effigie reproduite sur la couverture de la monographie que Natalie Barney vient de faire éditer chez Braun à la gloire de son amie Romaine Brooks?*
10. Brooks must have been pleased to find a London studio in Tite Street, knowing that Wilde and Whistler had shared the address. For an insightful discussion of Brooks's relationship to dandy-aestheticism, see Joe Lucchesi's article " 'The Dandy in Me': Romaine Brooks's 1923 Portraits," in Susan Fillin-Yeh, ed., *Dandies: Fashion and Finesse in Art and Culture* (New York and London: New York University Press, 2001), pp. 153–84.
11. Arsène Alexandre, "Exposition Américaine du Luxembourg," *Le Figaro*, October 20, 1919; Alexandre, "Les Salons de 1920: Société Nationale des Beaux-Arts," *Le Figaro*, April 14, 1920; image reproduced in *Bulletin de l'art* (April 1925), "Lit Tout, Renseigne Sur Tout" press service cutting, n.p.; 1923 image reproduced in *Revue de l'art* (April 1925), "Lit Tout, Renseigne Sur Tout" press service cutting, n.p.; image reproduced in *Sketch* (June 17, 1925), "Lit Tout, Renseigne Sur Tout" press service cutting, n.p.; Gustave Kahn, "Romaine Brooks," *L'Art et les artistes*, 37 (Mai 1923): 307–14; Jean La Porte, "Romaine Brooks Interprète de la Sensibilité Internationale," *Vogue* [Paris], June 1, 1925, pp. 34, 76; John Usher, "A True Painter of Personality," *International Studio* (February 1926): 46–50.
12. Louis Vauxcelles, Arsène Alexandre, Claude Roger-Marx, Guillaume Apollinaire, Albert Flament, cited in *Romaine Brooks: Portraits, tableaux, dessins*, pp. 48–52.
13. Guillaume Apollinaire, in "Les Peintresses, chroniques d'art," *Le Petit Bleu*, April 5, 1912. n.p.
14. Vauxcelles, *Gil Blas*, May 14, 1910; excerpted in *Romaine Brooks: Portraits, tableaux, dessins*, pp. 48–49.
15. Proust's *À la Recherche du temps perdu* was published in the 1920s when Brooks was painting her modern women.
16. Claude Roger-Marx, "Personnages d'une époque," n.p. *Ce chapeau haut de forme qui surplombe un visage feminin, ces mains gantées, ce costume viril rappellent certaines descriptions les plus effrontées de À la recherche du temps perdu.*Elisabeth Ladenson has convincingly argued that lesbianism bears the full representational burden, in Proust's work, of same-sex desire (*homo*-sexuality), in that sexual relations between men, in contrast to those between women, are described exclusively in terms of sexual inversion, which preserves the heterosexual schema. See Elisabeth Ladenson, *Proust's Lesbianism* (Ithaca: Cornell University Press, 1999).
17. See Eve Kosofsky, *Epistemology of the Closet* (Berkeley and Los Angeles: California University Press, 1990) for an elaboration of the argument that "the history, like the cultures, of same-sex desire is structured by its distinctive public/private status, at once marginal and central," i.e., an "open-secret structure," p. 22.

18. Natalie Clifford Barney, *Aventures de l'esprit* (Paris: Emile-Paul Frères, 1929), p. 180.
19. David Scott to Richard Wunder, undated memo, accession files, Brooks, AAM, Smithsonian.
20. Brooks to Wunder, August 10, 1966; accession files, Brooks, AAM, Smithsonian. Barney had earlier imposed upon Ambassador Bruce to help her find a London publisher for this manuscript. Bruce contacted Weidenfeld and Nicolson about this matter. Referenced in letter from Richard Wunder to Natalie Barney, July 29, 1966, accession files, Brooks, AAM, Smithsonian.
21. Letter dated December 15, 1934, NY, St. Moritz on the Park, NYC. FNCB, BLJD, Paris. Brooks, letters to Natalie Barney. NCB.2.2445, 86–107.
22. Letter dated December 15, 1934, NY, St. Moritz on the Park, NYC. FNCB, BLJD, Paris. Brooks, letters to Natalie Barney. NCB.2.2445, 108–28.
23. *Original Drawings by Romaine Brooks* (Chicago: Arts Club of Chicago, 1935), n.p.
24. Letter dated April 25, 1937. FNCB, BLJD, Paris. Brooks, letters to Natalie Barney. NCB.2.2445, 108–28.
25. Brooks, "No Pleasant Memories," Unpublished manuscript, c. 1930. AAA, Smithsonian, Washington DC, typescript p. 211.
26. Brooks, cited by Edouard MacAvoy, "Romaine Brooks," *Bizarre*, no. 46 (March 1968): 8.
27. Brooks, *Original Drawings by Romaine Brooks*, n.p.
28. Brooks, cited by Blandine Chavanne and Bruno Gaudichon, "Romaine Brooks Décoratrice," in *Romaine Brooks (1874–1970)* (Poitiers: Musée Saint-Croix, 1987), p. 78.
29. Pliny the Elder, *Natural History*, XXXV.
30. Montesquiou, "Cambrioleurs d'âmes," *Le Figaro*, May 1910, n.p. Clipping, Brooks's pressbook, AAA, Smithsonian, reel #5134. "Research Material on Romaine Brooks: Scrapbook, c.1910–35."
31. Montesquiou, "Cambrioleurs d'âmes," n.p.
32. Ferdinand Bac, "Le Blanc et noir de Romaine Brooks," *La Fin des "temps délicieux"* (Paris: Hachette, 1935), p. 111.
33. Brooks, *Original Drawings by Romaine Brooks*, n.p.
34. Otto Rank, cited by Victor I Stoichita, in *A Short History of the Shadow* (London: Reaktion, 1999), p. 138.
35. Montesquiou, "Cambrioleurs d'âmes," n.p.
36. Brooks, undated letter to Bryher (c.1938), Beinecke Rare Books and Manuscript Library, Yale University; Bryher Papers Gen Mss 97; Series I, correspondence (incoming); Box 5, Folder 191.
37. Charles Baudelaire, "Salon de 1859, Le Public moderne et la photographie," *Oeuvres complètes* (Paris: Bibliothèque de la Pléiade/Gallimard, 1954), p. 770.
38. The ancient Greeks employed the term with reference to painting.
39. William Henry Fox Talbot, notebooks, cited by Beaumont Newhall, *The History of Photography* (Boston, New York, Toronto: Bullfinch Press/Little, Brown and Company, 1993), p. 20. Fox Talbot, who conceived of a way of fixing images on a paper negative in 1835, titled his 1844 book of photographs

The Pencil of Nature. Light projected an image through the eye of the camera onto a chemically treated paper screen producing, in Fox Talbot's view, an unmediated image of the natural world, an indexical image.

40. Annamarie Jagose describes "the ambivalent relationship between the lesbian and the field of vision." See Jagose, *Inconsequence: Lesbian Representation and the Logic of Sexual Sequence* (Ithaca and London: Cornell University Press, 2002), pp. 2–3. Terry Castle argues that lesbians in our culture are hidden in plain sight, a premise upon which Jagose builds. See Castle, *The Apparitional Lesbian: Female Homosexuality and Modern Culture* (New York: Columbia University Press, 1993).
41. Invisibility, which serves as the enabling condition of visibility's coherence, closes the circuit of representation around legitimate modalities of gender and sexuality while denying representational space to potential alternatives. Yet, in so far as visibility implies legibility, achieving visibility necessarily calls for the reiteration (whether by opposition or affirmation) of established visual and social conventions—and therefore dominant power relations. See Peggy Phelan, in *Unmarked: The Politics of Performance* (London and New York: Routledge, 1993).
42. Martha Gever, *Entertaining Lesbians: Celebrity, Sexuality, and Self-Invention* (New York and London: Routledge, 2003), pp. 22–23.
43. *Les Chansons de Bilitis*, a collection of neo-sapphic poems that found favor with the members of Barney's circle, bore the dedication "to the young women of the future society." Pierre Louÿs, dedication, *Les Chanson de Bilitis* (Paris: Librairie de L'Art Indépendant, 1895), n.p. *Ce petit livre d'amour antique est dédié respectueusement aux jeunes filles de la société future.*

Chapter 3

"The Woman Who Does": A Melbourne Motor Garage Proprietor

Georgine Clarsen

In the years immediately following World War I, Alice Anderson ran a motor garage in the middle-class Melbourne suburb of Kew.[1] Over the next seven years—until her death in 1926—the women of the Alice Anderson Motor Service became the favored "machinists" and "chauffeuses" of wealthy eastern suburbs households and taught countless Melbourne women to drive. "Most people have seen her neatly uniformed chauffeurs leap briskly from the driver's seat, open the door and salute smartly," wrote one Melbourne newspaper.[2] The Alice Anderson Motor Service continued after her death, surviving into the early 1940s, when the staff left for military service in the next war.

This chapter presents Alice Anderson's garage as a site in which young Australian women sought meaningful work within a new technological domain and an emerging nexus of private consumption. In locating themselves within the domain of automobiles, which by the first decade of the twentieth century was becoming one of the sexiest of modern technologies, the women worked to make less viable men's exclusive claim to the fantasies of power and narratives of desire that so quickly came to adhere to automobile technology.[3] Most importantly, this chapter considers the Alice Anderson Motor Service as a place where new female identities were opened to public exploration and expression.

My reading of the garage relies on discontinuous scraps of evidence, as Alice Anderson and the other women who worked there left little indication of how they understood their lives and how they might wish to be remembered.

Newspaper reports, photographs, and recent oral testimony offered by Alice Anderson's sisters and women who had worked at the garage present the usual challenges to the feminist historian. Even more difficult is to retrospectively tease out a subtle and tentative thread of early twentieth-century lesbian history, without becoming paralyzed by impossible requirements to "prove" a fixed identity within what was a shifting field of sexual identities, discourses, and practices—a grounding in certainty, a which is rarely demanded of histories that assume a heterosexual subject.

What follows is a story, steeped in its own historical moment and location, of the ways in which the Alice Anderson Motor Service enabled, and for a brief time even made respectable, a highly public exploration of youthful female masculinity that was celebrated as stylish and enviable by contemporary observers in the immediate postwar years. It is a story of women engaged in a public performance, newly available to middle-class women, that revolved around the pleasures of self-reliant mobility, independence from men, escape from surveillance, new bodily comportments, access to valued knowledge, female solidarity, cross-dressing, playing with tools, the thrills of speed—in short, the joys of being daring, advanced, and outrageous. And for those "in the know," and those motivated to recognize it, their acts of gender-bending opened fresh conditions of possibility for the constitution of a new category of sexual identity. It was the garage that a new kind of lesbian subjectivity began to coalesce—not within the cramped space of the medical, moral, or criminal discourses that had captured the field, but around some of the possibilities and pleasures that characterized that moment of twentieth-century Australian modernity.

Garages such as the Alice Anderson Motor Service were not as rare as masculinist motoring histories would suggest. From the very earliest days, when the technology was unfamiliar to both men and women of privilege, numbers of women expressed great enthusiasm for automobiles. Women signed up for driving lessons, demanded courses in mechanical instruction, and tried to find ways to earn their living as chauffeurs, mechanics, tour operators, and car sales-women. And even though it is extraordinarily difficult to trace their ephemeral businesses so long after the fact, there is evidence to suggest that many Western cities could boast of at least one women's motor garage and taxi service from the 1910s until the 1930s, and occasionally beyond.

If women's early engagements with automobiles are only now being considered in automobile histories, the ways in which emergent lesbian identities were articulated through the pleasures and practicalities of automobility remains entirely neglected, though some literary accounts of lesbian identity explore the connections. In *The Well of Loneliness*, Radclyffe Hall invokes the motorcar as a vehicle of the aristocratic Stephen Gordon's movement from inchoate longings into a self-conscious knowledge of same-sex desire. Stephen's first love affair, at the turn of the twentieth century, was marked by her transition from accomplished horsewoman into early motorist. In practical terms, owning a motorcar that she herself was able to maintain and chauffeur, was central not only to her first encounter with Angela Crossby, but also to engineering their escape from the surveillance of Angela's husband. In Hall's narrative, Stephen's car enabled the women to meet frequently, alone, and to travel to "places where lovers might sit."[4] And years later, it was her work as an ambulance driver on the French front that led Stephen to Mary Llewellen, whom she would come to love and live with when the war was over.

War service, female masculinity, lesbian identity, and automobiles were also linked in the motor garages that prepared British women drivers and mechanics for military and civilian employment. Garages such as the Hon. Miss Gabrielle Borthwick's Ladies' Automobile Workshops in Brick Street Piccadilly, Miss C. Griff's Piccadilly Workshops in Dover Street, and the Women's Volunteer Reserve Workshop in Cromwell Mews operated throughout the war and were joined by new garages opened by women demobilized from military transport units. Such businesses were enabled by the discursive climate of "women's right to work" campaigns, the major focus of British feminism after suffragists suspended their demands for voting rights in favor of women's participation in the war effort. Feminist magazines, such as *Common Cause*, *Vote*, *Women's Industrial News*, and *Woman Engineer*, published feature articles about the garages, advertised their services, and helped to organize a union for women drivers, mechanics, and garage employees.[5]

In part, women's motor garages based their appeal on Victorian values, seeking to cater to older notions of elite female respectability—it being more "suitable" for women to be chauffeured or taught to drive by other women. But there were other distinctly forward-looking and modernist elements to those enterprises, which garage women and their customers deliberately courted. One of the most outrageous—"X Garage" as it was named in joking reference to its unknown quantity—was energized by the *frisson* of stylish female masculinity and sexual indeterminacy that characterized some of the wealthiest social circles in those years. Four women demobilized from the Women's Legion Mechanical Transport Section founded X Garage, located in a lane off Kensington's Cornwall Gardens, in the early 1920s. Standard Oil heiress Joe Carstairs, a flamboyantly butch lesbian, was its principle financier.[6] Brochures for X Garage advertised holiday tours throughout Britain and the Continent, and guided tours of the battlefields and war graves in France. Photographs of the garage women dressed in overalls at their repair work were published in the press with admiring stories of their celebrity clients and their adventures on the road. The women were familiar figures in the West End's more *louche* circles, where Joe Carstairs pursued affairs with various stage performers, including Tallulah Bankhead.

Such flamboyant forays into masculine territory extended the disparate expressions of female masculinities and gender-bending identities in which "deviation became entangled with the chic."[7] As they climbed on, in, and under their motorcycles, ambulances, delivery vans, taxis, private automobiles, and luxury touring cars, British garage women were exploring the transformative possibilities of a new technology, in which they could create themselves as new, ultramodern kinds of women. And as they engaged in assembling a vision of gender renewal that was distinctly *avant-garde* in its performative dimensions, their actions briefly meshed with the interests of the automobile industry, at that moment anticipating a postwar era of tremendous growth.

The war had established the viability of motor transport, introduced automobile technology across social classes, and had forced the reorganization of labor relations and factory design in ways suited to mass production. There was much hopeful talk of "cars for the millions," and motor manufacturers and their agents leaned heavily on advertising campaigns that employed images of energetic and accomplished young women motorists to promote that anticipated abundance.[8] Numerous advertisements depicted motoring women as archetypal modern consumers, carefree and confident, driving themselves (and frequently male passengers as well) into a pleasurable future. That invocation of a female presence worked to place an optimistic spin on technological progress, shifting automotive technology away from its recent associations with cataclysmic destructiveness wherein technology in male hands had spiraled entirely out of control.

Some advertisements used images of uniformed women drivers dressed in tunics, breeches, and high boots. Such postwar representations of women chauffeurs were distinctly different from those of the war years, however. Rather than rugged women in heavy coats and boots for the front, a serious and brave response to a grave national moment, post-war images of uniformed female chauffeurs were stylish and highly sexualized, suggesting pleasure, glamour, and optimistic modernity. During the 1920s and 1930s, for example, the large automobile accessory manufacturer Stewart-Warner used a uniformed female chauffeur, who they named "Miss Stewart Custombuilt," in countless advertisements for their products in Britain, Australia, and the United States. The power of such images, viewed so soon after the end of the war, spoke of a continued fascination with wartime gender-bending. They alluded to the "boyish look," then in high fashion, as well as to the ongoing aspirations of technologically accomplished women to retain the freedoms they had achieved during the war.

Alice Anderson was aware of professional women motorists in Britain. She corresponded with friends serving in Europe during the war, read English feminist magazines, motoring and engineering journals, and followed Australian press stories of the wartime changes in the gender order in Britain. And although Australian women's moves to form military units were thwarted, British women's successes helped to foster a transnational imaginary for Alice Anderson's motoring ambitions.[9] Her vision of the Australian female professional motor driver and mechanic, however, was somewhat different from its English expression. It was inflected by a belief in the superiority of colonial female resourcefulness and the more fluid class structure of Australian society, as well as by the distinctive role that automobiles played in Australian national life.

By early 1920s the rate of car ownership in Australia was one of the highest in the world, far beyond that of England. Measured against average wages, the initial purchase of a car in 1925 was less than at any time until 1965, though high ongoing costs ensured that ownership was largely restricted to prosperous middle-class families.[10] Statistics are not available for women's car ownership or driving licenses, but women were often featured in accounts of early motoring. They were prominent in stories of arduous, record-breaking trips across the Australian continent, in which pairs of women—kitted out in khaki bush suits, kodaks at the ready, automobiles fitted with long-range fuel tanks, water bags suspended from bumper bars, and camping supplies, spare parts, chains, and lengths of rattan matting roped to the running boards—set off to "discover Australia by car."[11] Alice Anderson's Motor Service was similarly taken to demonstrate the special resourcefulness of white colonial women in their ability to join with white men in claiming and taming a "new" country through modern technology.

Anderson was born in 1893, into an Anglo-Irish professional household impoverished by the 1890s depression. At a time when middle-class women were increasingly entering professional training at university level, her formal education was limited to a few terms at grammar school. But she did manage to acquire a thorough grounding in the mechanical arts. Qualifications in automobile work were not formalized until the 1920s, and that flexibility enabled her to receive mechanical training from sympathetic men, including her father. By sixteen, Anderson had learned to repair and drive charabancs, or unwieldy open buses, at a community transport cooperative near where she lived. She was given the deposit on her first car for her eighteenth birthday, leaving her to raise the £350 needed to complete the sale—a major challenge when female clerical wages were about £80 per year. After her office hours, she took touring parties on weekend picnics into the bushland she knew so well, chauffeured young women to dances, conducted shopping tours, drove women to hospital for their confinements, joined the convoys of Melbourne motorists who met troopships returning with wounded soldiers from the war, and continued her mechanical training at a city garage. Within four years Alice Anderson, then aged twenty-two, was able to open her motor garage. "I got the opportunity to vacate the office stool for the wheel—and I took it," she told a women's magazine.[12]

Though she only worked from the backyard of the house in which she lived in a rented room, the advertisement she placed in the *Melbourne Directory* of 1919 was bold and buoyant:

> MISS ANDERSON'S MOTOR SERVICE
> (KEW GARAGE.) Tel. HAWTHORN 2328
> 67 COTHAM ROAD, KEW.
> Seven-seater HUPMOBILE and Five-seater DODGE Touring Cars for Hire.
> Driving and Mechanism Taught.
> PETROL, TYRES, and all Motor Accessories Stocked.
> REPAIRS to all Classes of Cars.[13]

Her optimism paid off, and a year later she had borrowed enough money to place a deposit on a nearby block of land. The motoring press reported her plans in sympathetic terms, their description calling to mind some of the "New Woman" residential communities of the nineteenth century:

> Miss Anderson, who has taken up motoring as a profession, has made an unqualified success of her venture. Her garage work in Kew, Victoria, has grown so rapidly that a three storeyed brick garage is to be built to her special requirements.
>
> The first floor is to house the motors in for repairs; the second will be a workshop, where girls will be employed; the third will be used for sleeping and eating quarters for the staff.
>
> Miss Anderson has entered into the "game" in a business-like manner. Skirts and hair have gone; she has donned male attire, and a woman's chief worry, her hair, has been cut closely, and she will pass now for a youth of 18 or 19 years of age. Her interest and attention is devoted to her business, and she has proved that a woman can run a garage in good style with her staff of khaki-clad chauffeuses and mechanics.[14]

Alice Anderson's ambitious building plan was never realized, but she did open a single-story garage on a prominent corner of the main street of Kew [fig. 3.1, fig. 3.2]. And though her imagined community of female garage workers was reduced to a small bedroom for herself in a corner of the

MISS ALICE ANDERSON:
Motor Mechanic and Chauffeuse, Melbourne.

Fig. 3.1 Alice Anderson, Motor Mechanic, *Home*, December 1, 1920. Courtesy National Library of Australia.

garage, for the next seven years—until her death in 1926—newspaper and magazine articles reported it in warmly approving terms:

> Possibly no woman in Melbourne was better known. She pioneered the way to motor garages for women and made a greater success of it than most men could.[15]

Always a staunch advocate of motoring as a suitable career for middle-class women, Alice Anderson declared that a qualified woman mechanic could earn £5 per week and more—a good professional income for women at that time. Over the two decades of its operation, perhaps twenty-five women worked in the garage as professional chauffeurs and mechanics, though it is unlikely that any were paid £5. To secure their difference from, and even superiority to, male mechanics and chauffeurs, Anderson emphasized the women's social similarity to their customers,

Miss Anderson's assistants at work in the garage.

Fig. 3.2 Staff at the Kew Garage, *Home,* December 1, 1920. Courtesy National Library of Australia.

setting extraordinarily high standards of professional skill for female workers:

> Asked what type she looks to for her best assistants, she replies without hesitation. "The bright, intelligent, well-educated girl fresh from college. Education is essential. I can train a girl to be a good driver in a year; but if a girl is to qualify as a thoroughly competent garage assistant she must be in a position to undertake any repairs and to make spare parts if necessary. This involves a working knowledge of mechanics, chemistry and trig—an eight years course. My ambition is to turn a trade into a profession for women, and it is well within the grasp of those who have initiative and grit."[16]

Like most garages of the period, the Alice Anderson Motor Service provided an eclectic range of services. It had a driving school, which included mechanical instruction, a twenty-four-hour uniformed hire-car service, a fully equipped mechanical workshop, and petrol sales. Vehicles were stored for clients who were abroad, and wealthy Kew residents used the staff as part-time chauffeurs, garaging their cars in Anderson's premises, and calling them out by telephone as and when they were needed. They drove stock and station agents on tours of inspection through rural areas and organized holiday excursions during which Anderson's personal charm, bush knowledge, and cooking skills were a major draw.

This range of activities was broad enough to constitute a serious bid for a part of Melbourne's growing automotive service and repair industry. Her garage was registered with the Automobile Chamber of Commerce under several categories of membership, and Alice Anderson was amongst the first mechanics in Melbourne to apply for the newly established A-Grade certificate.[17] She had plans for expanding her business into forms of tourism and travel that would not be realized in Australia until the post–World War II decades and wrote a monthly motoring column called "Her Wheel" in *Woman's World* magazine.

While her garage had much in common with other motor garages of its day, her business represented much more than a foray into a technological domain wholly defined by men. Far from merely copying established business practices, Alice Anderson located herself as a creative participant in a growing and open field. She gained some fame as an innovator, particularly for what she called her "Get-Out and Get-Under" device, a fold-away creeper or platform on wheels, that allowed the stranded motorist to propel herself under the car without having to lie on the ground; her "patented radi-waiter" was a flask that used the heat of the radiator to keep drinks hot during a long trip.[18] Anderson also attracted a great deal of free publicity for her garage with her innovative "once-over for thirty shillings," a service in which the customer's car underwent a complete overhaul by her team of mechanics in eight hours.

More significantly, Alice Anderson developed services that were designed especially for women motorists, offering training programs at the garage that catered to women's lower incomes and their desires for mechanical knowledge. The *Australian Automobile Trade Journal* noted:

> A rather novel idea has been introduced by the Kew Garage . . . whereby girl car owners can wash, grease their cars and receive mechanical knowledge with the assistance of an apprentice from the garage at 2/6 per hour.[19]

In a more ambitious plan, women could attend the workshop as paying pupils for months at a time. They were supervised by the garage mechanics in a kind of minor apprenticeship or finishing school in the arts of technological modernity, which proved to be popular amongst school-leavers. The program was based on an appreciation of the impediments to automobility that were particular to women and drew its inspiration from London's feminist garages.

In the postwar years conservative elements of the Melbourne press, as elsewhere, identified female modernity with widespread social decadence, new vices, and the disinclination of women to become wives and mothers.[20] Some women's magazines, motoring journals, and popular daily press, however, adopted a more liberal view and reported the Alice Anderson Motor Service in terms that celebrated the ethic of exuberance and experimentation that the garage represented. Though their optimism about the demise of occupational barriers for women was premature, they registered a fascination with the garage as an expression of female masculinity, focusing particularly on the women's sartorial style. Reports never failed to describe the clothes the women wore, their hairstyles, masculine appearance and comportment.

Admiring reports about the garage and the women who worked in it suggested links between that enterprise and earlier feminist campaigns. The very image of a residential community of professional, single women recalled the "New Woman" communities of the turn of the century—the settlement houses, nursing schools, and colleges that had been central to the previous generation of feminists. When *Home* magazine described the garage building as "a roomy modern garage with sunlight streaming through lofty windows," it invoked a modern version of older female communities, religious, medical, collegiate, or military.[21]

That notion of collective feminist action, however, is not the best way to understand Alice Anderson's garage. The feminism that informed her enterprise can be better characterized as the kind of radical individualism frequently invoked by women who came to maturity in those interwar years.[22] Like other women of her generation, Alice Anderson distanced herself from feminism, with its connotations of a "sex war." Instead, she was inclined to emphasize individual accomplishments—unrelated to gender difference—and to boldly act as if sexual equality had already arrived. If her garage was a feminist enterprise, it was an implied, noncollective kind of feminism, one that did not seek to claim that name. In "Her Wheel," her motoring columns in *Woman's World*, she provided matter-of-fact technical advice to a motorist gendered, without comment, as "she." Anderson presented her actions as instances of individual initiative in which she and other singular women sidestepped the irrational restrictions of the time, rather than campaigning against them, and her garage can best be understood not as a space seeking to enhance the social status of women, but instead as one wanting to minimize the importance of the category altogether. That repudiation of oppositional feminist action and the downplaying of sexual difference went together with forms of female subjectivity more readily than earlier feminism did to embrace questions of female pleasure and female sexuality.

There are hints of the delight the garage women took in their ambiguous sexual positioning in the gender-bending stories told by women who worked at the garage. Gabrielle Fleury, a Frenchwoman who had been severely burnt while serving with the British Land Army in World War I, was named as one of the most memorable of the garage workers. She was remembered for her powerful build, short temper, florid language, inability to memorize the streets of Melbourne, as well as for her sexual ambiguity and scarred body, which made many assume she was a man. Jones, another long-term employee, was remembered as the heroine of an apocryphal story of gender confusion:

> One day Jones, who was tall and thin and not feminine looking, was working on a car when a man suddenly appeared asking, "Is there anywhere a bloke can have a leak?" The poor man was covered in confusion, but Jones did not bat an eyelid.[23]

Such stories of urbanity in the face of identity confusion—where traffic police stopped the garage's chauffeurs, believing them to be underage boys, where respectable Melbourne society was shocked by their androgyny, where unsuspecting men addressed them in crude language, or where scarring could appear to literally erase gender difference—were remembered with delight. The press could not resist jokes about a garage "manned" entirely by women, and Alice Anderson was most often described as an energetic and charming boy. The dearth of terms with which to represent a specifically female technical proficiency suggests the difficulties that adhered to women's claim to a place on the workshop floor, but it also opened a space for jokes at the expense of men. The women took great pleasure in the ways the garage could rattle the certainties of masculine entitlement to particular spaces, languages, comportments, and competencies. The jokes highlighted how their enterprise was not just a bid for meaningful work, but also a public declaration of defiance—a desire for change enacted at the most fundamental level of bodily signs and meanings.

Their masculine style, however, was a changing and unstable ground of signification over which they had little control. In 1919, the progressive Melbourne press had interpreted it as evidence of their admirable modernity, professionalism, and spiritedness—a sign they were advanced women, ready to step into a modern world. But during the second half of the 1920s, the permissive era of gender experimentation drew to a close, and a new sexual conservatism came to dominate. Increasingly, the garage worker's female masculinity risked signaling the disreputable and deviant instead of admirable modernity. Responding to that shifting ground of possibility was a delicate task that only escalated as the women grew older.

With her upper-class connections, lively personality, competence, and charm, Alice Anderson was able to generate goodwill and free publicity for her garage, at least in public forums. She wore a Joan of Arc tiepin on her uniform as a public symbol of her earnestness. A malleable symbol of female rebellion, Joan of Arc—courageous, fervently Christian, mobile, bob-cut, cross-dressed, sexually ambiguous, and single-mindedly prepared to risk all for a just cause—provided the women of the garage with an instantly recognizable, even respectable means of representing their masculine activities.

Their attempts to present their actions in such high-minded terms were only partially successful, however, and the pleasure they took in creating that particular version of female masculinity sometimes threatened to overwhelm the business of the garage altogether. As a magazine aimed at a sophisticated female readership headlined a feature article on her, Alice Anderson was "The Woman Who Does." Apparently an approving headline, it simultaneously resonated with the title of Grant Allen's scandalous "New Woman" novel of 1897, *The Woman Who Did*. In that novel, Herminia Barton, the feminist heroine and an advocate for free love, has a child out of wedlock and a tragic death. As Sally Ledger has argued, Allen's novel was an example of a genre in which male writers pathologized feminist aspirations by linking them to sexual decadence and emerging homosexual identities.[24] So while the banner "The Woman Who Does" ostensibly celebrated her as a practical "do-er," a woman who put into action feminist precepts of sex equality, it also carried a hint of scandal, a whiff of a question. What else did Alice Anderson and her "gallant little band" of khaki-clad mechanics and chauffeurs do?

Alice Anderson's adult life was dogged by scandal. She was suspected of the full range of sexual transgressions—of living with men, of having abortions, and of being a lesbian. Her dramatic death at the garage of a gunshot wound to her head only served to create even more gossip about her. She died only days after returning from a much-publicized trip into Central Australia in a "Baby" Austin Seven with Jessie Webb, the first woman lecturer in the Department of History at the University of Melbourne. While no hint of scandal emerged at her inquest and a verdict of accidental death was returned—the death determined to be caused by a faulty pistol she was cleaning—persistent rumors of suicide brought about by financial worries or an unhappy love affair continued to circulate for decades.

Whispers of lesbianism were never far away from the garage, and in that broadly libertarian milieu, a circle of lesbians were associated with the business. Some of Alice Anderson's close friends as well as some of her staff and customers were identified as members of a lesbian friendship network that centered on the garage. But while her sisters freely acknowledged that association, they declared that she attracted the sexual interest of women inadvertently. Alice merely "walked with the girls," as they put it, though members of the next generation of the family were more inclined to believe she was a lesbian.

Whatever Alice Anderson "did," or however she identified, there can be little doubt that she played with and greatly enjoyed the transgressive elements of her professional and sexual positioning. A striking family photograph, carefully preserved because it was said to provide a perfect likeness of Alice's cheeky charm, shows her in chauffeur's uniform, sitting on a sand-hill with an unknown woman of much more feminine appearance [fig. 3.3]. The two are shown self-consciously playing with the possibilities implicit in their difference. Alice looks at her companion with a smile, holding her hand, an arm about her waist. It is a pose devoid of ironic comment at masculine pretensions, a parody that cross-dressing portraits frequently express with relish.[25] Instead, it appears as a playful and flirtatious gesture, however uncertain in its wider import. Is Alice flirting with her apparent masculinity, even as she remains transparently feminine? Is she flirting with the young woman, who acknowledges the camera and smiles with the joke? Certainly, they are both flirting with the camera, the photographer, and the possibility of transgression. The caption on the back of the photo, supplied by a sister, directs an innocent interpretation: "Alice pretending to be the 'boyfriend' of a polio victim she had taken on an outing."

The photograph represents a moment that resists resolution. It is a fragment that reminds us of the joke as well as the seriousness of women's desires for masculine license. For in spite of Alice Anderson's buoyant personality and capacity for both social and physical mobility, apparently in contrast to her disabled client/friend, the position she occupied was fragile. She died too young, under circumstances that will always remain uncertain, by a firearm she had been urged to carry to protect herself and her companion from both black and white men on their trip to Alice Springs. Neither can we know how Alice Anderson might have continued her business had she lived longer.

We do know, however, that the climate in which her garage operated was undergoing rapid change. The automobile service and repair sector was becoming increasingly regulated, formalizing it as a male, working-class trade unwelcoming to women. With technical improvements, cars became more reliable, making it easier for people with no mechanical knowledge to be confident motorists and further working to consolidate mechanical knowledge as a masculine specialization. Growing mass consumption was transforming cars into an everyday technology in which owners opted to drive themselves rather than be chauffeured. That democratization of automobility fostered an ethic of "driving" that replaced the more snooty practice of "motoring." Such changes in the culture of automobility placed the style and rationale of the Alice Anderson Motor Service out of step—an old-fashioned response to a version of automobile technology that no longer pertained.

Fig. 3.3 Alice pretending to be the 'boyfriend' of a polio victim she had taken on an outing. Courtesy Anderson family.

The business declined after Anderson's death. It rarely rated a mention in the Melbourne press, and though the driving school continued to flourish, the chauffeuring and mechanical work came to rely on a dwindling base of clients. The garage became a curiosity in the local community and was sometimes mocked, as the staff, clients, and equipment aged. Far from being considered modern and advanced, their uniforms were called "frumpy," and the women dismissed as a remnant of an earlier era of class superiority, feminist pretension, and lesbian deviance.

Memories of Alice Anderson and her garage have now been largely erased, though in some social circles in eastern Melbourne questions of whether Alice Anderson was a lesbian who deliberately killed herself in the back of the garage continued to be asked well into the post–World War II years. The businessman who purchased her garage in the 1950s to expand his luxury-car dealership summed up the elision when he wrote to me, "Alice Anderson Motors, was, I understand, a hire-car service operated by the two Anderson sisters prior to World War II and rumor has it that they committed suicide in the building."[26]

That bald version of events, a masculinist narrative of impossibility, works to write over and write out the fluidity and exuberance of the gender experimentation of the early 1920s. It replaces it with the standard story of women out of place in a man's world, women who must inevitably come to a doubly unpleasant end. In its misremembered version of literal sisterhood, however, the story inadvertently returns to the atmosphere of lesbian sorority that once surrounded the Alice Anderson Motor Service. My attempt to recuperate those forgotten erotics of sisterhood draws attention to the expression of lesbian desires and lesbian subjectivities embodied in the playful, ex-centric, but also dangerous embrace of the pleasures of being modern.

Notes

I would like to thank Barbara McBane, Laura Doan and Jane Garrity for their helpful comments on this paper. The material is expanded in my *Auto-Erotics: Early Women Motorists' Love of Cars* (Johns Hopkins University Press, forthcoming).

1. Much of the material in this chapter was gained from interviews with Alice Anderson's three sisters, Frances Durham, Kathleen Ball, and Claire Fitzpatrick. I am indebted to Mimi Colligan for her earlier work on Alice Anderson, and for generously allowing me access to her files. Frances Durham and Kathleen Ball were interviewed by Mimi Colligan in 1981. During 1995–1997, I interviewed her younger sister Claire Fitzpatrick numerous times, as well as other women who worked at the garage. See Mimi Colligan, "Alice Anderson: Garage

Proprietor," in Marilyn Lake and Farley Kelly, eds., *Double Time: Women in Victoria—150 Years* (Melbourne: Penguin Books, 1985), pp. 305–11.
2. *Melbourne Herald*, September 18, 1926, p. 1.
3. Sean O'Connell, *The Car in British Society: Class, Gender and Motoring, 1896–1939* (Manchester: Manchester University Press, 1999). Wolfgang Sachs, *For Love of the Automobile: Looking Back into the History of Our Desires* (Berkeley and London: University of California Press, 1992). Virginia Scharff, *Taking the Wheel: Women and the Coming of the Motor Age* (New York: The Free Press, 1991).
4. Radclyffe Hall, *The Well of Loneliness*. 1928 (New York, Anchor Books, 1990), p. 147.
5. B. P., "A Women's Motor Garage," *Common Cause*, August 4, 1916.
6. Kate Summerscale, *The Queen of Whale Cay* (London: Fourth Estate, 1997), pp. 56–60.
7. Laura Doan, *Fashioning Sapphism: The Origins of a Modern English Lesbian Culture* (New York: Columbia University Press, 2001), p. xiv.
8. May Walker, "A Woman's Point of View: Good Times Ahead for the Lady Who Drives Her Own Car," *Autocar*, May 17, 1919. J. Owen, "Motors and Motoring: Shall We Go Back to Animal Traction?" *Westminster Gazette*, December 23, 1920.
9. Jan Bassett, "Ready to Serve: Australian Women and the Great War," *Journal of the Australian War Memorial* 2 (1983): 8–16.
10. John Knott, "The 'Conquering Car': Technology, Symbolism and the Motorization of Australia before World War Two," *Australian Historical Studies* 114 (2000): 4–7.
11. Georgine Clarsen, "Tracing the Outline of Nation: Circling Australia by Car," *Continuum: Journal of Media and Cultural Studies* 13, no. 3 (1999): 359–69. Georgine Clarsen, "The 'Dainty Female Toe' and the 'Brawny Male Arm': Conceptions of Bodies and Power in Automobile Technology," *Australian Feminist Studies* 15, no. 32 (2000): 153–63.
12. *Woman's World*, February 1, 1922, p. 13.
13. Sands and McDougal's *Directory of Victoria*, Melbourne, 1919.
14. *Australian Motorist*, June 2, 1919.
15. *Melbourne Herald*, September 18, 1926, p. 1.
16. *Woman's World*, February 1, 1922, p. 13.
17. *Australian Automobile Trade Journal*, February, 1921. Victorian Automobile Chamber of Commerce, Melbourne, Records of the 'A' Grade Certificate Board of Examiners, 1926.
18. "A Clever Invention," *Australian Motorist*, September 1919, p. 20. *Woman's World*, February 1, 1922, p. 13.
19. *Australian Automobile Trade Journal*, January 1920.
20. Dennis Shoesmith, "The New Woman: The Debate on the 'New Woman' in Melbourne 1919," *Politics* 8, no. 2 (1973). Patricia Grimshaw, Marylin Lake, Ann McGrath and Marian Quartly, *Creating a Nation* (Melbourne: McPhee Gribble, 1994), pp. 205–29.
21. *Home*, December 1, 1920, p. 74.

22. Barbara Caine, "Women's Studies, Feminist Traditions and the Problem of History," in Barbara Caine and Rosemary Pringle, eds., *Transitions: New Australian Feminisms* (Sydney: Allen and Unwin, 1995), pp. 1–14.
23. Letter from Lucy Johnstone to Mimi Colligan, April 1, 1983.
24. "The Woman Who Does," *Home*, December 1, 1920, p. 74. Grant Allen, *The Woman Who Did.* 1895 (Oxford: Oxford University Press, 1995). Sally Ledger, *The New Woman: Fiction and Feminism in the Fin de Siecle* (Manchester and New York: Manchester University Press, 1997).
25. Mandy Merck, " 'Transforming the Suit': A Century of Lesbian Self-Portraits," in Mandy Merck, ed., *Perversions: Deviant Readings* (New York: Routledge, 1993), pp. 86–100.
26. Letter from Bib Stillwell to author, May 7, 1996.

Part 2

The Sapphic Body in Space: Leisure, Commodity Culture, Domesticity

Chapter 4

Sapphic Smokers and English Modernities

Penny Tinkler

The cigarette dominates the twentieth-century history of smoking, and, according to this historiography, the adoption of cigarette smoking by Western women was used, and widely interpreted, as a sign of their emancipation and modernity.[1] As Michael Schudson explains: "In modern societies, people mark themselves not only in social space but in social time. Through goods, they indicate their relationship to one another and also accent their relationship to the spirit of the times. They display their modernity or their resistance to modernity."[2] In England, the phenomenon of cigarette smoking among women was established from the 1880s, although pipe smoking among women pre-dates the nineteenth century.[3] Evidence suggests that between 1880 and 1920 smoking gained in popularity among upper-class women, but prior to 1920 the level of smoking among women was too low to record.[4] During the interwar years tobacco consumption increased rapidly among upper- and middle-class women although only cigarette smoking was sufficiently high to be recorded. In 1921 annual consumption of manufactured cigarettes per woman aged 15 and over was only 13; this rose to 90 by 1925, 270 by 1933 and to 500 by World War II.[5]

The association of women's smoking with modernity was well established in early twentieth-century England. However, the signification of the cigarette, or indeed of any tobacco product, was not independent of social context. Moreover, modernity was "not one discourse, but the site of intersection of several, which do not sit easily together."[6] The diverse meanings of smoking practices stemmed from a range of discourses on smoking and on modernity, and on the ways in which they interrelated within different social and cultural contexts. Modernity is, however, not just a discursive category, it is also "the experience of living through and making sense of" the processes of modernization, the "practical negotiation of one's life and one's identity within a complex and fast-changing world."[7] Women, Rita Felski argues, have experienced modern processes in gender-specific ways and these experiences "have been further fractured, not only by the oft-cited hierarchies of class, race, and sexuality but by their [women's] various and overlapping identities and practices as consumers, mothers, workers, artists, readers, and so on."[8] Exploration of English women's experiences of modernity has begun, and some of the specifically lesbian dimensions have been teased out by Laura Doan.[9] However, though smoking is frequently accorded a prominent place in women's modernity, the place of smoking in lesbian engagements with modern life remains underexplored. Blanket statements about women's smoking, emancipation, and modernity do not engage with the significance of lesbian contexts of smoking, the diversity of tobacco products consumed by lesbians, and the importance of sexuality. How did lesbians utilize smoking practices in the presentation of identities, and were they modern ones?

This chapter begins to explore the smoking practices of lesbians and women engaged in "lesbian-like practices."[10] Due to the paucity of sources on working-class and lower-middle-class lesbian smokers, the discussion focuses primarily on upper- and middle-class women, especially the artist Gluck, the motorboat racer Joe Carstairs, and the writers Radclyffe Hall and Vita Sackville-West. An examination of lesbian smoking practices reveals the limitations of focusing only on cigarette smoking and interpreting this simply as a marker of "women's modernity." Lesbians used a broader range of tobacco products in complex ways to articulate social and temporal aspects of their identities; they were used in the effort to pass as a man, to make statements about gender and sexuality, and to symbolize acceptance into male society. Smoking was an articulation of modernity for many lesbians, but this was not universal and working-class lesbians were almost completely excluded. The association of smoking with modernity was also varied and complex. Smoking could signify modernity in relation to different aspects of identity, for example, sexual practice, intellect, and sartorial style. More generally, smoking practices represented an engagement with modernity from several vantage points in terms of gender and sexuality. There was "women's modernity," and sometimes a distinctively "sapphic modernity," and, for lesbians passing as men, male modernity.[11] In some contexts, these could be inherently conservative forms of modernity.[12]

Smoking and Passing

Smoking and chewing tobacco were almost the exclusive preserve of men in nineteenth- and early twentieth-century England. Not surprisingly the consumption of tobacco products was often key to the performance of masculinities. Male impersonators smoked cigars and cigarettes in their performances.[13] Even men used smoking as evidence of their maleness as seen in a photo from 1918 of three young men sporting pipes even though they did not smoke.[14] Not surprisingly, tobacco products were also used as signs of masculinity by passing women. Women who passed as men adopted male attire, posture, behavior, and activities; they "exploited all possible symbols of masculinity."[15] Such women of the nineteenth century notably included "Bill" Chapman who chewed tobacco and "squirted tobacco juice" and Mary Newall who stole and smoked cigars.[16] In the interwar years there was "William Sidney Holtom," a timber carter, who smoked "two to three ounces of tobacco weekly in a clay pipe."[17] To them, tobacco consumption represented a means of reinforcing the impression of masculinity and, when the gender of these women came into question, it was widely interpreted as evidence of their maleness.

Passing women tended to use tobacco products that were unambiguously masculine. In the nineteenth century, chewing tobacco and pipe and cigar smoking were distinctly masculine practices, although the type and quality of product consumed varied according to the social class of the smoker.[18] From the late nineteenth century, cigarette smoking became increasingly popular with men although it was frequently regarded as having lower status than cigar or pipe smoking and as slightly effeminate: "The increased prevalence of the cigarette, available in mass-produced form in the 1880s, was incomprehensible to the more 'manly' smokers of the pipe and cigar."[19] In the twentieth century the meaning of cigarettes shifted as they became popular with men across social classes and, increasingly, with women, but cigars and pipes (especially the briar pipe) remained unambiguously masculine. This gender differentiation of tobacco products was vigorously promoted in interwar England. Publicity for International Pipe Week, in 1930, featured a woman smoking a cigarette and declaring "This is pipe week—and I like to see a man smoke a pipe"; another publicity feature proclaimed that the pipe is "the everyday sign of manhood."[20]

Smoking by cross-dressed lesbians was not an expression of a modern female or sapphic identity because it was an acknowledgment and acceptance of the lack of change in the position of women; significantly, cross-dressing was a strategy adopted principally by poor women.[21] For cross-dressed women smoking could, however, be an expression of a modern masculinity.

Although passing as a man was not a form of sapphic or female modernity, access to opportunities to *play* at being men was a response to modern processes, in particular women's increased access to the public sphere and the demise of the practice of chaperonage. A desire to be experimental with identities was also a very modern phenomenon.[22] Playing with gender identities was obviously attractive to some lesbians,[23] but it is unlikely that this was exclusive to lesbians. In the context of far-reaching changes in society, the desire to experiment with gender was also attractive to heterosexual women. Occasional photos from family albums suggest that pipes and cigarettes were used playfully by women as symbols of masculinity. Bessie Clinton, a middle-class young woman from a fairly wealthy and respectable family, posed for the camera during World War I dressed in the army uniform of her sister's fiancé with a cigarette in her mouth; the only sign of her femininity were her dainty shoes.[24] Whether or not Bessie's desire to dress up as a man suggests unrest with her feminine gender and heterosexuality is difficult to determine given that the photo was ostensibly "a joke."

Smoking as an aspect of playfully passing as a man could, however, be a specifically lesbian practice and an expression of sapphic modernity. Vita Sackville-West's account of her love affair with Violet Trefusis refers to smoking facilitating their sexual encounters. In what she described as her "best adventure," which took place in 1918, Vita dressed in male clothes as "Julian" strolled around Mayfair smoking a cigarette: "I stepped off the kerb, down Piccadilly, alone . . . I walked along, smoking a cigarette, buying a newspaper off a little boy who called me 'sir', and being accosted now and then by women."[25] Vita was not recognized as a woman and she therefore had the freedoms of a man. "Julian" could smoke in the streets without attracting anything other than the attention of admiring women; this at a time when a woman smoking in Oxford Street could make headlines in the London *Evening News*.[26] This masquerade was not essential to Vita's sexual liaison with Violet (Vita had a flat in London from which she and Violet commenced their adventure), but it clearly added to the sexual frisson as, following her parade around London, Vita escorted Violet to a boarding house to make love.

Statements

Passing as men, or playing at passing, involved the use of tobacco products in masquerade. However, consistent with the modern emphasis on the importance of outward appearance as an expression of identity,[27] many lesbians, and women more generally, consciously exploited the visuality of smoking to make complex statements about gender and sexuality. Smoking was clearly a source of pleasure for some lesbians, but it was also an important aspect of self-image. Even for those who did not like tobacco, smoking could still be a valuable sign. Joe Carstairs, for example, admitted that she smoked "merely for effect; she never inhaled."[28] Lesbians visually recorded their smoking in amateur photos and in commissioned portraits. The appearance of a cigarette was usually significant. Vita Sackville-West was never photographed wearing her spectacles but was, from the mid-1930s, invariably shown with a cigarette,[29] and Joe Carstairs, according to her biographer, paraded her smoking in almost every photo: "For the camera, she frowned a little, squared her shoulders, held a cigarette in one hand and placed the other in a jacket pocket."[30] These photos were used for private purposes such as gifts to friends and, in the case of celebrities, as publicity material. The artist Gluck completed a self-portrait in 1926 in which she depicted herself with a cigarette protruding from the corner of her mouth. This painting was reproduced in the society magazine, *Eve*, and later as a Christmas card that Gluck sent to her friends in 1930.[31]

But what did these smoking practices mean? Smoking any form of tobacco was a specifically gendered statement of modernity for middle- and upper-class women. It was a sign of gender rebellion and it signaled a break from traditional forms of femininity. More specifically, smoking represented a rejection of the passive, subordinate, and domesticated "angel in the house" and the embrace of an identity characterized by qualities such as intellectuality, an active sexuality, and physical prowess, previously assigned exclusively to men. Smoking served as a visual critique of dominant notions of femininity. Crucially, this only worked if done from the vantage point of a female identity; smoking could not represent rebellion and a claim to equality if the woman was passing as a man.

Smoking as a statement of modernity for women drew upon the long-standing association of smoking with masculinity. In engaging in a practice that was previously the preserve of men, women smokers laid claim to male privileges and asserted their right to equality in all spheres of social life: " 'liberation' was understood by the dominant culture to mean the ability and opportunity to act (and smoke) like men."[32] The capacity of smoking to signify gender rebellion and liberation was further accentuated by the use of tobacco by groups of "radical" women from the 1890s; cigarettes were advertised in the suffrage press, and some women's clubs provided smoking rooms for their members.[33] The association of smoking with a demand for equality was sufficiently common to constitute the humor in various forms of advertising in the 1890s. An advert for Beecham's products, for example, portrayed a woman dressed in stiff collars, a tie, and breeches, brandishing a lit cigarette; the text proclaimed that "Beechams can make a New Woman of you."[34]

Women's smoking as liberation also drew on the long-standing, but less obvious, association of tobacco with female sexuality. Tobacco products were often anthropomorphized into a wife or lover.[35] The involvement of women in the production of cigars contributed a further layer of sexual associations,[36] as did the depiction of women on tobacco packaging.[37] Cigarette adverts often highlighted the sexuality theme. A 1920s advert for Kiamil cigarettes, for example, depicted a young woman smoking while seated at her dressing table, her bodice strap hung off her shoulder as she looked round provocatively; these cigarettes, the advert proclaimed, are "alluring and seductive."[38] The association of smoking with an active female sexuality was potentially liberating for women from social elites, and although in these contexts women's sexuality was intended to be read as heterosexual, it was open to reinscription within a lesbian framework.

Commissioning a photograph of oneself smoking was quite radical for an interwar woman and also highly meaningful. Professional portraits of society women and their middle-class sisters did not usually feature cigarettes, even if the women were smokers, and the cigarette was also invisible in working-class portraiture.[39] Photographs of literary women were notable exceptions and included Radclyffe Hall, Sylvia Townsend Warner, Vera Brittain, Daphne du Maurier, Virginia Woolf, and Vita Sackville-West.[40] Literary women used smoking to communicate their intellectual modernity and equality with men. The association of smoking with contemplation and intellectuality was well established in the masculine history of smoking, and one that was also promoted in the antics of fictional male characters such as the detective Sherlock Holmes.[41] In most portraits of lesbians smoking the focus is on the head or upper body of the subject, usually with the forehead illuminated, and the sitter conveys, partly by use of the cigarette, a meditative or pensive demeanor. Although smoking as a statement of intellectuality was not exclusive to literary lesbians, it was usually only heterosexual women, or women who passed as straight, who adopted smoking poses that drew on aspects of glamour photography.[42] Publicity photographs of models and actresses smoking contrasted starkly with portraits of lesbian intellectuals. Close-up facial shots were common in these glamour photographs in which the emphasis was on the mouth; alternatively, full-body shots were used in which the woman-sitter, attired in a figure-hugging dress, adopted a languid pose and draped herself over various props.[43] The composition of photos of literary women located smoking in the context of the sitter's professional identity, but it was not only literary lesbians who located their smoking in professional contexts. Gluck chose to be photographed dressed in her artist's smock (a masculine costume) and holding a cigarette.[44] Other photos of Gluck painting in her studio also depict her with a cigarette in her mouth or hand. The modernity of Gluck and other lesbian professionals was inextricably bound up with their work, which represented entry into the public domain on "equal terms" with men.

Cigarettes were particularly favored as indicators of fashionable modernity by middle- and upper-class lesbians. This is not surprising as the cigarette was, at the turn of the century, regarded as the modern form of smoking. For women and men the cigarette, like the motor car, signaled an engagement with the spirit of the times. Cigarettes were a relatively new product in 1900 and not weighed down by tradition. They were mass produced and available in a standardized form. The mode of consumption was also compatible with the demands of modern, urban lifestyles in that it was "convenient": "The cigarette is the standardized, reliable, quick and easy smoke. It is the McDonald's of the tobacco trade, the fast food of smoking . . . the preferred smoke for people aiming for a streamlined, cultural modernity, involved in the fast pace of city life."[45] Cigarettes, smoked with or without a holder, became a fashion accessory for stylish affluent women. Fashion images of women smokers emphasized femininity; moreover, as magazines recognized that some women reached for a "gasper" there were reminders about how to do this in gender-specific ways. Assuming that readers "should hate to be boys . . . even the most masculine-minded—are girls at heart" and that matrimony was desirable, readers of one magazine in 1926 were advised to give smoking the "girlish touch": "He doesn't like you to look professional, as it were . . . That is his prerogative!"[46] While a languid grip and a dainty puff may have been the most feminine way to smoke, particularly with the use of a cigarette holder, fashionable smoking styles also included sporting the cigarette between the teeth or drooping it from the corner of the mouth. As seen in the pages of *Vogue*, the cigarette accompanied anything from the boyish/masculine look of the late 1920s, to the ultrafeminine style of the 1930s. Not surprisingly, it was the cigarette, rather than the pipe or cigar, that figured most prominently in the smoking statements of lesbians intent on proclaiming their fashionable status. Radclyffe Hall, for example, attired in a black Spanish-style cape, tailored jacket or smoking jacket with cigarette in hand or clenched between her teeth represented a dashing example of the masculine look. Her partner, Una Troubridge, looked fashionable smoking a cigarette while attired in a soft-fitted dress and a fur stole.[47]

Cigarettes were the most popular and fashionable smoke among interwar women, including lesbians. Cartoons in *Punch* suggest that modern women were sporting pipes in the 1920s, but this practice was not common among heterosexual or lesbian women;[48] these cartoons merely represent anxieties about the limits of "modern" ways and the implications of these for gender and gender relations. Some lesbians did indulge in pipe and cigar smoking. Cigar smoking was described in 1897 by the sexologist, Havelock Ellis, as a lesbian practice and one not shared by straight women.[49] It is not possible, however, to gauge the extent of pipe and cigar smoking by lesbians, or indeed by heterosexual women, because this practice seems to have been more private than cigarette smoking. This may be, in part, because pipes and cigars were usually smoked indoors in leisure contexts and because, in upper-class circles, pipe smoking was considered rather vulgar even among men. In 1914 pipe smoking was often prohibited in restaurants and other public places even where the smoking of cigars and cigarettes was allowed; though it was acceptable for a laborer, or a man in "a bowler hat and a lounge suit," to smoke a pipe in the streets, it was considered "bad form" for upper-class men to do so.[50] Celebrity lesbians did, however, provide sporadic evidence of these consumption practices. Joe Carstairs smoked cigars, cheroots, and pipes,[51] but it was the cigarette that she posed with in photographs. Cigars were smoked by Gluck, she also enjoyed puffing on a clay pipe. Aged 21 in 1916, Gluck lived in Lamorna, a village in Cornwall famous for its colony of artists, and was painted as a gypsy girl smoking a small clay pipe that she owned. In a letter to her brother Louis in 1918, Gluck described the importance of her pipe: "My dear my pipe is a boon and a blessing to me . . . I have some gorgeous moments with it. It is going a perfectly lovely color and is the envy of Lamorna."[52] Pipes and cigars were not, however, statements of fashion even if they could be used as statements of rebellion and of individuality. Take, for example, Gluck's clay pipe. Whilst in 1900 a few older working-class women smoked clay pipes, this practice was restricted almost exclusively to lower-class men.[53] Smoking a clay pipe was, therefore, a statement of gender and class rebellion for Gluck. It was also a sign that Gluck belonged to a particular community because in the early twentieth century the clay pipe enjoyed a renaissance in certain artistic circles; Gluck's artist friend Ella Naper also smoked one when attired in her "workman's corduroy trousers."[54] Although Gluck was depicted with a clay pipe in 1916, the images of herself that she promoted most assiduously in the interwar years were of a woman who smoked cigarettes and the occasional cigar.

While for some middle- and upper-class lesbians smoking was a means of critiquing traditional conceptions of womanhood and of fashioning a modern femininity, for others smoking served as a more radical disassociation from femininity and a visual alignment with masculinity. Gluck dressed in men's clothing and she publicly engaged in a range of smoking practices some of which were still regarded in the interwar years as the preserve of men. Carstairs similarly dressed like a man and smoked as a visible means of being masculine and modern. A photograph taken around 1926 of Carstairs in her boat, Newg, portrays her with a cigarette protruding from her mouth, wearing a beret, scarf, jacket, and trousers; there was no sign in this photo that Carstairs was a woman.[55] This and other photos of Carstairs with her motorboats were for public consumption and at the time Carstairs's appearance was just about contained within the fashion for boyish or mannish looks; press descriptions refer to her as "boyish," "school boyish," "tomboyish," "modern." However, Carstairs engaged in practices such as swearing and spitting that must have been hard to contain within a modern version of 1920s womanhood. She even smoked "incessantly . . . not with languid and feminine grace, but with the sharp decisive gestures a man uses."[56] Carstairs also had photos taken for private use in which she posed with a cigarette. One photo portrayed her dressed in trousers, cigarette in the corner of her mouth, and with shirtsleeves rolled up to reveal well-developed biceps and tattoos. It is difficult, however, to pinpoint a style of smoking that was exclusively lesbian. In themselves, pipe and cigar smoking, or a masculine style of cigarette smoking, were not indicative of sexuality;[57] a range of smoking styles were fashionable among women. However, masculine smoking practices, in combination with masculine clothes and a lack of feminine signifiers, were probably significant statements of sexuality for lesbians such as Carstairs, Gluck, and Hall.

The capacity of the cigarette to serve as a statement of modernity was always context dependent and not all women smokers were therefore regarded as "modern." Some working-class women in the decades from 1900–1939 smoked,[58] but it is usually impossible to judge whether these were lesbians. However, the symbolism of the cigarette differed markedly among women smokers from different social classes. Smoking accentuated the modernity and sophistication of the middle- and upper-class young woman but, stemming from the prewar association of smoking with prostitution, it symbolized promiscuity and a lack of refinement and respectability among the working-class woman. Arising from this it is rare to see working-class women depicted as smokers in the media.[59] In everyday life, the sexual associations of smoking among working-class women also came to the fore and it was widely seen as being incompatible with respectability.[60] According to Felski, the courtesan in France was a symbol of "eroticised modernity";[61] in Britain the slightest hint of sexual impropriety debarred a working-class woman from the status of "modern." The author Vera Brittain, herself a smoker at the time, fired a maid in 1918 because she wore makeup and smoked expensive Turkish cigarettes; together these practices indicated to Brittain that the maid was a prostitute rather than a "modern woman."[62] The opportunities for working-class lesbians to use smoking as a statement of female or sapphic modernity were slim although, as we have seen, a masculine engagement with modernity was a possibility for working-class lesbians who passed as men.

Male Acceptance

Schudson suggests that cigarettes were valuable "social currency" for women as they engaged in modern social practices in the 1920s. Although he specifically addresses American women, his observations apply equally to women in England.

> Women were newly public people and needed, more than before, social currencies acceptable in the public world defined by men. The cigarette was one such coin and a particularly convenient one: cheap, visible, an identifying mark, both easily flaunted and easily hidden, a topic of talk, a token of comradeship and, to boot, a comfort in anxious moments.[63]

Negotiating the public sphere and engaging with men without the presence of chaperones were just some of the ways in which women's lives changed in England after 1914 and cigarettes facilitated women's management of this. Advertising and fiction commonly portrayed women and men smoking together in new social contexts; women were depicted smoking with men in bars, cafes, at sporting and other cultural events, and in moments of intimacy.[64] But whereas the dominant version of the cigarette's social currency was in promoting heterosexual relations, for lesbians the exchange of tobacco products with men could have different meanings. Certain smoking practices, or rituals, were perceived and utilized by lesbians as symbols of male acceptance.

Diana Souhami describes Gluck as getting on well with "establishment men": "They commissioned her to do their portraits and shared with her their conversation, brandy and good cigars."[65] The reference to brandy *and* cigars is interesting because these two items are often cited as aspects of upper-class male bonding rituals. Souhami does not cite evidence for her claim, but this account is interesting irrespective of whether or not this did occur. Either Gluck was offered cigars and brandy as statements of acceptance into a specific gender and class community or she, or someone else, thought that she should have been offered them.

Cigar sharing as a motif of acceptance into male company also has a prominent place in the biography of Joe Carstairs. According to her biographer, Kate Summerscale, Carstairs often recounted stories about sharing cigars with men, at least one of which was clearly very important to her. The earliest story that Carstairs narrated concerned her stepfather, Roger de Perigny. Carstairs claimed that when she was fifteen years old Roger treated her like a boy by "adapting his racing cars, a Peugeot, so that she could drive it, offering her his cigars and introducing her to his many mistresses."[66] The second and most precious story was of meeting her biological father,

Colonel Carstairs in 1918. According to this story, "Carstairs bought her a drink and gave her a cigar."[67] Summerscale doubts the veracity of this account as the dates are inconsistent. Moreover, at the time this encounter was supposed to have taken place, Carstairs, who was only eighteen, would not have been mistaken for a man because she still wore a skirt and had long hair worn in a bun. Whether the stories about being offered cigars are true or not is immaterial, they obviously meant a lot to Carstairs because they symbolized male acceptance. According to another story Carstairs, aged eight, was caught smoking one of her stepfather's cigars. "He punished her by ordering her to sit down in his study and smoke one," but Carstairs, who according to Summerscale had been stealing his cigars for some time, "sat down and calmly smoked her way to the end."[68] In this story cigars feature as a sign of Joe Carstairs's emergent masculinity and as a claim to equality with her despised stepfather.

Sharing cigars with men was also symbolic in other ways that are conducive to bonding. While both "an adept smoker and a novice smoker can get about the same satisfaction from a cigarette, . . . this is much less so with a pipe or cigar": "With a pipe, the quality of the smoke is more dependent on the skill and patience of the smoker and, to a lesser extent, this is true of cigars as well."[69] Sharing cigars represented an acknowledgement of an elite skill. It was also a sign that a woman could tolerate the stronger types of tobacco that were usually appreciated only by men. The consumption of cigars, like that of brandy, was also associated with being a connoisseur and, in this respect, of having a refined and educated palate.[70] Women's smoking of cigars and pipes therefore signaled a complex relationship to modernity. Good cigars represented a celebration of craft skills and tradition, they embodied a critique of the standardization which characterized modern forms of cigarette production. While cigarette smoking was often presented as in rhythm with the bustle of the modern city, the cigar and pipe were seen as an antidote. The *Morning Post*, for example, noted the "soothing influence" of the briar pipe in the context of the "nervous strain to which our town dwellers are submitted in this mechanically-driven age [1924]."[71] Pipe and cigar smoking aligned lesbians with both gender modernity and the embrace of tradition; these consumption practices were, to use Alison Light's phrase, representative of a conservative form of modernity.[72]

Smoking and Modernities

In England, lesbian smoking practices were clearly more diverse than is suggested by the prevailing history of women's smoking. Pipes and cigars feature in lesbian smoking history alongside the cigarette, although the cigarette was the main smoke for lesbians as for women smokers generally in the early decades of the twentieth century. The purposes served by these smoking practices were also more varied than is commonly recognized. Some lesbians utilized smoking to pass as men in their daily lives or as experimentation and/or sexual play. Cigar smoking was also, for some lesbians, a highly symbolic ritual of acceptance into male society. More commonly, smoking was a means of making visual statements about gender and sexual identity.

For many lesbians, smoking signified modernity but this was a more complex matter than is suggested by usual interpretations of women's smoking. There were different articulations of modernity and, with one exception, these were available only to women smokers of the middle and upper classes. Smoking as a statement about gender and/or sexuality was commonly an expression of modernity for middle- and upper-class lesbians. In their hands, the cigarette represented the forging of a modern womanhood and could, for instance, denote a modern intellect and/or sartorial style. The capacity of smoking to signify modernity was dependent on social context and working-class women were unable to make statements about a modern female or sapphic identity through tobacco use prior to World War II. Smoking as an aspect of passing as a man was not a sign of engagement with modern processes, and it did not usually express a modern identity. The exception was where, through passing as a man, lesbian smokers (including working-class passing lesbians) represented a masculine engagement with modernity. Play passing could, however, be an expression of women's modernity and, in the context of lesbian sexual practice, of sapphic modernity. Lesbian smoking practices as symbols of male acceptance also had a complex relationship to modernity. In this instance, the modern aspects of women's smoking were overlaid with other, often conservative, meanings.

The place of smoking in expressions of, and engagements with, modernity were varied and complex, and distinctively sapphic dimensions are often difficult to pinpoint. This is particularly so with smoking practices as statements about gender and sexuality. However, for some lesbians, pipe and cigar smoking, or a masculine style of cigarette smoking, could in combination with masculine clothes and a lack of other feminine signifiers, serve as a marker of lesbian sexuality. Style of smoking was less telling for those lesbians who adopted a feminine mode although even then it could, when juxtaposed against the masculine style of a female partner, suggest differential roles within a lesbian relationship and thereby contribute to a specifically lesbian statement.[73] The sapphic possibilities of certain smoking practices would have been discerned by other lesbians, as well as by those who were aware of female homosexuality. Following media coverage of the trial of *The Well of Loneliness* in 1928, this signaling entered public consciousness and the realms of popular culture.[74]

Notes

1. Bobbie Jacobson, *The Ladykillers: Why Smoking Is a Feminist Issue* (London: Pluto, 1981); Michael Schudson, *Advertising, the Uneasy Persuasion* (New York: Basic Books, 1985); Lorraine Greaves, *Smoke Screen: Women's Smoking and Social Control* (London: Scarlet Press, 1996); Matthew Hilton, *Smoking in British Popular Culture 1800–2000* (Manchester: Manchester University Press, 2000), chapter 4; Rosemary Elliot, " 'Destructive but Sweet': Cigarette Smoking Among Women 1890–1990." Unpublished PhD thesis, University of Glasgow, 2001; Penny Tinkler, " 'Red Tips for Hot Lips': Advertising Cigarettes for Young Women in Britain, 1920–1970," *Women's History Review* 10 (2001); Penny Tinkler, "Rebellion, Modernity and Romance: Smoking as a Gendered Practice in Popular Young Women's Magazines, Britain 1918–1939," *Women's Studies International Forum* 24 (2001); Penny Tinkler "Refinement and Respectable Consumption: the Acceptable Face of Women's Smoking in Britain, 1918–1970," *Gender and History* 15, no. 2 (2003).
2. Schudson, *Advertising*, p. 196.
3. George Latimer Apperson, *The Social History of Smoking* (London: Martin Secker, Ballantyne Press, 1914).
4. Nicholas Wald, Stephanie Kiryluk, Sarah Darby, Sir Richard Doll, Malcolm Pike and Richard Peto, *UK Smoking Statistics* (Oxford: Oxford University Press, 1988), p. 13, table 2.1.
5. Ibid.
6. Alan O'Shea, "English Subjects of Modernity," in Alan O'Shea and Mica Nava, eds., *Modern Times: Reflections on a Century of English Modernity* (London and New York: Routledge, 1996), p. 19.
7. Ibid., p. 11.
8. Rita Felski, *The Gender of Modernity* (London: Harvard University Press, 1995), p. 21.
9. Laura Doan, *Fashioning Sapphism: The Origins of a Modern English Lesbian Culture* (New York: Columbia University Press, 2001).
10. See Judith M. Bennett " 'Lesbian-Like' and the Social History of Lesbianisms," *Journal of the History of Sexuality* 9, nos. 1–2 (January/April 2000): 1–24.
11. On "women's modernity" see Felski, *The Gender of Modernity*; on "sapphic modernity" see Doan, *Fashioning Sapphism.*
12. On "conservative modernity" see Alison Light, *Forever England: Femininity, Literature, and Conservatism between the Wars* (London and New York: Routledge, 1991).
13. Sara Maitland, *Vesta Tilley* (London: Virago, 1986); see also discussion in Marjorie Garber *Vested Interests: Cross-dressing and Cultural Anxiety* (Harmondsworth: Penguin, 1993), p. 156.
14. Greater Manchester Records Office, 1632/103.
15. Alison Oram and Annmarie Turnbull, *The Lesbian History Sourcebook: Love and Sex between Women in Britain from 1780 to 1970* (London: Routledge, 2001), p. 12.

16. Ibid., p. 22.
17. Ibid., p. 44.
18. Hilton, *Smoking.*
19. Ibid., p. 28.
20. Ibid., p. 122.
21. Oram and Turnbull, *The Lesbian History Sourcebook*, p. 11, point out that pre-1900 cross dressers also included women from higher social class backgrounds.
22. Jeffrey Weeks, "History, Desire and Identities," in Richard G. Parker and John H. Gagnon, eds., *Conceiving Sexuality: Approaches to Sex Research in a Postmodern World* (London: Routledge, 1995).
23. Martha Vicinus, "Fin-De-Siécle Theatrics: Male Impersonation and Lesbian Desire," in Billie Melman, ed., *Borderlines* (London: Routledge, 1998). See also images of Carstairs in Kate Summerscale, *The Queen of Whale Cay* (London: Fourth Estate, 1998).
24. Greater Manchester Records Office, 377/75.
25. Nigel Nicholson, *Portrait of a Marriage* (London: Phoenix, 1996), p. 22. See also Victoria Glendinning, *Vita: The Life of V. Sackville-West* (Harmondsworth: Penguin, 1984), p. 95.
26. *Evening News*, March 24, 1920, p. 2.
27. See discussion in O'Shea, "English Modernity," pp. 22–26.
28. Summerscale, *The Queen*, p. 91.
29. Glendinning, *Vita*, p. 103.
30. Summerscale, *The Queen*, p. 68.
31. Diana Souhami, *Gluck: Her Biography* (London: Pandora, 1988), p. 70.
32. Greaves, *Smoke Screen*, p. 20.
33. Peter Gordan and David Doughan, *Dictionary of British Women's Organisations 1825–1960* (London and Portland, OR: Woburn Press, 2001).
34. Reproduced in Diana and Geoffrey Hindley, *Advertising in Victorian England, 1837–1901* (London: Wayland Publishers, 1972), figure 4.5.
35. Hilton, *Smoking*, p. 32.
36. Ibid., pp. 25–26, and on the popularisation of this notion in the opera, *Carmen*, pp. 140–41.
37. On American tobacco packaging, some of which would have been distributed in Britain, see Mitchell Dolores Mitchell, "Images of Exotic Women in Turn-of-the-Century Tobacco Art," *Feminist Studies* 18 (Summer 1992).
38. *Eve*, January, 1920, p. xvi.
39. This observation is based on an examination of photographs of women from across the social-class spectrum that are archived in the National Portrait Gallery Heinz Archive and Library and in the Documentary Photography Archive located in Greater Manchester Record Office.
40. All photographs referred to are in the National Portrait Gallery with the exception of du Maurier's portrait which is reproduced in Ethel Mannin, *Young in the Twenties* (London: Hutchinson, 1971). Fiction also provides examples of smoking signalling a modern intellect and professional identity. See Radclyffe Hall, *The Well of Loneliness* (London: Virago, 1982), p. 210.

41. On smoking and contemplation see Wolfgang Schivelbusch, *Tastes of Paradise: A Social History of Spices, Stimulants and Intoxicants* (New York: Pantheon Books, 1992), pp. 107–110. On Sherlock Holmes see Hilton, *Smoking*, pp. 19–20.
42. For example, portrait of Rosamond Lehmann, National Portrait Gallery Heinz Archive and Library.
43. Photographs of the actress Gertrude Lawrence by Paul Tanqueray and Cecil Beaton in the early 1930s (in the National Portrait Gallery Heinz Archive and Library) are good examples. In the 1940s, and out of the limelight, Lawrence was Daphne du Maurier's lover. See Margaret Forster, *Daphne du Maurier* (London: Arrow, 1994), p. 252.
44. Thanks to Laura Doan for loan of these images.
45. Schudson, *Advertising*, p. 199.
46. *Girls' Favourite*, October 23, 1926, p. 271.
47. See painting by Glady Hynes, 1937, reproduced in Katrina Rolley "Cutting a Dash: The Dress of Radclyffe Hall and Una Troubridge," *Feminist Review* 35 (1990): plate 1.
48. *Punch*, June 15, 1921, p. 470, cited in Doan, *Fashioning Sapphism*, p. 106.
49. Havelock Ellis, *Studies in the Psychology of Sex*, vol. 2, *Sexual Inversion*, cited in Sheila Jeffreys, *The Spinster and Her Enemies. Feminism and Sexuality 1880–1930* (London: Pandora, 1985), p. 106.
50. Apperson, *The Social History of Smoking*, pp. 195–96.
51. Summerscale, *The Queen*.
52. Souhami, *Gluck*, p. 42.
53. Apperson, *The Social History of Smoking*, pp. 215–16.
54. Souhami, *Gluck*, p. 43.
55. Reproduced in Summerscale, *The Queen*. See also photograph of Carstairs in an advert for spark plugs featured in *Tatler*, August 4, 1926, p. 11.
56. Summerscale, *The Queen*, p. 114.
57. See also Doan, *Fashioning Sapphism*.
58. See occasional letters in working- and lower-middle-class young women's magazines, for example: *Our Girls'*, November 27, 1915, p. 623; *Girls' Friend*, April 4, 1925, p. 4.
59. Discussed further in Tinkler, "Respectable Consumption."
60. Elliot, "Destructive but Sweet," pp. 300, 302.
61. Felski, *Gender of Modernity*, p. 20.
62. Vera Brittain, *Testament of Youth* (London: Virago, 1981), p. 429.
63. Schudson, *Advertising*, pp. 182–83.
64. Tinkler, "Red Tips for Hot Lips."
65. Souhami, *Gluck*, p. 81.
66. Summerscale, *The Queen*, p. 24.
67. Ibid., p. 43.
68. Ibid., p. 18.
69 Schudson, *Advertising*, pp. 181, 199.
70. Hilton, *Smoking*, pp. 28–29.

71. Ibid., p. 120.
72. Light, *Forever England.*
73. Rolley, "Cutting a Dash," argues that there were sartorial indicators of the respective roles of Hall and Troubridge within their relationship. Some images of the couple suggest that smoking styles may also have been markers of difference.
74. Doan, *Fashioning Sapphism.* See also Summerscale, *The Queen*, p. 112.

Chapter 5

"Woman's Place *Is* the Home": Conservative Sapphic Modernity

Laura Doan

And around her a posthumous halo has developed.

The halo in question hovers above the famously cropped head of the writer Radclyffe Hall, whose 1928 novel *The Well of Loneliness* thrust, quite suddenly, the subject of lesbianism into British public discourse.[1] Hall's determination to use her novel for political ends (as seen by her demand for the social tolerance of, and the right to existence for, the intermediate sex or "inverts") bestowed on her a special status in the familiar progress narrative of homosexual rights—when, during the late nineteenth and early twentieth centuries, only a few "outrageous" sexual radicals likewise put their reputations and livelihoods at risk through their open association with what might inelegantly be termed nonnormative sexualities, or same-sex love.[2] Like the playwright Oscar Wilde, arguably Hall's male counterpart in the modern English history of homosexual emancipation, the lesbian novelist gained notoriety through a collision with the legal system; in her case, during the autumn of 1928 at London's Bow Street magistrate's court, when the conservative government at that time prosecuted *The Well* for obscene libel. A name notably absent from a letter sent to various national newspapers to protest the government's actions, and signed by forty-five leading figures in "literature, the drama, art, religion, education and science," was that of the prominent novelist (and married sapphist) Vita Sackville-West, who, according to a teasing Virginia Woolf, was not approached for her signature because her own "proclivities" were "too well known."[3] Sackville-West did take a keen interest in the case, however, and attended both the initial hearing and subsequent appeal.

Prior to the uproar and massive media coverage, in fact on the very eve of the publication of *The Well*—tame in literary style but daring in its elitist vision of the future of the intermediate race—an interview Hall gave to the (lesbian) journalist Evelyn Irons appeared in the London *Daily Mail*, entitled provocatively "Woman's Place *Is* the Home."[4] Hall acknowledged that even though the interviewer—and readers—would "doubtless" think her "rather old-fashioned," she nevertheless believed that, "generally speaking, woman's place is the home." For several paragraphs Hall reflects with grave seriousness on the importance of being "a good wife and mother," for this is "the finest work": "A woman who brings up her children, dresses well, and looks after her servants and treats them as they ought to be treated, is doing quite as useful work as she would ever be able to do in an office." Expressions of sympathy for the stay-at-home mum and concern for those women burdened with the arduous task of managing household servants seem odd sentiments indeed from an author clamoring for sexual emancipation in the same month that the Equal Franchise Act granting full female suffrage on equal terms with men became law.

On December 10, at the height of the public controversy surrounding the government's prosecution of *The Well* (the hearings took place on November 9 and 16, and the unsuccessful appeal on December 14), Sackville-West recorded with the novelist Hugh Walpole her thoughts on the subject of "The Modern Woman," a broadcast that had been organized by Hilda Matheson, the director of talks at the BBC. No transcript of this exchange exists, it seems, but Sackville-West's biographer informs us that Vita hardly said a word since she seized up with "stage-fright."[5] Though Sackville-West was frustrated and disappointed with her inarticulacy, the event had one happy result: in a matter of days, the two women had become lovers.[6] In June of 1929, Matheson persuaded Sackville-West and her husband, the diplomat Harold Nicolson, to address BBC listeners on the subject of marriage—a most curious topic in light of the interesting marital agreement the pair had negotiated for themselves, which was, according to Evelyn Irons, that Vita "should have her girlfriends while [Harold] had his boys."[7] Sackville-West was by no means public about her lesbianism, but such knowledge was hardly a secret, particularly in Bloomsbury circles, because of her sensational affair some years earlier with Violet Trefusis and, more recently, with the publication of Woolf's *Orlando* (1928), a celebration of Sackville-West, androgyny, and sapphic desire. Still, Sackville-West was concerned that "her public image as a respectable married woman" remain intact, which may account in part for some of the narrow views advanced in this exchange between wife and husband.[8] Sackville-West, for instance, declares emphatically: "It is scarcely possible to devote yourself adequately to a husband and children and follow a profession at the same time. One or the other must suffer."[9] And how feminists of the late 1920s must have suffered to see such public personalities contribute blithely to the undermining of the ability of most women to strike some sort of balance between the spheres of home and work, as critic Alison Light observes: "Central to any discussion of the interwar years must be the ambiguous place of home and private life in the period, and the problematic and contradictory ways in which it signaled the feminine."[10] Mired in conventionality, one wonders if the dreary commentary on the role and status of modern women vis-à-vis the domestic by two powerful and influential women of the literary marketplace might mask another sort of cultural work. In imparting to readers, listeners, and fans a few tantalizing details of their private feminized space as well as of their personal opinions on modern womanhood and marriage, these cultural documents may work on several levels at once: as honest expressions of conservative political views, as clever marketing strategies on the part of successful writers, or simply as smokescreens to draw attention away from their own unconventional lifestyles. In any case, what these writers accomplish through public disclosure achieves much more than merely the blurring of the boundaries between the private and public. Their pronouncements reveal the strategies of self-fashioning and self-exposure as politically charged and ideologically motivated, enabling us to question whether these private/public boundaries—within some expressions of sapphic modernity—are meaningful categories of cultural analysis at all.

At a time when public awareness of same-sex relations between women in England was increasing, Hall and Sackville-West, lesbians from privileged backgrounds, voiced opinions for public consumption informed by a strange ideological amalgam: an idiosyncratic version of feminist ideals, filtered through conservative values, inflected by class prejudice, and, in the case of Hall, religious fervor. Feminism's demand for equality with men, while seductive, held obvious dangers for such women whose position in the gender hierarchy was far from straightforward. Thus Hall's early ambivalence toward feminism would later evolve into antipathy, as she became "traditionalist and patriarchal," and "instinctively sided with the Establishment and held to the hierarchical view of society to which her class subscribed."[11] The same could be said for the "blatantly and unashamedly anti-working class" Sackville-West whose own writing, literary critic Suzanne Raitt observes, "fed the nostalgic and snobbish hunger of the middle-class reading public to revisit and commemorate that decaying aristocratic order."[12] While the "English, conservative side of her . . . nature" would not blossom fully until the mid-1930s, her views on feminism could at best be described as inconsistent.[13] For example, in the BBC discussion, she complains that marriage is "assumed to be a woman's natural profession" and that men's "growth [is] at the expense of . . . [women's] vitality," and yet—in the same broadcast—adamantly denies she is an "extravagant feminist."

Sackville-West wasn't particularly "extravagant" when it came to religion, either ("I am not, myself, what is called a 'religious' person in the orthodox sense of the phrase"[14]), unlike many other lesbian writers and artists of the interwar period, especially Hall, who was a convert to Roman Catholicism and extremely devout. The bohemian and artist Beresford Egan hit the nail on the head when he cruelly caricatured Hall as a crucified martyr in his lampoon, *The Sink of Solitude*: "Maligned by Beresford Egan, the Conservative government, the *Daily Express*, her mother, called obscene and disgusting, humiliated and reviled, [Hall] responded by showing them all how high-minded she was. She, not they, was close to God."[15] With her ascendance to literary stardom in 1927, Hall may also have sought to affirm her purity at a time when lesbianism had been linked in parliamentary debate with cultural pollution ("a most disgusting and polluting subject"[16]); the social pressure placed on self-respecting lesbians to protest otherwise must have been immense. By her public endorsement of middle-class standards of hygiene, even though such values were mocked by those "real" writers and artists who believed that "filth meant freedom from oppressive bourgeois standards," Hall set about sanitizing her sexuality.[17] Although a sexual radical who moved in bohemian circles, Hall eschewed the bohemian ethos that rejected "the rituals of domestic perfection, including cleanliness itself."[18] For Hall cleanliness represented social respectability as an upper-middle-class lesbian artist increasingly in the public eye. Neither Hall nor Sackville-West observed the rules of established gender norms and hetero-normativity, thinking themselves somehow exceptional and thus exempt, yet their accomplished performances of domesticity and wifeliness suggest an underlying unease, a recognition of the necessity to shore up their "respectability" credentials as a model homemaker or as a woman in a monogamous marriage.[19]

Hall's chatty "good housekeeping" interviews (the one in 1928 and another that appeared a year earlier) and Sackville-West's BBC discussions provide a good focal point from which to investigate the complicated relationship between sapphism, feminism, and modernity between the wars in English national culture. As Light notes, one result of the social changes that came about after World War I was a "move away from the formerly heroic and officially masculine public rhetorics of national destiny . . . to an Englishness at once less imperial and more inward-looking, *more domestic and more private*—and, in terms of pre-war standards, more 'feminine.' "[20]

Out of these contradictions, Light observes the evolution of what she terms "conservative modernity," one that.

> could accommodate the past in the new forms of the present; it was a deferral of modernity and yet it also demanded a different sort of conservatism from that which had gone before. It is the women of an expanding middle class between the wars who were best able to represent Englishness in both its most modern and reactionary forms.[21]

To Light's notion of "conservative modernity"—with its distinctive combination of "popular modernism and a lively traditionalism"[22]—I propose to introduce the concept of sexuality, to see how sapphism complicates the interplay between deviance and conformity, rebel and reactionary, dissident and dominant. An examination of the sapphic turn toward conservatism within modernity will show that our reading strategies of transgression have been extremely limiting, in terms of foreclosing the multiplicity of interpretive possibilities, by ignoring the ways that sexual radicalism may coexist with a certain class-based political conservatism.

My specific focus on the negotiation of the mass media by women such as Hall and Sackville-West also invites us to rethink the ways in which our models of sexual radicalism have too often been uncritically allied with a liberal social agenda to the exclusion of cultural specificity. Some of the sexually progressive in England at a particular point in time (the very individuals we usually judge as *ahead* of their time) may have found it possible to present themselves to large audiences as wholly modern and—at the same time—as the antithesis of politically progressive. Even more disturbing is the apparent willingness of these writers to claim special rights for themselves but relegate the majority of women to traditional, even backward, roles. As career women immersed in the highly visible and masculine world of work, their public embrace of modernity is, as we will see, fraught with ambivalence and equivocation. These privileged modern women, aligned with the "masculine" realm of authorship, fully exploit the technologies of mass culture—such as the women's pages of a widely circulated London daily or the radio broadcast—to espouse not feminist ideals but the values of a male-dominated culture, as evident in these examples of a peculiarly English—and profoundly conservative—expression of sapphic modernity. Unlike "sapphic modernism," which, according to literary historian Shari Benstock, "constitutes itself through moments of rupture in the social and cultural fabric," the contours of what I term "conservative sapphic modernity" represent less cultural rupture than complicity and appropriation.[23]

Past Time as Pastime? The Abandonment of Feminism

Speaking of a cultural moment one generation earlier than Hall's and Sackville-West's, Rita Felski, in *The Gender of Modernity*, writes: "Women's affinity with the temporal dynamics of the modern was . . . shaped as much by their particular ideological affiliations as their material and social circumstances . . . . [F]irst-wave feminism encouraged many women to identify themselves as historical subjects and to present themselves as liberatory agents of the new."[24] These New Women saw the rejection of the past as a radical gesture, one consequence of which was to separate them from the domestic role to which they had been traditionally assigned. This "liberation from the tyranny of the past," as Felski puts it, meant turning one's back on the home and looking ahead with a "quintessentially modern time awareness."[25] If the social forces within English modernity were favorable to women in general, as Light and others have argued, such changes (including greater access to the professions or the dissemination of sexual knowledge) were especially favorable for the creation of a visible sapphic subculture among a small group of upper- and middle-class lesbians located primarily in the country's capital.[26] Thus it is curious that Sackville-West, with her commitment to the institution of marriage, and Hall in particular—a trendsetter in the London social scene—would be such vigorous proponents of conventional constructions of femininity and traditional domesticity relegated to a bygone era by many in the vanguard. How could a thoroughly modern woman such as Hall remain ideologically tethered to familiar formulations of the domestic and yet call strenuously and urgently—and, above all, publicly—for the emancipation of a social outcast, the lesbian or female invert? Hall's narrow and apparently hostile attitude toward women's emancipation sits uneasily beside her forceful and outspoken advocacy of sexual liberation for women such as herself.

Part of the answer to this paradox can be found in a strange 1927 interview published by the *Daily Mail* in which Hall, a recent recipient of the prestigious Femina Prize, offers a glimpse into the inner life of the novelist.[27] In this gossipy interview—two parts banter and one part hype—the journalist Evelyn Irons presents a few select, though less than intimate, details of the living arrangements of Hall, with an emphasis on fashion and fashionable living. We learn, for instance, that the popular writer adores roses, bathrooms, and the color yellow. There is nothing particularly surprising in Hall's exploitation of the publicity apparatus, as she was a woman considered by many commentators of her day to be, as one newspaper phrased it, "a most arresting personality," with an "aura . . . of highbrow modernism."[28]

Such prominence in print—the "new mass media" symptomatic of modernity[29]—would have been designed to capitalize on the buzz generated by her award and to consolidate the writer's status as a celebrity figure, though Hall's readers may have expected an author noted for sporting the ultrachic "severely masculine mode" of dress to plug the pleasures of automobile ownership or exotic travel rather than to prescribe the cultural imperatives of conventionality. In fact, on the eve of the publication of a book that would change profoundly the public's perception of female inversion, Hall presents herself to *Daily Mail* readers as a contradiction: modern *and* old-fashioned—her fashionable, modern appearance was no guarantee of fashionable, modern ideas.

The interview's exclusive revelations concern not the writer's literary technique or views on the contemporary novel, but her effusive interest in the domestic (Hall, we are told, polishes her antique oak furniture "with beeswax and turpentine") and her keen attentiveness to the mundane details of everyday life: "I love my house . . . I am a fussy housekeeper with a perfect mania for cleanliness." Newsworthiness was obviously beside the point of a women's page feature article that, through layout and photographic illustration, displays the "personality" of the week as someone with whom the average *Daily Mail* reader could identify. The upshot of this kind of media exposure, of course, was primarily to stimulate consumers' interest in Hall as a public persona with sexual glamour and thereby increase the sale of her books (the titles of three of Hall's novels appear in the caption beneath her photograph). Yet the overall message conveyed exceeds the sum of its parts. On the left-hand side of the four-column article is a large, somewhat austere photograph of the author, hair shingled and cigarette in hand. Nothing of her surroundings can be glimpsed, but Hall's highly tailored jacket and stiff collar situate her as an unquestionably important representative of 1920s English modernity. This photo of the sleekly elegant modern woman contrasts starkly with Hall's enthusiasm for the therapeutic value of physical exertion in vigorous housework: "when I feel jarred and disgruntled, I work it off in a bout of polishing," an act she ecstatically declares is the "greatest" of her "household joys." Even the interviewer acknowledges bafflement at this seeming contradiction: "Coming from this businesslike woman in tweeds and polo collar, with her fair Eton-cropped hair brushed straight back from her forehead, this was a surprising statement." Perhaps one explanation is that Hall approaches the "art" of domesticity as an entirely modern woman by using a professionalism that was de rigueur during the interwar years. At a time when "efficiency and management increasingly became the new watchwords of upper-middle-class women who no longer saw themselves as simply wives at home but 'housewives,' something altogether more professional," Hall appeals to the house-proud.[30] In the absence of a husband or children, the Hall/Troubridge household is no locus of heterosexual marital bliss, sexual reproduction, or family responsibilities, but instead an object of professional interest for Hall's housekeeping instincts.

Hall strives to convince readers that—like them—she is utterly scrupulous about such activities as dust removal, and, indeed, at the time, this "very high standard of housekeeping was expected"; as historian Jane Lewis explains: the conscientious housewife "felt that it was necessary to mop daily and dust pictures and skirtings, electric light fixtures and cupboard tops thoroughly once a week."[31] Hall accordingly tells her readers that she diligently patrols every inch of her house on the lookout for disorder: "I often write for twelve hours at a stretch. If during that time I spy specks of dust I have to control my itch to remove them, for I have the housewife's 'seeing eye.' " Closer examination of the way Hall runs her home, however, shows that she is not like other upper-middle-class women, who would have been consulting "household manuals . . . [that] advised" them to apply "the principles of scientific management used by industry, including time and motion studies, to increase their efficiency."[32] Hall, though thorough and meticulous, did not meet (and did not *have* to meet) modern standards—a really modern housewife would have taken advantage of the greater availability of small household appliances designed to make housework a far simpler affair. Hall's failure to mention the helpfulness of mechanical devices, along with her emphasis on good old-fashioned elbow grease, positions her as a homemaker of an earlier era and suggests that her "mania" for cleanliness was working to suture ties that were dangerously close to fraying. Public exposure of the upper-middle-class Hall/Troubridge household becomes an opportunity to affirm respectability, to pass as normal and unexceptional. If "dirt is essentially disorder," and if lesbianism connotes the loss of cleanliness, Hall's performance of domestic femininity disassociates her and her partner from cultural pollution: "In chasing dirt, in papering, decorating, tidying we are not governed by anxiety to escape disease, but are positively reordering our environment, making it conform to an idea."[33] The concern for dirt, as anthropologist Mary Douglas argues, represents "care for hygiene and respect for conventions."[34] Hall's own investment in convention, her claim to the moral high ground, surfaces when it is most likely to be lost.

More significantly, Hall admits that her urge to clean house is little more than, as she puts it, a "hobby" or "recreation"—in other words, a simple pastime. For some successful career women, modern life facilitates the reconfiguration of domestic work as plaything rather than as "science" or drudgery. Hall's new literary status gives her—and a few others like her—the luxury, quite literally, to play house. This stance, however, is privileged, as Hall does not speak to the potential for *all* women to regard the home as a hobby. Modern life, for instance, still divides into discrete polarities (masculine/feminine, public/private, work/recreation, career/home, modern/domestic): "It is seldom," Hall notes, "that my career and my home come into conflict." Thus the one realm in the house to elude domestication is the writer's "Spartan little study"—amid the clutter of books, files, and papers, Hall banishes the soft feminine colors and scents of flowers. One of modernity's achievements is that it allows certain creative women to establish a new relationship with the traditional feminine sphere and align with the masculine world of work or public life, but such progress is not in the cards for every woman. Hall's home is not the traditional comfortable refuge from public life, as she has invited the media to intrude into her private world in order to put it on display to a wide readership. Hall's insistence that she refuses to "let the house run itself—I must supervise it personally and do my accustomed 'chores,' " also signals to readers that she is independent and autonomous. Hall thus differentiates herself in terms of class and gender from ordinary *Daily Mail* readers, women who, presumably, had sole responsibility for the upkeep of the home. Not for her the "ridiculously high standards" that left women "little time to wonder whether their lives might have been better spent than in this endless round of domestic ritual."[35] The interview itself, for all its "findings," works on behalf of another agenda seen even more vividly in Hall's second interview. While in 1927 Hall had spoken generally of "woman," in the following year the novelist uses the phrase "these women." This strategic shift posits a crucial distinction between "the majority of women—the 'wife and mother' type," and "exceptional women [who] are very strong physically, or intellectually brilliant." Hall continues to refine these categories by arguing that "there is no reason to suppose that all women are potential amazons or scholars. It is very noticeable that in our postwar world there are more and more women who are not of the wife and mother type. They are perfectly happy and efficient doing men's work." But, Hall bluntly states: "Very few women can do it!" Here we see an emerging political stance that is rather more unsettling because it rests on exclusionary notions of femininity.

A similar sentiment is echoed by Sackville-West who, at the outset of her BBC discussion, dismisses both the superrich and those who earn a mere thirty-five shillings per week, in favor of the "professional classes," a group she further subdivides into active and passive women. Despite their numbers, Sackville-West regards the nonactive as undeserving of any social concern or pity, as they "*are* content to find their fulfillment in devotion to their husband and home and children; it is very lucky for them, and very nice for their husbands." Active women need hardly spare a moment's commiseration for their passive sisters, because the latter are merely responsive to the dictates of their inner nature, in accordance with their biological drives: "it probably even satisfies some need of [the passive woman's] nature to subordinate herself entirely to the service of her family." The active type of woman, on the other hand, "has interests beyond her home . . . [and] may even have a profession." Neither amazons nor scholars, Sackville-West conceives of these modern women as "barristers, doctors, politicians, even Cabinet Ministers." This group deserves greater consideration, Sackville-West contends, due to the failure of the government or employers to provide services and amenities to enable such women to pursue both a career and a home life; after all, the "picture of a man pushing a pram is grotesque." Sackville-West's sympathies obviously lie with those active women who face a bleak future in which they either "must give up the happiness of home, or . . . must sacrifice [their] . . . career." Like Hall, Sackville-West willingly abandons feminist principles of inclusivity to create a space for that rare breed known as the exceptional woman, separated from her bourgeois sisters by the English class system and tolerated, because of her class, in a male-dominated culture in order to confirm "the mediocrity of other women."[36] Ultimately, the promise of modernity is not for the "majority" of English women, whose place most assuredly "*is* the home"—the majority asks for nothing more and deserves nothing less.

"The Home Speaks"

Hall—like her contemporary, the popular writer Mrs. Ethel Alec-Tweedie—sees "home life" as "an idyll: everything should be done to make it beautiful and its surroundings worthy. The home speaks."[37] In other words, the home makes visible to the visitor aspects of its owner's habits, and, like Eve Sedgwick's definition of the "closet," Hall's house speaks volumes, while it remains stubbornly silent. Sedgwick writes: "the relations of the closet—the relations of the known and the unknown, the explicit and the inexplicit around homo/heterosexual definition—have the potential for being peculiarly revealing."[38] In this way, Hall and her way of living are both seen and unseen, on public view and yet secret. The explicit and inexplicit aspects of Hall's lifestyle are best revealed in her house tour, which teases and beguiles the reader and makes "public" an invented domesticity that speaks to certain normative values and ideals. Where Irons mentions, almost casually and in passing, that Hall "shares" her fashionable Kensington house with "Una Lady Troubridge," Hall paints a picture of cozy domesticity, with a clear-cut division of labor not between husband and wife or homeowner and staff, but between two housewives: "Lady Troubridge sees to the food. I am not really interested in that side of housekeeping . . . . My province is the house itself."

Troubridge's busy engagement with meal planning and food shopping gives Hall the freedom not only to work, but also to perform house *work*, which is not really work at all, but, as she puts it, "a relaxation." Troubridge never speaks directly to the interviewer, so we can only assume that she acquiesces to this arrangement, happy in the knowledge that these assigned tasks allow her partner to get on with other, more important, jobs. Hall alone makes the key decisions concerning home improvements: the "only alteration I made in the house when I took it" was in ordering the mantelpieces to be ripped out. In favoring an authoritarian approach to household management, Hall rejects an egalitarianism more congruent with those feminist values that would typically divide jobs into "fairly equal divisions" and endorses a more conventional heterosexual division of labor within the gender hierarchy.[39] Hall's lifestyle is not a role model to feminists, but one of refinement facilitated by superb taste, where every aspect of her home life is subject to her control: "The very papers on the desk," Irons comments, "were meticulously ordered." Hall's participation in the upkeep of the home is, in effect, a policing effort in which she is constantly on the lookout for disorder, and where she rules over Troubridge and the staff. How many of Hall's readers swallowed this spin is hard to gauge, but it is important to remember that in 1928 any reference to house sharing might have been interpreted in any number of ways, including—but not necessarily denoting—same-sex intimacy. Hall's glib aside that she entrusts the care of her "beautiful old oak furniture" only to long-time staff is the only indication that, like many women of their social class, the couple actually did very little themselves around the house; we know, for example, that the couple employed "a personal maid, four house servants, a gardener and gardener's boy."[40]

Both women, according to Troubridge's memoirs, thrilled in their home life and continuously searched for the "perfect home."[41] For Troubridge, the home and its furnishings—full of "every comfort and convenience that our hearts could desire"—were almost a source of erotic pleasure, as seen in this description of a spending spree after moving into their first home together: "we enjoyed our first orgy of selecting and discarding the furniture."[42] The purchase of "really beautiful" and "unquestionably genuine" furniture was not simply a practical necessity, but "evoke[d] wonderful thrills."[43] Irons too observes in the first interview how Hall could be seen "fingering the worn wood [of a] toilet-table . . . lovingly," while one bedroom contained "Hall's special pride—two beds of an early period with lovely linenfold paneling." Sexual frisson emanates not from the bedroom, even with this revealing glimpse into an inner sanctum, but from the house itself that Hall anthromorphosizes as a flirtatious mistress, requiring all of Hall's willpower to resist its seductive power: "The minute my house begins to 'vamp' me—houses do become vampires sometimes—I run away from it." Hall's allusion to vampire appears to be an acknowledgment of sorts of a lesbian relationship between home and homeowner, since in feminizing the house Hall becomes the lover pursued, if also the lover who resists pursuit.[44] Rather than flee *to* a hotel to partake in illicit lovemaking, the lesbian writer runs "away from" her own home: "Somehow the household arrangements of an hotel don't clamor for my attention: that happens only in my own home."

Mass-media exposure promises readers a tantalizing glimpse of the world behind closed doors, but Hall maneuvers—as a not yet public lesbian—between the "real" private, that is, her life in a committed relationship with her female partner, and an alternative "private," which functions as a commodity for readerly consumption. That alternative "private"—via the interview—purportedly shifts her private feminized space into the male-dominated public space, but that gesture is a mere masquerade. The interview thus allows the award-winning writer to expand her readership by marketing a version of the private sphere as public. The home speaks, but on many levels and to different audiences. Ironically, within weeks of the 1928 interview, the then *Sunday Express* editor, James Douglas, would accuse Hall and others of her ilk of residing not in a cleansed, pure, and sanitized space, but in a realm of pollution, pestilence, and contagion.[45]

"They're Here, They're Queer—They're Conservative!"

My analysis of these cultural documents shows that, if modernity is "the practical negotiation of one's life and one's identity within a complex and fast-changing world," then these formulations of the "modern" woman by Hall and Sackville-West represent one sort of negotiated settlement with a postwar world undergoing radical change.[46] At the same time, both writers were surely aware that publicity of this kind would not be detrimental to their commercial prospects, and they tailored much of their commentaries to please their respective readerships and audiences among the "professional" classes. Hall, for instance, could not have found a more ideal readership than the one on offer with the *Daily Mail*, which "presented a vision of stable femininity and peaceful domesticity that harnessed the latest modern developments, but respected the traditions of the past."[47] In Sackville-West's case, Raitt speculates, the "conservatism" of the married couple's "conversation could be seen as a defense, but it seems likely that they believed most of what they said. (Their letters suggest that they took the broadcast seriously.)"[48] Raitt's supposition seems on target, as evident when, frustrated by her dismal performance in the first BBC "discussion" with Walpole,

Sackville-West clarifys her position in private correspondence with her husband, exclaiming: "Woman *cannot* combine careers with normal life . . . . They love too much; they allow love to override everything else. Men don't."[49] We can also gauge something of Sackville-West's attitude toward feminism in a passage of her 1931 novel *All Passion Spent*, in which the female protagonist reflects: "Yet she was no feminist. She was too wise a woman to indulge in such luxuries as an imagined martyrdom. The rift between herself and life was not the rift between the worker and the dreamer."[50] As Raitt points out, "Sackville-West's anxiety to repudiate feminist politics demonstrates her need, or her desire, to protect the institution of marriage, and her unwillingness to accept that it could be amended or even abandoned," an institution that protected her and Nicolson from scandal and disgrace.[51] Their marriage was, by every standard of measure, highly unusual, but it worked, and the pair even found it possible to fashion a plausible formula for marital success to offer their BBC listeners.

That marriage, of course, was not all that it seemed—and neither was the exquisite construction of domesticity Hall peddled to readers. Oddly enough, Hall was not possessed with nesting instincts—she never settled down and, throughout her life, continually bought and sold houses: "It was a pattern . . . to house herself in style, extensively refurbish, purchase antique furnishings, take on all the paraphernalia and responsibilities of domesticity—servants and pets—get the whole place just so, and then sell up . . . . At root was a subversion, a restlessness."[52] Hall was not much of a homebody either and, in reality, cared little for the daily routines of homemaking. As early as 1926 commentator Beverley Nichols observed that Hall was known to "boast that she knew nothing about housekeeping. She must have regarded this as a sign of virility, because she often referred to it."[53] Another of Hall's biographers points out that "neither [Hall] nor Miss Irons had any illusions: the [1927] article was a piece of journalistic 'hype.' Privately, [Hall] confided to her interviewer that Una looked after the house and that if any dusting or polishing was necessary, she simply rang for the maid."[54] Sackville-West, incidentally, would not attempt housework until World War II, when she told her husband: "I am still polishing with great effect . . . but it is hell doing the brass hinges on the Coromandel cabinet. . . . I am beginning to see what housemaids mean, when they talk of 'dust-traps.' "[55]

Hall and Sackville-West (and no doubt other prominent upper-class and upper-middle-class lesbians who sought and were sought after by the mass media of the interwar period) knew little and could not care less about the everyday running of their households—but none dared risk alienating potential readers, and this entailed creative self-fashioning to always appear respectable and acceptable to their readers. Hall and Sackville-West, highly visible personalities of London's literary and artistic circles, both exploited the public platform to tell other women how they should balance career and home life, or abandon a career altogether; however, for all the fluidity of boundaries enabling the modern woman to move with ease in the masculine world, the march of progress was not to be for "the majority of women." Still, Hall and Sackville-West were by no means on the radical fringe of conservatism—the lesbian writer Clemence Dane's homophobic tirade against the "sexually abnormal" might be viewed as even more reactionary—but their appropriation of conservative modernity, in which "the same old private life—the sphere of domestic relations, and all which it encompassed had . . . changed" was at once pragmatic and self-serving.[56] By enabling the construction of a different kind of domestic life, Hall could include her lesbian partner *and* lay claim to respectability, even as she excluded most other women. In this way, she co-opted conservative modernity to "break with tradition and [imagine] new futures."[57] In much the same way, Sackville-West co-opted the institution of marriage to accommodate her alternative lifestyle. In cautiously reserving the options and opportunities of these "new futures" for a select few, rather than all or even most other, women, their agenda was, arguably, to curtail the emancipation of modernity and to deny others what modernity had allowed them. In recasting the feminine, domestic sphere of a past time as a *pastime* for a lesbian elite, such women courted the hostility of feminists, as seen in some of the responses in feminist publications toward Hall's groundbreaking novel. In *Time and Tide*, for instance, feminist Vera Brittain welcomed Hall's radical call for tolerance of the sexually abnormal, but sharply criticized her conservative investment in conventional gender roles, calling the novel's female heterosexual characters "clinging and 'feminine' to exasperation."[58] Brittain astutely recognized that Hall's representation of "true womanhood" was at odds with the lives of average "wives and mothers," women who were of little concern to Hall.

Hall's ideological linkage with antifeminist conservative forces suggests that the author of *The Well of Loneliness* was a clever tactician in seizing on the eve of the novel's publication the opportunity to reassure readers that she was by no means radical and that, on the contrary, she was eager to endorse the social values of the dominant culture. The accompanying photograph of the 1928 interview—a headshot in a different pose than the 1927 photograph, but in the same outfit—underscores the high seriousness of the businesslike author. Under the headline, "Woman's Place *Is* the Home," the subheading announces: "An interview with Miss Radclyffe Hall, whose new novel . . . appears tomorrow." The timing of Hall's alignment with conservative forces ("these women don't honestly prefer their jobs to their homes") was no coincidence. As a professional writer who also constructed herself as a modern homemaker, Hall fully understood a fundamental condition of conservative English modernity, with all the privileges of her class: that, in its ability to negotiate both the past and the future, one could locate a safe haven for a few exceptional women. Hall constituted the home either as a pastime or a place for the inferior mother-and-wife type and, in so doing, elevated those who were unable to retreat safely each evening to a traditional family and those who, unless privileged with a private income, would be forced to join the ranks of working men. In yoking the majority of women to the "tyranny of the past," to return to Felski's terms, and in reserving modernity's "liberation" for the few, Hall and Sackville-West envisioned a new and better world for an elite minority, whether inverted or exceptional. The politics of such sapphic conservatism are bold, but also elitist; even, in Hall's case, what might be termed "homosexist." Under the influence of women such as Radclyffe Hall and Vita Sackville-West, sapphic modernity evolved in England as a deeply conservative affair, suspicious of feminism and reluctant to challenge the cultural imperatives represented by the very men keen to silence the dangerous modern woman.

Notes

Many thanks to Jane Garrity and Bev Skeggs for thoughtful comments on early versions of this essay.

1. This heading of the essay's opening section appears in Jeffrey Weeks' *Coming Out: Homosexual Politics in Britain from the Nineteenth Century to the Present* (1977; reprint, London: Quartet Books, 1990), p. 111. Radclyffe Hall, *The Well of Loneliness*. 1928 (New York: Anchor Books, 1990).
2. Weeks, *Coming Out*, p. 97.
3. *Daily Herald*, November 11, 1928. The phrase—probably tongue-in-cheek—about Sackville-West's "proclivities" appears in a letter from Virginia Woolf to Vita Sackville-West. See Nigel Nicholson and Joanne Trautmann, eds., *The Letters of Virginia Woolf*, vol. 3, 1923–1928 (New York and London: Harcourt Brace Jovanovich, 1978), p. 520.
4. *Daily Mail*, July 26, 1928, p. 4. This interview was the second conducted by Irons with Hall—an earlier one had appeared the previous year. No further references to the article "Woman's Place *Is* the Home" will be cited, unless the context is unclear.
5. Victoria Glendinning, *Vita: The Life of V. Sackville-West* (London: Weidenfeld and Nicolson, 1983), p. 208.
6. Ibid., pp. 209–10.
7. Ibid., p. 240.
8. Suzanne Raitt, *Vita and Virginia: The Work and Friendship of V. Sackville-West and Virginia Woolf* (Oxford: Clarendon Press, 1993), p. 7.
9. See "Marriage: A Discussion between Victoria Sackville-West and Harold Nicolson," *Listener* 1, June 26, 1929, pp. 899–900. No further references to the article "Marriage" will be cited, unless the context is unclear.

10. Alison Light, *Forever England: Femininity, Literature, and Conservatism between the Wars* (London and New York: Routledge, 1991), p. 217.
11. Michael Baker, *Our Three Selves: The Life of Radclyffe Hall* (New York: Morrow, 1985), p. 49.
12. Raitt, *Vita and Virginia*, pp. 10–11.
13. Glendinning, *Vita*, pp. 283–84.
14. Ibid., p. 285.
15. Diana Souhami, *The Trials of Radclyffe Hall* (London: Weidenfeld and Nicolson, 1998), p. 239.
16. *Hansard*, Lords, 5th ser., 14 (1921): 568.
17. Virginia Nicholson, *Among the Bohemians: Experiments in Living 1900–1939* (London: Penguin Books, 2002), p. 201.
18. Ibid., p. 195.
19. See Bev Skeggs' chapter on "Becoming Respectably Heterosexual" in *Formations of Class and Gender: Becoming Respectable* (London: Sage, 1997), pp. 118–38.
20. Light, *Forever England*, p. 8. Emphasis mine.
21. Ibid., pp. 10–11.
22. David Glover and Cora Kaplan, "Editorial," Special issue: "Conservative Modernity," *New Formations: A Journal of Culture/Theory/Politics* 28 (Spring 1996), p. 2.
23. Shari Benstock, "Expatriate Sapphic Modernism: Entering Literary History," in Karla Jay and Joanne Glasgow, eds., *Lesbian Texts and Contexts: Radical Revisions* (New York: New York University Press, 1990), p. 198.
24. Rita Felski, *The Gender of Modernity* (Cambridge: Harvard University Press, 1995), p. 145.
25. Ibid., pp. 146–47.
26. See, for example, Light, *Forever England* and Janet Wolff, *Feminine Sentences: Essays on Women and Culture* (Berkeley: University of California Press, 1990).
27. *Daily Mail*, May 11, 1927, p. 19. No further references to the article "How Other Women Run Their Homes" will be cited, unless the context is unclear.
28. *Newcastle Daily Journal and North Star*, August 22, 1928, p. 8.
29. Mica Nava and Alan O'Shea, "Introduction," in Nava and O'Shea, eds., *Modern Times: Reflections on a Century of English Modernity* (London and New York: Routledge, 1996), p. 4.
30. Light, *Forever England*, p. 218.
31. Jane Lewis, *Women in England 1870–1950* (Brighton, Sussex: Wheatsheaf Books, 1984), p. 116.
32. Ibid.
33. Mary Douglas, *Purity and Danger: An Analysis of Concepts of Pollution and Taboo* (London and Henley: Routledge, 1979), p. 2.
34. Ibid., p. 7.
35. Nicola Beauman, *A Very Great Profession: The Woman's Novel 1914–39* (London: Virago, 1983), p. 110.
36. Anthea Trodd, *Women's Writing in English: Britain, 1900–1945* (London: Longman, 1998), p. 22.
37. Mrs. Ethel Alec-Tweedie, *Women and Soldiers* (London: John Lane, 1918), p. 148.

38. Eve Kosofsky Sedgwick, *Epistemology of the Closet* (New York: Harvester Wheatsheaf, 1991), p. 3.
39. Gillian A. Dunne, "A Passion for 'Sameness'? Sexuality and Gender Accountability," in Elizabeth B. Silva and Carol Smart, eds., *The New Family?* (London: Sage, 1999), p. 66.
40. Una, Lady Troubridge, *The Life and Death of Radclyffe Hall* (London: Hammond, Hammond, 1961), p. 63.
41. Ibid., p. 61.
42. Ibid., p. 62.
43. Ibid., p. 63.
44. For an interesting discussion of the linkage between "lesbian" and "vampire," see Sue-Ellen Case, "Tracking the Vampire," *differences: A Journal of Feminist Cultural Studies* 3, no. 2 (Summer 1991).
45. James Douglas's editorial of August 19, 1928, "A Book That Must Be Suppressed," is reprinted in Laura Doan and Jay Prosser, eds., *Palatable Poison: Critical Perspectives on The Well of Loneliness* (New York: Columbia University Press, 2001), pp. 36–38.
46. The headline "They're here, they're queer-they're conservative" appeared recently on the cover of the *Nation* magazine, as reported in the *Guardian*, July 8, 2002, p. 14. O'Shea, "English Subjects of Modernity" in *Modern Times*, p. 11.
47. See Deborah S. Ryan, " 'All the World and Her Husband': The *Daily Mail* Ideal Home Exhibition 1908–39," in Maggie Andrews and Mary M. Talbot, eds., *All the World and Her Husband: Women in Twentieth-Century Consumer Culture* (London: Cassell, 2000), pp. 10–11.
48. Raitt, *Vita and Virginia*, p. 7.
49. Quoted in Glendinning, *Vita*, p. 209.
50. Vita Sackville-West, *All Passion Spent* (London: Hogarth Press, 1931), p. 164.
51. Raitt, *Vita and Virginia*, p. 8.
52. Diana Souhami, *The Trials of Radclyffe Hall* (London: Weidenfeld and Nicolson, 1998), p. 120.
53. *Sunday Herald*, March 26, 1926.
54. Baker, *Our Three Selves*, p. 195.
55. Glendinning, *Vita*, pp. 322–23.
56. Clemence Dane, "Two Million Women," *Britannia and Eve* (May 1929), p. 22 and Light, *Forever England*, p. 10.
57. Sally Alexander, "The Mysteries and Secrets of Women's Bodies: Sexual Knowledge in the First Half of the Twentieth Century" in *Modern Times*, p. 163.
58. Vera Brittain, *Time and Tide*, August 10, 1928; rpt. in Doan and Prosser, eds., *Palatable Poison*, p. 60.

Chapter 6

Art Deco Hybridity, Interior Design, and Sexuality between the Wars

Two Double Acts: Phyllis Barron and Dorothy Larcher/ Eyre de Lanux and Evelyn Wyld

Bridget Elliott

Tracing the emergence of female interior decorators around the turn of the twentieth century, Peter McNeil notes that the issue of the designer's sexuality has been suppressed in most of the design literature, perhaps because during the interwar years so many leading figures in the field were women who pursued same-sex relationships. To demonstrate his point, McNeil draws our attention to the interior decorator Elsie de Wolfe, the florist Constance Spry, the painter and frame-maker Gluck, the furniture historian and advisor Margaret Jourdain, the designer and architect Eileen Gray, and the designing couple Elizabeth Eyre de Lanux and Evelyn Wyld.[1] Starting from McNeil's observations, this chapter considers the practice of two such designing couples: Phyllis Barron and Dorothy Larcher, who specialized in hand-block printed textiles and worked in London before moving their studio to rural Gloucestershire, and Eyre de Lanux and Wyld, who produced furniture and rugs first in Paris and later in Cannes. Both couples were active during the late 1920s and early 1930s, when they combined their work (sometimes with that of other artists) to produce remarkably innovative interior decoration schemes. This chapter investigates their sources of inspiration, technical practices, and esthetic tenets as well as their desire to redesign everyday life for the modern woman. In particular, it examines some of their better known and more fully developed room schemes, including Barron and Larcher's home in Painswick, Hambutts House, which was furnished and decorated over many years, and their commission to decorate the common rooms of Girton College, Cambridge (1932–1934), as well as Eyre de Lanux and Wyld's room schemes for the Société des Artistes Décorateurs (1928) and the Salon d'Automne (1929) and their decoration of Mrs. Forsythe Sherfesee's Paris apartment (1930).

Focusing on the work of these two couples helps us reconceptualize an aesthetic field that has been governed by an opposition between modernism and art deco (or art *moderne*) with its attendant binaries of avant-garde/historicist, exterior/interior, structural/decorative, industrial/handmade, mass/elite, and male/female. Traditionally, art deco has been cast as the stylistically impure, superficial and commercially contaminated counterpart to the modernist avant-garde and condemned for its unholy combination of streamlined forms and decorative details based on zigzag jazz-age motifs or stylized historical patterns.[2] This impure or hybrid space was one that seems to have suited experimental women artists and designers particularly well, especially those working in small-scale workshops who sold their work through a series of women's networks. As explained later in this chapter, the division between modernist and *moderne* (or deco) was complicated in the world of design, where, as McNeil stresses, esthetic, social, and sexual experimentation tended to flourish during the interwar years. Instead of denigrating both couples' practices as not being modernist enough and excluding it from the canons of art and design, I suggest that its hybridity is what makes the work so engaging and not only from an esthetic point of view. As I argue, the social and sexual effects of the two couple's esthetic collaboration present interesting challenges and opportunities for the recently charted field of sapphic modernity, by stretching its parameters and adding further layers of complication.[3] Here I deliberately invoke the vocabulary of Pierre Bourdieu whose cultural force-fields function as paradigms for organizing messy and recalcitrant material traces from other times and places.[4] While some historical case studies neatly occupy the center of a field, others haunt its margins, moving in and out of the space in ways that reinforce and undermine its explanatory power. These are case studies whose liminality and ambiguity suggests that the boundaries between lesbian, bisexual, and straight have been more fluid than our current use of these terms implies.

From the outset, it should be stressed that, despite the fact that one couple remained lifelong partners, these women designers do not seem to have self-identified as lesbian, sapphic, or even primarily women-oriented in ways we would recognize now—at least in the archival material that I have examined. Instead they appear to have been reticent about questions of sexuality, perhaps to avoid the sorts of negative stereotyping that followed the 1928 trial of Radclyffe Hall's *Well of Loneliness* or perhaps because they were more absorbed in the practice of art than in sexual politics. Writing as an art historian, this is something that I have opted to respect given the struggles women artists and designers have faced in trying to secure adequate professional recognition for their work. Rather than interrogating private lives, I have focused on collaborative esthetic practice, considering its implications for the fields of both modernist design and sapphic modernity.

Phyllis Barron and Dorothy Larcher started working together in 1923. Barron trained as a painter at the Slade School of Fine Art and had been cutting blocks for printing textiles since 1915. Like Barron, Larcher had also studied painting but at the Hornsey School of Art. After completing her painting course, Larcher spent several years in India recording the Buddhist frescoes of the Ajanta Caves.[5] Both women would continue to draw inspiration from earlier "primitive" art forms—ranging from eighteenth- and nineteenth-century French and Russian examples to African and Indian patterns—and together they amassed a large historical collection of old printing blocks, which they often exhibited with their fabrics and which Barron illustrated in an essay she published in 1928 on the subject of block printing.[6]

Block printing involves cutting patterns either into a linoleum inset or else directly into a woodblock itself. The block is dipped in a thickened dye and hand pressed onto the fabric. Smaller units can be combined in an infinite variety of ways, and were often overprinted.[7] More typically, however, Barron and Larcher executed fairly simple designs in a limited range of natural dyes—indigo, black (oak galls), brown (iron rust and cutch), and later in the 1930s, reds (pure alizarin, an extract of madder, and German chrome) were introduced. The couple also experimented with indigo discharge, which involves dying a fabric blue in a vat and then printing in nitric acid to discharge or bleach out the design, which then appears in white on the blue ground. They printed in larger or smaller blocks on a wide variety of fabrics, including cotton, linen, organdie, crepe de Chine, wool, velvet, and silk, according to the intended use of the fabric in furnishing or clothing. The work, all done by hand, was physically demanding, involving various female apprentices and assistants, who helped print, dip, hoist, steam, and hose down fabric not to mention cutting, sewing, and fitting garments and slip covers. Such work proved difficult in the confined space of their first Hampstead studio and their relocation to the village of Painswick in rural Gloucestershire was motivated partly by their desire for more studio space and a reliable pool of local village women who could work as assistants.[8]

The Cotswold area appealed to Barron and Larcher, because they had friends there and the region had long been associated with the arts and crafts movement.[9] Their female staff at the workshop added a new feminist and sapphic layer to the antiindustrialist, guild production of earlier and better known craftsmen such as William Morris at Kelmscott, Charles Robert Ashbee at Chipping Camden, and Ernst Grimson and Ernest and Sidney Barnsley at Pinbury Park in Saperton.[10] The fact that many thriving small-scale workshops remained in the area enabled Barron and Larcher to incorporate the production of these highly skilled artisans into some of their own commissions.

It is important to stress that Barron and Larcher worked in spaces directly adjacent to their own living quarters and many visitors and friends commented on their close relationship and the intertwining of art and life. When Robin Tanner first met the couple in 1938 in the splendid garden that inspired many of their designs, he could not help noticing Barron's tall, large, handsome, and commanding figure, closely cropped silver hair and men's brogues. He was even more struck by her "long linen garment, printed in one of her favorite designs which she called 'Guinea,' in the galled iron black she was so fond of . . . . And all down the front were old silver Dutch buttons." Larcher's smaller figure was no less striking, because she too was most beautifully dressed in "cotton printed in iron rust in her own design called 'Old Flower' the very first she ever cut. . . . [She] was a most distinguished embroideress. I observed at once the immaculate stitchery and the embroidered collar and cuffs of her dress, and the amber glass buttons chosen with perfect appropriateness." Tanner found the inside of their house to be as lovely as the garden and their clothing along with their curtains, covers, and cushions to have their own patterns. He concluded that "[e]very small detail of every object in that room seemed right. . . . I thought, if ever there was a marriage of true minds it was here in this room."[11] Tanner's impression is confirmed by photographs of their home taken by Dietrich Hanff after Barron's death in 1964 (fig. 6.1) and a jacket owned by Phyllis Barron (fig. 6.2) that survives in the collection of the Crafts Study Centre. The black cotton jacket has a discharge print in "Eagle" overprinted in brown with a positive version of "French Dot". A red running stitch picking out the pattern echoes the soft red cotton lining. Six carved mother of pearl buttons in three pairs forming the front closure adds further sensual appeal. This mingling of discipline and pleasure, employment and domesticity was typical. Household implements including rubber car mats, nailbrushes, and pastry cutters created various textiles patterns and textures. Part of the attraction of their fabrics was their handcrafted appearance: mottled colors (achieved with different varieties of gum) and printing irregularities created visual interest, a point of human contact and a sense of exclusiveness.

Fig. 6.1 Photograph by Dietrich Hanff of a corner of Phyllis Barron's study at Hambutt's House, 1964 © Crafts Study Centre.

Fig. 6.2 Jacket worn by Phyllis Barron © Crafts Study Centre.

This hybrid sensibility was further developed in their interior designs, such as their commission to decorate the Fellows' Dining Room and Combination Room for Girton, the first Cambridge college exclusively for women (fig. 6.3). For these multifunctional rooms used for both working meetings and daily relaxation, Barron and Larcher proposed simple Cotswold crafted furniture in a range of woods by Fred Gardiner and Eric Sharpe, pierced vellum paper light shades, and Khelim rugs from Lady Colefax's shop in Mayfair. The heavy linen curtains, slip covers, and cushions printed in "Winchester" and variations of "Feather," were the most expensive items. Both their pale appearance and expense worried some members of the Furnishing Subcommittee, who would have preferred more traditional antique furniture and velvet curtains had they not been well beyond their budget. Despite some initial wrangling with the Subcommittee, Barron and Larcher's designs ended up being much appreciated, as a 1935 article in *Homes and Gardens* attests.[12]

Despite the fact that the Girton College commission involved large public rooms, it recalls Barron and Larcher's treatment of their own domestic space. The dramatic accents of the room were provided by the bold "primitive" patterns of textiles in the curtains, cushions, and slip covers of the large overstuffed sofas and chairs. The floors and walls tended to be unobtrusive in color and made of smooth-surfaced, lightly grained and stained wood. The plain Arts and Crafts furniture constructed in a variety of domestic and exotic wood was easily moved and dusted. Such low maintenance was a virtue championed by other leading furniture designers of the day, such as Betty Joel whose room schemes often resembled those of Barron and Larcher, as a 1934 photograph of Joel's own London flat indicates.[13]

Lightness, flexibility, and practicality characterized the designs of Elizabeth Eyre de Lanux and Evelyn Wyld also. In 1924, as an American living in Paris, Eyre de Lanux started designing modern furniture with the encouragement of Wyld who invited her to join the Atelier de Tissage in 1927. Wyld, a former cellist and English expatriate, had moved to Paris around 1907. A family friend of Eileen Gray, Wyld produced daringly abstract rugs, which she initially sold through Gray's Galerie Jean Désert. The two designers soon teamed up producing unusual combinations of the "primitive" and "ultramodern" as seen in their room at the 1928 Paris exhibition of the Société des Artistes Décorateurs (fig. 6.4). Described as the bay window of a forty-ninth floor studio apartment in New York, their room traded on the French obsession with Manhattan, by placing the furniture against a photograph of a night-lit New York skyline. The floor-lighting reflecting from Eyre de Lanux's stacked glass table made the photograph seem real by extending the dramatic chiaroscuro in the virtual space of the photograph into the real space of the exhibit. The perception of a continuous space

Fig. 6.3 Barron and Larcher, a corner of the Combination Room at Girton College, Cambridge, with curtain and cushions by Dorothy Larcher, standard lamp by Eric Sharpe and table by Fred Foster, c. 1934. Courtesy of Girton College Archives.

Fig. 6.4 Eyre de Lanux and Wyld, Baie d'un studio au 49ᵉ étage, with a glass table by Eyre de Lanux and rug by Evelyn Wyld, Salon des Artistes Décorateurs, 1928. Courtesy of RIBA.

intensified the striking contrast between the urban modernity of the photograph and the "primitive" pattern of Wyld's rug with its American Indian design. The starkly cubic chairs with their functionalist lines, black and white reversals, and geometrically woven backs were decidedly up-to-the-minute.

The following year at the Salon d'Automne of 1929, Wyld and Eyre de Lanux presented a "Terrasse dans le Midi" with blue sky, white walls, thick black tiles, and thick white rugs. Again the sparsely arranged furniture had restrained lines despite the richness of its pony skin, cowhide, lacquer, and African patterns. Reviewers were struck by the dramatic intensity that was achieved with so little in the way of furnishings.[14] This minimalist elegance was precisely what clients wanted when they commissioned the couple, as Mrs. Forsythe Sherfesee's Paris apartment demonstrates. Discussing the project, Eyre de Lanux explained, "the chic of . . . [the] apartment is hoped to be its "simple extravagance." . . . There is almost nothing, but it is of the very best . . . There is practically no color . . . The result is a cool and disciplined smartness . . . expensive bareness." She also noted that they had used "large and serene forms balanced by areas of super alert patterns."[15] Once again the patterning of Wyld's rugs offset the plain but very expensive walnut paneling and leather furniture. In one room, Wyld's "Pelican" rug was positioned in front of a table with a display of Mexican terracotta pottery in a way that evoked earlier religious altar-pieces. Like the furniture, a few unusual artifacts were carefully choreographed for maximum impact.[16]

At this point I should explain why I have drawn the work of these two couples together despite their many differences. We might recall that Barron and Larcher worked in the rural countryside of their native England and in many respects continued a long Arts and Crafts tradition. Their lifelong partnership involved a very close collaboration producing various textile designs and running the workshop, which employed apprentices such as Enid Marx and Susan Boscence as well as local village women. In contrast, Erye de Lanux and Wyld were expatriates attracted to the metropolitan centers of Paris and Cannes. Uniting their separate areas of expertise when designing room schemes, they at the same time continued to work alone in their respective fields of furniture and carpet design. Although they remained lifelong friends, their shorter affair and professional collaboration between the years of 1923 and 1933 seems to have been more strategically motivated. And yet, despite these important differences, there are several common threads running through their practices.

Most striking is the fact that the work of these couples has all but disappeared from the canons of art and design, probably because it does not fit the prevailing patterns of gendering interior space, which are neatly illustrated in two of Osbert Lancaster's cartoons from his 1939 book, *Homes, Sweet Homes* (figs. 6.5 and 6.6). In the functionalist (i.e., modernist) interior we see a slight man on a small stool with book in hand, while in the "modernistic" (or *moderne* or art deco) interior we see a large woman on an ample sofa not far from a box of chocolates. Admittedly, both images send up their subject matter but the masculine functionalist interior is more intellectual with its books, "primitive" sculptures, and Bauhaus and Swedish furniture. As Gillian Naylor suggests, the functionalist interior is treated with more respect, echoing the sentiments of one of England's leading critics of the 1930s, Nicholas Pevsner, who championed modernist "cleanness, directness and precision" over the "sham splendor" of the 1925 Paris Exhibition.[17] As we know, such sentiments had long been espoused by male avant-garde figures, such as Adolf Loos and Le Corbusier, who denounced both ornamentation and femininity.

Analyzing some of the more heated rhetoric in Le Corbusier's 1925 book, *The Decorative Arts of Today*, Tag Gronberg notes that he wanted the design of the home removed from the influence of women, whose consumer orientation and shopgirl esthetic had led them to create illogical spaces and ostentatious displays particularly associated with the Victorian period and movements such as Art Nouveau. According to Le Corbusier, this sad state of affairs provided male ensembliers and architect-engineers with an opportunity to rationally redesign domestic interiors by making them functional, emphasizing their unity, balance, proportion, and harmony.[18] His pavilion for L'Esprit Nouveau at the 1925 Paris Exhibition, with its industrial drinking vessels and tubular steel furniture, was to lead the way by rebuking the

Fig. 6.5 Functionalist Interior from Osbert Lancaster, *Homes Sweet Homes* (London: J. Murray, 1939).

consumer-oriented displays in the pavilions of the department stores and leading artist-decorators such as Emile-Jacques Ruhlmann.

But what about Lancaster's rather more sensually indulgent "modernistic" interior? Some aspects of its conspicuous femininity, such as the curvilinear overstuffed furniture and mantelpiece, resemble elements in Barron and Larcher's Girton commission, just as the theatrical devices of the drapery, recessed lighting, and mirror recall certain details in Eyre de Lanux and Wyld's 1928 room for the Société des Artistes Décorateurs. Yet we should not judge too hastily since many functional features are present in their designs, including the open form of the chair, the boldly patterned geometric rug and curtains, as well as the "primitive" sculpture. Instead of a system of binary oppositions, our two couples evidently embraced a more interesting hybrid complexity.

This is something that seems to have characterized the work of those women designers involved in same-sex relationships who appear in Peter McNeil's article. We might expand his list by adding the names of Marion Dorn, Betty Joel, and Syrie Maugham who, although they lived with men at various points in their lives, largely directed their energies toward

Fig. 6.6 Modernistic Interior from Osbert Lancaster, *Homes Sweet Homes* (London: J. Murray, 1939).

redesigning the home for the modern woman. Placing their work within the rubric of a sapphic modernity enables us to think about women's relationship to the home in ways that echo some aspects of the industrialized rationality championed by critics such as Le Corbusier, Pevsner, and Lancaster while at the same time also departing from it in significant ways.

Working with the modern woman in mind—the woman who lived without servants in smaller spaces, sometimes on her own or with other women instead of a traditional family—designers such as Barron and Larcher and Eyre de Lanux and Wyld wanted to rid domestic spaces of an accumulated clutter that was difficult to clean and did not fit comfortably into the smaller-scale flats and houses that characterized the interwar years. Hence the elimination of moldings and cove ceilings, and the introduction of streamlined furniture. They also used lighter color schemes, or just one colors as in the case of Syrie Maugham's famous all-white room. This reduction of color was probably fuelled by a desire to distance themselves from traditional feminine stereotypes, which since the Renaissance had associated color with the sensual, irrational, and intuitive in contrast to the more cerebral qualities of line.[19] But here the resemblances between their work and that of the architect-engineers such as Le Corbusier ended.

For many of the women working during this period the functionalism celebrated in avant-garde modernist circles seemed unappealingly cold, sterile, and even disembodied. Eileen Gray, for one, grappled with this problem in 1929 when she complained that Le Corbusier's structures were governed by intellectual formulas rather than the human needs of their inhabitants. As Caroline Constant has argued, the tactile and highly embodied sensual pleasures, which were an integral part of Gray's designs, differentiated her work from that of her better known and more heroically modernist male counterparts.[20] Several years later, in 1935, Joel expressed her own reservations when she asserted that a "great deal too much is talked about functionalism."[21] In her view, women did not need to sacrifice either comfort or a sense of beauty when having a modern interior designed for them. According to Joel, it was important for women to retain a sense of their own personality by having their cherished old possessions and furnishings harmoniously integrated into the new schemes they commissioned.[22] Design historian Penny Sparke stresses that historicist or eclectic tendencies were recast as feminine during this period because one of the duties of women in the "era of modernization was to act as guardians of the past, maintaining a sense of continuity by keeping one foot in the pre-industrial world."[23] Encouraged not to sever their connections with the past, women designers such as Joel lamented the fact that architects were becoming more like engineers instead of remaining craftsmen, all of which led to a loss of feeling that she attributed to the desire to mass produce cheaper goods.[24] Although Joel acknowledged that mass production had improved the range of goods available to the multitude, she worried that "[t]oo much office-designed planning about our homes also kills the joy which we may derive from the gradual perfecting of our surroundings." The craftsman (or, we might add, crafts woman) had the important function of "adding the personal touches which correspond to the owner's taste and views." For Joel, what was more important than the "so-called 'modern movement' in design" was the taste of the individual female owner who should be encouraged to select an eclectic mix of furnishings that appealed to her.[25]

Although I do not have space to enumerate all of the connections between the women mentioned in this chapter, a few will suffice to evoke a larger set of networks that still needs to be fully traced. Just as Romaine Brooks purchased her rugs by Wyld from Eileen Gray's gallery and Barron and Larcher bought rugs from Lady Colefax, Syrie Maugham regularly used Marion Dorn's rugs and Constance Spry's floral arrangements in her interiors. Elspeth Little's gallery, Modern Textiles, supplied many textiles used by Syrie Maugham and Elsie de Wolfe.[26] Like Wyld and Eyre de Lanux, who showed with Gray, Barron and Larcher used a number of small galleries and exhibition spaces run by women such as Little's Modern Textiles, Dorothy Hutton's Three Shields Gallery, Muriel Rose's Little Gallery, and Margaret Pilkington's Red Rose Guild. In these venues they exhibited with other women, including a number of important lesbian artists such as their close friends, the potter Katherine Pleydell-Bouverie and the designer Enid Marx. These small-scale crafts outlets were well suited to a growing number of skilled entrepreneurial women and flourished during the interwar years.

Along with the works of craftswomen (and a few craftsmen such as Michael Cardew and Bernard Leach) products from rural workshops and various ethnic crafts were also exhibited. For instance, Muriel Rose's Little Gallery included anonymous textiles and artifacts from South America, Eastern and Western Europe, India, and China, as well as examples of Welsh and Durham quilting, a craft that the Rural Industries Bureau encouraged amongst women in the depressed mining communities of north-east England and the Rhondda Valley Bureau.[27] Although there was clearly a hierarchy separating the work of signed craftswomen and craftsmen from that of the anonymous or collective producers, there was also a shared sense of working outside the mainstream by producing works that were more alive than those of the conventional fine arts. As well as being an integral part of daily life, craftswomen seemed to use more direct and expressive mark-making forms that they had experimented with, first on an individual basis and later in institutions such as the Central School of Design.[28]

Typical of many craftswomen during this period, one of Enid Marx's favorite collections as a student was one that was known in the 1920s as "the Savage Gallery" (now the Museum of Mankind), which she described as "one long magnificent gallery with beautiful prints on bark-cloth, leather puppets from Java and inlaid wood carvings decorated with shells. All this could be seen in one long exhilarating visit."[29] According to design historian Cynthia Weaver, Marx's early fascination with this collection and other "primitive" works led to he own remarkable collection of British popular and naive art and her publications on the subject, both of which were undertaken collaboratively with her partner, Margaret Lambert.

Although there is an extensive literature tracing how avant-garde male artists appropriated the ethnic arts of other cultures,[30] little attention has been paid to the way women artists and designers responded to these artifacts. Can a range of "primitive" enthusiasms that were differently inflected according to gender be traced? One suspects that, given their own relative marginalization, the middle-class women mentioned in this chapter, who were already more closely associated with premodernity, domesticity, amateurism, and handicraft than their male counterparts, might have been predisposed to look at the anonymous handcrafted production of other cultural classes and societies with a different eye. The apparently lesbian orientation of our two couples and many of the women designers discussed here adds further complications to any questions of primitivism, exoticism, and otherness because, as Robin Hackett observes in scientific writing about sexuality during the period, "markers of race, class and sexuality overlap" as "lesbianism and male homosexuality, blackness, disease, criminality, working-class status, taint, pollution, and prostitution coexist as multiple features of the trope of degeneracy."[31] While engaging the "primitive" ran the risk of appearing degenerate, it also offered inviting possibilities for challenging the traditional tenets of Western academic art.

As noted earlier, Barron and Larcher's collection of woodblocks from other cultures and different historical periods were often combined with their own contemporary blocks creating a fusion of time, space, and cultural identity on the surface of the fabric. Eyre de Lanux and Wyld's hybridity was achieved on a different level by combining pieces that were individually more consistent. Eyre de Lanux's furniture designs and materials, such as the stacked glass table, were usually modern, although sometimes she used materials with rich historical association such as galuchet (or shark-skin), which had been popular in eighteenth-century aristocratic circles, another period associated with decadence and degeneracy. Wyld's carpets introduced patterns and techniques borrowed from a wide range of sources including African, Celtic, and indigenous North American. It is worth stressing that in both cases the designer's engagement with these other cultures was less superficial than many during this period, as they devoted considerable time and energy to learning complicated local methods of manufacture in order to reproduce these same labor intensive practices in their own work. For instance, Barron illustrated a model of an Indian calico printer from the collection of the Victoria and Albert Museum in order to demonstrate her own practice in her 1928 article on block printing[32] and around 1907 Wyld traveled to North Africa with Eileen Gray in order to learn from Arab women the process of weaving and dyeing wools with natural colors.[33] The multiplicity of the sources (including some from earlier periods of Western history and others from cultures outside Europe) that influenced their choice of motifs, media, and working process seems rather different from, say, Picasso's appropriation of African masks in *Les Demoiselles d'Avignon* (1909), which he had seen in various Paris collections.

Although both of our couples also sold directly to individual buyers, their participation in these larger collective ventures provided them with additional sources of financial and moral support. Furthermore, both couples seem to have deliberately chosen to work in organizations controlled by other women rather than men. Eyre de Lanux participated regularly in Natalie Barney's well-connected lesbian salon, meeting many leading figures in the fields of literature, theatre, dance, and the visual arts, and when she joined forces with Wyld, the two worked together in the Atelier Tissage. In a similar vein, Barron recorded that early in her career she had refused Roger Fry's invitation to join the Omega Workshops, an invitation that many would have considered a good opportunity.[34] As Marjorie Orpin Gaylard explains, Barron feared that she would have been overshadowed by and unable to extricate herself from the older and better-established figures of Roger Fry, Duncan Grant, and Vanessa Bell. Furthermore, Barron believed in executing her own textiles rather than shipping them to France to be printed commercially as the Omega group did.[35] One cannot help wondering whether Roger Fry harbored any lingering resentments that might have found expression in a 1926 *Vogue* review of Barron and Larcher's textiles that began by stressing the distance between the pure and applied arts. Quoting Bergson, Fry noted that "any poet could be a wit by being less than his complete self, and we might say likewise that any artist-painter could be a decorator by confining and restricting his full powers."[36] It is worth stressing that, by this point, thanks to their extensive networking with other women, Barron and Larcher did not need Bloomsbury's stamp of approval. Although Fry was generally very positive about their work, he concluded by complaining about the timidity of some of their arabesque and floral patterns, urging them to vary the scale of their designs by introducing larger and bolder geometric forms such "big diamonds, squares or circles of some Negro and Byzantine materials."[37] Espousing positions that would subsequently become modernist orthodoxy, Fry seems not to have appreciated the hybrid aspects of their work that appealed to many of their women buyers, a point I will return to develop more fully in a moment. Two years later, in 1928, Barron and Larcher entered into a close commercial relationship with Muriel Rose's Little Gallery, where their work was permanently displayed and commissions were taken. Evidently this was a lucrative arrangement as their order book spanning the years from 1938 to 1944 in the collection of the Crafts Study Centre reveals.

The outbreak of World War II, however, curtailed this form of upscale artisanal production since the necessary raw materials became very scarce. For instance, Barron and Larcher were no longer able to secure the fine fabrics they needed for block printing. Furthermore, after the war, the market for such custom-designed arts and crafts goods never fully recovered, thanks to declining interest and dwindling disposable incomes. None of the flourishing English interwar outlets cited above reopened and craftswomen such as Barron and Larcher ceased production.[38]

Returning to the question of the sapphic elements in these designs, Sandra Gilbert and Susan Gubar provide a useful starting point in their study analyzing early twentieth-century lesbian and female bisexual writers.

There they suggest that one of the most important survival strategies for these writers was to work collaboratively in order to offset the isolation they experienced in relation to heterosexual norms and a literary tradition that provided them with little, apart from Sappho, in the way of precedents. Thus the double speak of their collaboration is represented as a defense mechanism even in the case of those expatriate women who had moved to relatively tolerant centers such as Paris.[39] Considering a diverse group of writers including Renée Vivien, Gertrude Stein, Virginia Woolf, H. D., and Djuna Barnes, Gilbert and Gubar stress also the curiously doubled temporality of much of the writing that dealt with the trials and tribulations of the present either by harking back to a mythic sapphic past or by anticipating an "apocalyptic post-patriarchal future."[40] Throughout their examples, they point to the particular pleasures and perils of the lesbian writer speaking "to," "with," "as," or "for" a lover who so closely resembles herself.

Fusion and loss of identity is certainly something that lesbian painters such as Gluck addressed, particularly in her portrait entitled *Medallion* (1937) in which she superimposed her own profile over that of her lover Nesta Obermer. Gluck tellingly described the work as the "You We" picture that commemorated their "marriage" and exchange of rings in 1936.[41] As Gluck's biographer Diana Souhami observes, the "gaze of aspiration and direction and the determined jaws have something of the feel of social revolutionary art. Nesta's fair hair forms a halo around Gluck's dark head. There is no 'setting.' "[42] Indeed such extreme idealization suggests that Gluck may have imagined the couple transcending history and standing on the threshold of a "postpatriarchal future" of the sort envisioned by Gilbert and Gubar's lesbian writers.

However, such apocalyptic gestures seem oddly out of place in the profession of interior design, where many of the leading designers were women and gay men, despite the fact that, during the 1920s and 1930s, both a "Wildean" estheticism and a "shopgirl's" esthetic were increasingly castigated by design reformers such as Le Corbusier and Nicholas Pevsner. Perhaps having recognizable predecessors in the profession, as well as effective networks for exhibiting and marketing their work, enabled our designing couples to quietly set up shop and produce an innovative body of experimental work that seems less agonized than the literary corpus described by Gilbert and Gubar. This is not to say that their works were unmarked by their sexual orientation. As Christopher Reed has perceptively argued, queerness is not just constituted in the body of the queer, "in his/her inhabitation, in his/her gaze," instead it leaves its traces in spaces that queers have designed and occupied for others to discover—much to their delight or discomfort.[43] In the case of our two couples, such traces were historically inflected by the specific early twentieth-century conditions in which they worked, this is another way of saying that such traces contained discreetly sapphic echoes of the lives they led.

We might follow these traces by considering how both couples emphasized the role of textiles in their room schemes by using bold patterns and textures. During this period, accentuating the textiles was an innovative professional move that, in many cases, drew attention to the femininity, practicality, and modernity not only of the design but also of the designer. These were issues that the critic Derek Patmore raised in 1933 in a discussion of Betty Joel's work. "Since the advent of apartments and flats, the small room has become one of the principal problems of the interior architect, and frequently the best scheme of decoration will be obtained by concentrating all the color in such a room in the fabric used for the curtains and covers."[44] Patmore's term "interior architect" tellingly undermines the binary opposition of masculine exterior structure and feminine interior decoration by foregrounding the fact that both architecture and design address human relationships to space.

Although this new spatial approach often resulted in designers being subordinated to architects, whose buildings set the tone for all that followed,[45] the textiles of Barron and Larcher and Wyld seem to have been an exception. Unlike Marion Dorn (dubbed the "architect of floors" in a 1933 article by Dorothy Todd) who preferred to design her rugs working closely with individual architects and specific locations,[46] our two couples tested their ideas on each other rather than taking their cues from a particular architect or site. One might speculate that this relatively autonomous artistic practice stemmed from both an initial training in the fine arts, where individuality is highly prized, and a strongly artisanal orientation with its concern to control all aspects of production. Indeed Barron and Larcher's block prints have been described as having the "strong architectural feeling" needed in large spaces such as Girton College and Westminster Cathedral.[47] This architectural sensibility was achieved by using highly textured natural fabrics whose surface pattern played an important role in the final effect; by printing with unflocked blocks, where in the absence of a wool cover created unevenly printed surfaces; and by creating spatial complexity through varying the printing direction from straight to diagonal and overprinting different patterns.

The practice of overprinting also reveals the extent of Barron and Larcher's collaboration and returns us to Gilbert and Gubar's issue of lesbian fusion. In a number of textiles, the final effect was achieved by overprinting each other's patterns, for example, the case where the reverse side of Larcher's "Basket" was overprinted with Barron's "Diagonal." Since both patterns were executed in black, residual hints of the former bled through entangling the latter.[48] However, unlike most of the lesbian writers that Gilbert and Gubar consider, neither partner's work seems to predominate and both took equal credit for the designs, as their friend Robin Tanner stressed:

> It has not always been possible to say whether a design was Barron's or Larcher's; it would be wrong to imagine that one used geometrical forms as her main source and the other natural forms, though it is of course easy to attribute certain very characteristic designs. What is so notable and so rare is the marvelous harmony of attitude—to the choice and printing of textiles and to living with them—that existed between these two designers.[49]

According to numerous critics, this fusion was one of the most appealing aspects of their practice, as Roger Fry stressed when he described some of their residual forms lingering on a level that the viewer was only vaguely conscious of perceiving.[50]

From one perspective, the hybrid spatial designs of Barron and Larcher and Eyre de Lanux and Wyld might be seen as not modernist enough given their combinations of primitive and modern, handmade and industrial, smooth-surfaced and highly patterned. But to me this reading seems sadly reductive. Instead, I prefer to see their work as part of an exciting and flexible period of experimentation and art deco hybridity that we are only just beginning to appreciate as we discover a wider variety of responses to modernity. For instance, in textile and wallpaper design, Lesley Jackson has noted how "rampant decoration flourished alongside emergent Modernism during the 1910s and 1920s," a period of "great diversity and innovation for pattern design" prior to the entrenchment of Bauhaus and Le Corbusier's ideas in avant-garde circles.[51] Evidently such diversity continued to be valued by Barron and Larcher's contemporaries as an anonymous review of their work published in the *Times* in 1929 indicates: "Working mostly in sprigged patterns—though some are geometrical—and for the most part in sober colors, they keep, in style, a happy medium between naturalism and abstraction. At one end of their range they will please those brought up in the Morris tradition, and at the other they will at least be tolerated by the 'modernists.' "[52] This leads me to argue that the networks and collaborations established by craftswomen and interior designers ensured that the world of design retained a measure of esthetic hybridity and polymorphous play throughout the 1930s, marking off a sphere that was sufficiently separate and self-confident to take what it wanted from modernism without sacrificing its pleasures and comforts to modernism's increasingly functionalist tendencies. Furthermore, as we have seen in these two case studies, the sexual diversity and experimentation that was associated with such art deco practices also generated a number of intriguing sapphic esthetic effects.

Notes

Thanks to Jean Vacher of the Crafts Study Centre and Sally North of RIBA for help locating archival materials, Adam Stead for research assistance, and the SSHRC for ongoing support.

1. Peter McNeil, "Designing Women: Gender, Sexuality and the Interior Decorator, c. 1890–1940," *Art History* 17, no. 4 (December 1994): 635.
2. Tag Gronberg, "Décoration: Modernism's 'Other'," *Art History* 15, no. 4 (December 1992): 547–52 and Richard Striner, "Art Deco: Polemics and Synthesis," *Winterthur Portfolio* 25 (Spring 1990): 21–34. Art Moderne is more correctly used as a later, streamlined manifestation of Art Deco although the two terms are often used interchangeably.
3. Laura Doan, *Fashioning Sapphism: The Origins of a Modern English Lesbian Culture* (New York: Columbia University Press, 2001), pp. xvii–xviii.
4. Bridget Elliott and Jo-Ann Wallace, *Women Artists and Writers: Modernist (im)positionings* (London: Routledge, 1994), pp. 1–2.
5. Marjorie Orpin Gaylard, "Phyllis Barron (1890–1964). Dorothy Larcher (1884–1952). Textile Designers and Block Printers," *Journal of the Decorative Arts Society* 3 (1979): 32–33.
6. Phyllis Barron, "A Note on the Block Printing of Cover Papers," in Allen W. Seaby, ed., *Color Printing with Linoleum and Wood Blocks* (Leicester: Dryad Handicrafts, 1928), pp. 33–36.
7. Their textile patterns can be found on the Arts and Humanities Data Service website (http://ahds.ac.uk) in the collection of the Crafts Study Centre.
8. Hazel Clark, "Eccentric and Indefatigable: Phyllis Barron (1890–1964) and Dorothy Larcher (1884–1952)," *Quilter's Review* 17 (Summer 1994): 6–7; Barley Roscoe, "Phyllis Barron and Dorothy Larcher," in Mary Greensted, ed., *The Arts and Crafts Movement in the Cotswolds* (Stroud: Alan Sutton, 1993), pp. 122–39, and idem, "Phyllis Barron and Dorothy Larcher," in *Pioneers of Modern Craft*, pp. 61–70; and Alan Powers, *Modern Block Printed Textiles* (London: Walker Books, 1992), pp. 32–37.
9. Greensted, ed., *The Arts and Crafts Movement in the Cotswolds.*
10. Most histories of the British arts and crafts movement ignore the generation of craft producers during the interwar years, many of whom were women such as Ethel Mairet, a weaver, who gave Phyllis Barron much advice about dyeing.
11. Roscoe, "Phyllis Barron and Dorothy Larcher," p. 123.
12. Barley Roscoe, "The Biggest and Simplest Results," *Crafts* 144 (January/February 1997): 31–35.
13. Christopher Wilk, "Who Was Betty Joel? British Furniture Design Between the Wars," *Apollo* 141 (July 1995): pl. 4; Betty Joel, *Designs by Betty Joel 'Token' Hand-Made Furniture* (London: Betty Joel Ltd., 1937).
14. "La saison de Cannes," *Décor* (unpaginated clipping dated August 25 in the Evelyn Wyld file in the RIBA Library).

15. Cited in Isabelle Anscombe, "Expatriates in Paris: Eileen Gray, Evelyn Wyld and Eyre de Lanux," *Apollo* 115 (February 1982): 118.
16. Photographs of this commission are in the Drawings Collection of the RIBA.
17. Gillian Naylor, "Conscience and Consumption: Art Deco in Britain," in Charlotte Benton, Tim Benton and Ghislaine Wood, eds., *Art Deco 1910–39* (London: V & A Publications, 2003), p. 234.
18. Gronberg, "Décoration," p. 551.
19. McNeil, "Designing Women," p. 643.
20. Caroline Constant, "The Nonheroic Modernism of Eileen Gray," *Journal of the Society of Architectural Historians* 53 (September 1994): 265–79; idem, *Eileen Gray*; and idem and Wilfried Wang, eds., *Eileen Gray: An Architecture for All Senses* (Boston: Harvard University Graduate School of Design, 1996).
21. Betty Joel, "A House and a Home," in John de la Valette, ed., *The Conquest of Ugliness* (London: Methuen, 1935), p. 90.
22. Ibid., p. 88.
23. Penny Sparke, *As Long As It's Pink: The Sexual Politics of Taste* (London: Pandora, 1995), p. 4.
24. Joel, "A House and a Home," pp. 91–93.
25. Ibid., p. 94.
26. Hazel Clark, " 'Modern Textiles': 1926–39," *Journal of the Decorative Arts Society* 12 (1988): 52.
27. Hazel Clark, "Selling Design and Craft," in Jill Seddon and Suzette Worden, eds., *Women Designing: Design in Britain Between the Wars* (Brighton: University of Brighton, 1994), p. 60.
28. Mary Schoeser, "Following the Thread," in Sylvia Backemeyer, ed., *Making their Mark: Art, Craft and Design at the Central School 1896–1966* (London: Herbert Press, 2000), pp. 49–51.
29. Cited in Cynthia Weaver, "Enid Marx at the Central School in the 1920s," in *Making Their Mark*, p. 102.
30. See, for example, James Clifford, *The Predicament of Culture: Twentieth-Century Ethnography, Literature, and Art* (Cambridge, MA: Harvard University Press, 1986); James Gilroy, *The Black Atlantic: Modernity and Double Consciousness* (Cambridge, MA: Harvard University Press, 1993); Sieglinde Lemke, *Primitivist Modernism: Black Culture and the Origins of Transatlantic Modernism* (Oxford: Oxford University Press, 1998); Sally Price, *Primitive Art in Civilized Places* (Chicago: University of Chicago Press, 1989); "Primitivism" in James Rubin, ed., *Modern Art: Affinity of the Tribal and the Modern*, 2 vols. (New York: Museum of Modern Art, 1984); Marianna Torgovnick, *Gone Primitive: Savage Intellects, Modern Lives* (Chicago: University of Chicago Press, 1990).
31. Robin Hackett, *Sapphic Primitivism: Productions of Race, Class, and Sexuality in Key Works of Modern Fiction* (New Brunswick, NJ: Rutgers University Press, 2004), pp. 8, 36.
32. See Barron, "Note on the Block Printing of Cover Papers," pl. 4.
33. Peter Adam, *Eileen Gray, Architect Designer: A Biography* (New York: Harry N. Abrams, 2000), p. 62. Early in her career Eileen Gray perfected the art of making lacquer furniture from Seizo Sugawara, a Japanese artist working in Paris.

34. Robin Tanner, *Phyllis Barron 1890–1964 and Dorothy Larcher 1884–1952: A Record of Their Block Printed Textiles*, vol. 1 (Chippenham: Hand-Printed, 1968), p. 23.
35. Gaylard, "Phyllis Barron. Dorothy Larcher," p. 32.
36. Roger Fry, "Hand Printed by Phyllis Barron and Dorothy Larcher," *Vogue* (April 1926): 68.
37. Ibid., p. 96.
38. Clark, "Selling Design and Craft," p. 63.
39. Sandra Gilbert and Susan Gubar, " 'She meant what I said': Lesbian Double Talk," in *No Man's Land: The Place of the Woman Writer in the 20th Century*, vol. 2 (New Haven and London: Yale University Press, 1989), pp. 222–23.
40. Ibid., p. 223.
41. Diana Souhami, *Gluck 1895–1978: Her Biography* (London: Pandora, 1988), pp. 121–23.
42. Ibid., p. 122.
43. Christopher Reed, "Imminent Domain: Queer Space in the Built Environment," *Art Journal* 55, no. 4 (Winter 1996): 64.
44. Derek Patmore, *Color Schemes for the Modern Home* (London: The Studio, 1933), pp. 21–22.
45. Christine Boydell, "Textiles in the Modern Home," *Twentieth-Century Architecture* 2 (1996): 51–64.
46. Madge Garland, *The Indecisive Decade: The World of Fashion and Entertainment in the Thirties* (London: Macdonald, 1968), p. 17; Valerie Mendes, "Marion Dorn, Textile Designer," *Journal of the Decorative Arts Society* 2 (1978): 27; Christine Boydell, "The Decorative Imperative: Marion Dorn's Textiles and Modernism," *Journal of the Decorative Arts Society* 19 (1995): 32.
47. Powers, *Modern Block Printed Textiles*, p. 37.
48. Such patterns can be found in Tanner, *Phyllis Barron and Dorothy Larcher*, vol. 1.
49. Ibid., foreword.
50. Fry, "Hand Printed by Barron and Larcher," p. 96.
51. Lesley Jackson, *Twentieth-Century Pattern Design: Textile and Wallpaper Pioneers* (New York: Princeton Architectural Press, 2002), p. 35.
52. "Printed Textiles," *Times* (December 4, 1929) in the collection of the Crafts Study Centre.

Part 3

In and Out of Place: History, Displacement, and Revision

Chapter 7

Impossible Objects: Waiting for the Revolution in *Summer Will Show*

Heather K. Love

> *As in Hamlet, the Prince of a rotten State, everything begins by the apparition of a specter. More precisely by the waiting for this apparition. The anticipation is at once impatient, anxious, and fascinated: this, the thing ("this thing") will end up coming. The revenant is going to come. It won't be long. But how long it is taking.*
>
> —*Jacques Derrida, Specters of Marx*

> *"And how do I desire it?" he thought. "I want to feel it on every side, more abundantly. But I want to die first".*
>
> —*Sylvia Townsend Warner, Mr. Fortune's Maggot*

One of the most significant challenges faced by scholars in the field of the history of sexuality is a persistent doubt about whether or not sexuality has a history. The field has constituted itself against such disbelief, against claims that sexuality is too private and too idiosyncratic to constitute an object of sustained historical inquiry; that the evidence for a history of same-sex relations is slender; and that any look at the history of queer experience is inevitably a projection of a current state of affairs, a matter of "special pleading."[1] Despite the growth of this discipline over the last several decades, the validity of the history of sexuality as an object of study can still never be assumed, but must always be argued. The construction of queer existence as an "impossible object" of historical inquiry suggests an analogy between the epistemological disadvantage of queer studies in the academy today and the epistemological disadvantage of individual queers, those "impossible people" who, over the course of the twentieth century, have been marginalized not only through moral censure but also through silence and disregard. In this sense, we might say that the history of the field recapitulates the history of the community, and that the demand for the recognition of queer history as a viable practice is charged with a long history of similar claims for the viability of certain "hard to believe" modes of existence and desire. The inventiveness of a whole range of queer historical practices might be understood as a result of the paired necessities of having to "fight for it" and to "make it up."[2]

Through such highly charged encounters, the past itself is transformed: it becomes, in the words of Leila Rupp, a *desired* past—not a neutral chronicle of events, but rather an object of speculation, fantasy, and longing.[3] The historical moment called "sapphic modernity" has been especially charged with such desires. The phrase refers to the emergence of new gender identities and new sexual cultures that emerged in the early twentieth century. The spaces of sapphic modernity—from Harlem rent parties to Paris salons to women's ambulance units in World War I—have taken on tremendous significance, as they have come to represent the sources of a recognizably modern lesbian community. In part because of the significant role it plays in such origin stories, sapphic modernity is difficult to describe as a traditional historical period. Like any form of modernity, it is characterized by a kind of untimeliness: it designates not only a period, but also a principle—of constant renewal, of revolutionary dissolution, of resistance to historicity itself. Sapphism too is untimely: it yokes a modern form of desire to the name of a poet dead for centuries who may or may not have had erotic relations with other women. The history of longing and isolation that is evoked by "sapphism" is not dissolved but rather amplified by its conjunction with "modernity." While modernity reaches forward to an ever brighter future, sapphism pulls backward toward the past, toward a legacy of female same-sex desire that is at best uncertain.

This essay explores the contradictions of sapphic modernity in Sylvia Townsend Warner's 1936 novel *Summer Will Show*.[4] Written in the years leading up to the Spanish Civil War, the novel chronicles the growing intimacy between two women against the background of the failed Paris revolution of 1848. Warner's attention in this book to dissident sexuality and to the fate of social outsiders more generally make the book an important contribution to the literature of sapphic modernity. At the same time, it is a novel in which the untimeliness and cross-temporal longing characteristic of sapphic modernity are particularly evident. The ostensible subject of *Summer Will Show* is the desire for a worker's revolution and for the transformation of everyday life. While the transformative energies of revolution are invoked in the novel, these energies are short-circuited again and again. Through exploring revolution and its failures, Warner imagines a form of expectancy linked to a vision of history that is permeated by loss. She imagines a revolution fueled by despair and by desire. Warner's figuring of the revolution as an "impossible object of desire" is significantly at odds with a forward-looking, scientific Marxism; but it is at the heart of the novel's attention to a politics of affect.

At the center of such reflections in the novel is the bohemian artist, Minna Lemeul. Orphaned by a pogrom in Lithuania, Minna makes a living as a storyteller in Paris, while supporting the work of the revolution. On the night of the February uprising, a salon in her apartment is interrupted by workers demanding carriages for the building of a barricade in the street. As Minna looks on from her window, her new friend Sophia Willoughby feels a sense of flatness in the proceedings; she casts a glance at Minna, who says:

> You think I am not very enthusiastic? I have not given them my carriage, have not exclaimed . . . Perhaps you think I am not very sincere. But if you have ever longed for a thing, longed for it with all that is noblest in you and worked for it with all that is most base and most calculating, you would understand with what desolation of spirit one beholds the dream made flesh. (146)

Summer Will Show is, like several of Warner's other novels, set against a backdrop of failed revolution. However, Minna speaks these words in the early days of the uprising, before the alliance between the workers and the bourgeoisie was broken. The desolation that her comment registers is a response not to the failure of a particular dream, but rather the disappointment implicit in the realization of *any* dream.

The subject of the novel is revolutionary hope; at the same time, Warner traces a number of darker feelings—desolation, despair, regret, fear—that attach to the desire for social transformation. Gillian Beer captures this element of Warner's fiction well when she writes that she is "rare among writers of the 1930s in producing work at once skeptical about belief and wholehearted in its relish of the possible. The Utopian reach of her fictions of the 1930s is, over and over again, undermined sardonically from within."[5] Tracing this mixture of utopianism and disappointment throughout Warner's writing, Beer argues that in these novels "escape is investigated rather than celebrated. The hoped-for alterity—of island life in *Mr. Fortune's Maggot* (1927), of revolution in *Summer Will Show* (1936), of Spain in *After the Death of Don Juan* (1938)—is bared to view, with all its catastrophic losses."[6] In its narration of a failed revolution, the novel suggests the compatibility of feelings of despair and political activity. In fact, despair in the novel appears as a kind of resource as necessary as hope to make change happen. Such a structure of feeling is grounded, I would argue, in a history of queer experience: in the association of same-sex desire with the impossible, and in a history of longing for recognition in an impossible elsewhere. Linking revolutionary longing to this history of queer longing, Warner explores the dark affects that fuel social change. Dreams of revolution in *Summer Will Show* are not utopian. Warner imagines a form of politics that is bound not to the image of the world after revolution but rather to the damaged world that it aims to repair.

* * *

Critical responses to *Summer Will Show* tend to present it in extremely polarized terms: they see it either as a Marxist novel, concerned with class politics and relatively uninterested in questions of romance, fantasy, and sexuality; or it is a sapphic text in which the workers' revolution becomes secondary to Warner's representation of an intimate relation between two women.[7] The novel obeys many of the dictates of the historical novel as Georg Lukács outlined it in his work of the 1930s; it returns to a crucial moment of social upheaval and explores the "historical psychology" of its characters—the historicity of their "inner motives and behaviour."[8] Work that has emphasized this aspect of the novel has tended to disregard its plot of same-sex desire. For instance, in her introduction to the 1987 Virago reprint of *Summer Will Show*, Claire Harman asserts that "[l]esbianism was not Sylvia Townsend Warner's theme in this book," and that that the novel's plot of "anarchic" love forms the backdrop to its central concern—class politics.[9] Terry Castle has made the strongest argument for the fantastic element of the novel in "Sylvia Townsend Warner and the Counterplot of Lesbian Fiction."[10] Castle argues that *Summer Will Show* is aligned with Warner's more explicitly fantastic fiction (such as her popular first novel, *Lolly Willowes*); according to Castle's reading, the novel breaks with conventions of verisimilitude in order to imagine a world in which lesbian love would be unexceptionable, a part of everyday life.

In a more recent article, Janet Montefiore attempts to reconcile these two critical approaches, but fails.[11] She ends by suggesting that the difference between these two readings "is, finally, political":

> for [Castle's] lesbian-feminist reading, what is important about the book is that it goes beyond plausibility; it 'dismantles the real, as it were, in a search for the not-yet-real, something unpredicted and unpredictable'. My own

> socialist-feminist interpretation values the novel for the way it enables the reader to share in the transformation of a woman's consciousness, not only of her erotic desires (though these are crucially important) but of the material world of political struggle . . . These opposed interpretations are, so far as I can see, irreconcilable: either *Summer Will Show* engages with history, or it does not. (212)

Such a description seems out of touch with the place of history in the novel. *Summer Will Show* is probably best described as a historical novel imbued with strong elements of fantasy. While it is possible to describe its peculiar tone as the product of a confluence of genres, I would argue that it is better understood as an effect of Warner's understanding of history as bound up with fantasy. History in the novel is not simply a neutral chronicle of events, nor is it a ground for the working out of the dynamics of class conflict. Rather, history—like the future—is a medium for dreaming about the possibility of the complete transformation of social life. Such dreams bear little resemblance to the predictions of a scientific Marxism: they are wild dreams, desires so powerful that they disrupt the linear temporality of progressive history. Castle in her treatment of sexuality in the novel describes such temporal warping as an effect of desire. But for Warner, a desire for another "impossible" world aims to transform not only sexual relations but all aspects of the social. While the presence of a fantastic element within history has become a familiar concept in recent queer historiography, Warner borrows from intimate experience to introduce this fantastic element into a representation of class struggle.

When *Summer Will Show* opens, Sophia Willoughby is living alone with her two children on her family estate. Conservative and independent, she is estranged from her husband and isolated from those around her. In the novel's first pages, Sophia and her two children spend a hot summer afternoon walking up to the limekiln on the property; Sophia's children have developed whooping-cough and, repeating the treatment that her parents gave her, she takes them to breathe the fumes of the kiln. Soon thereafter, the routine at Blandamer is upset by the arrival of Sophia's nephew Caspar, the illegitimate son of an uncle working in the West Indies. Sophia is seduced by his beauty, and falls into a "holiday frame of mind" (43). Soon, however, she recovers her composure and begins to feel that Caspar's presence is a threat to domestic tranquility; she accompanies him to a nearby boarding school and drops him off. When she returns, the children have fallen ill; as it turns out, the encounter with the kiln-man has left them with fatal cases of smallpox. Sophia's husband Frederick returns from Paris to see the children, who die soon afterward.

The death of the children marks a turning point in the novel. In a state of numbing grief, Sophia decides to try to have another child. First she walks to the limekiln one night and makes an overture to the man who had infected her children; after he rejects and insults her, she decides that she will travel to Paris to find Frederick and have another child with him. When she arrives, she fails to find Frederick at his hotel and so finds her way to Minna's apartment, where a mixed company of artists, bohemians, and revolutionaries is gathered together. At first put off by the disorder of the scene, Sophia is soon absorbed by the story that Minna is telling of her parent's death by pogrom. When workers come requesting carriages for the barricades, all the guests leave except Sophia, who sleeps over. The women spend the whole next day talking and begin an intimacy that is at the center of the rest of the narrative. Sophia becomes increasingly estranged from Frederick, who eventually cuts off her access to his money; she moves in with Minna and begins working for the Communists.

Late in the novel, Caspar reappears; he has left boarding school, and Frederick has paid his subscription in the counterrevolutionary force of the Gardes Mobiles. Sophia once again shuffles him off, asking him to move out of the apartment. The novel ends several months after it began, during the failed June uprising. Minna and Sophia go to fight together on the barricades; Caspar reappears for the last time and stabs Minna with his bayonet. Sophia herself is captured, and though nearly executed, she is released at the last minute. She searches for Minna's body without success, finally returning to their apartment. Finally, Sophia sits down and begins to read the pamphlet she had been distributing the day before—it is *The Communist Manifesto.*

The choice of 1848 is an important one in terms of the generic status of the novel. It was, to begin with, a turning point in the history of class relations and in the history of modern homosexuality. In terms of class relations, the revolution of 1848 seemed to promise a productive alliance between the bourgeoisie and the working class; however, in the bloody suppression in June, these hopes were crushed, and the counterrevolutionary force of the bourgeoisie revealed. In terms of sexuality, the birth of modern homosexuality is usually dated to the birth of the term in medical literature later in the century; however, the importance of the figure of the lesbian as a counter in French literary and artistic circles should not be underestimated. It was, after all, in response to Charles Baudelaire's mid-century sapphic writings that led Walter Benjamin to name the lesbian the "heroine of modernity." Reading Lukács as well as Marx's *Eighteenth Brumaire,* Thomas Foster describes the way that 1848 fell short of its revolutionary potential, remarking that "the February revolution released desires for emancipation that European society was not ready to fulfill or at least created a social space where these desires could be expressed, and for Warner that social space includes lesbian desire."[12]

The conjuring up of unfulfilled desires in the revolution of 1848 has made it one of the most ghostly and fantastic moments in modernity. In the opening of the *Manifesto* that is cited at length at the end of Warner's novel, Marx and Engels call for a manifestation of the dream of Communism: "A spectre is haunting Europe—the spectre of Communism. All the powers of old Europe have united in a holy alliance to exorcise this spectre . . . It is high time that the Communists should lay before the whole world their point of view, their aims and tendencies, and set against this spectre of Communism a Manifesto of the Party itself" (406–7). What Marx and Engels call for is the dream made flesh: the replacement of ghostly potential with manifest reality. Like so many crucial moments in modernity, 1848 split reality into two: a future taken up with the progressive realization of this dream, and a past in which the ghost of what might have been continued to walk. Warner's concern with the ghostly, backward-looking aspect of history in *Summer Will Show* renders the novel fantastic. History is, more than anything, a way dreaming about alternative pasts and possible futures. The gap that opens between potential and reality is a space for speculation, fantasy, and desire.

* * *

The novel takes on questions of genre and the relation between "historical faithfulness" and fantasy in Minna's narration of her childhood in Lithuania. This story is a piece of historical fiction set in the 1848 present of the novel. In this account, Minna describes her political awakening; in this sense, her narrative serves not only as a model for Sophia's imminent awakening, but also as a kind of allegory of the emergence of the historical within the novel itself.

Before describing the murder of her parents, Minna recalls the spring when her mother took her out to see the river breaking up in the thaw.

> On either side it was still frozen, the arched ice rearing up above the water like opened jaws. But in the center channel the current flowed furiously, and borne along on it, jostling and crashing, turning over and over, grating together with long harsh screams, were innumerable blocks of ice. As the river flowed its strong swirling tongue licked furiously at the icy margins, and undermined them, and with a shudder and a roar of defeat another fragment would break away and be swept downstream. It was like a battle. It was like a victory. The rigid winter could stand no longer, it was breaking up, its howls and vanquished threats swept past me, its strongholds fell and were broken one against another, it was routed at last.
>
> I wept with excitement, and my mother comforted me, thinking I was afraid. But I could not explain what I felt, though I knew it was not fear.

> For then I knew only the wintry words of my race, words such as exile, and captivity, and bondage. I had never heard the word Liberty. But it was Liberty I acclaimed, seeing the river sweeping away its fetters, tossing its free neck under the ruined yoke. (122–23)

The passage describes the taking up of a landscape into allegory. In the image of the raging river with its "icy margins," the young Minna reads a whole narrative of the inevitable defeat of the "rigid winter" by the irrepressible force of Liberty. While her mother is only able to read her emotion as fear—seeing it only in the framework of the "wintry words of her race"—Minna remembers feeling an emotion that she could not name, a name that promises to break *her* out of a Jewish narrative of diasporic endurance and move her toward a socialist narrative of redemption.

Continuing her narrative, Minna flashes forward to the next spring, when she sees the aftereffects of her dream of Liberty made flesh. In her return to the scene of this awakening, everything looks different: it is a pestilence year, and a fog hangs over the landscape. The "thunders and crashings" of the previous year can still be heard at the riverbank, but the scene is quite different. While the first view of the river offered an image of a landscape wholly absorbed into allegory, in the second view, allegory has reverted back into material reality. The river itself is visible again, along with the raw materials that go into the production of human liberty.

> A mist hung over the water, flowing with the river, the glory of the year before was not there. Then, as I looked, I saw that on the hurried ice-blocks there were shapes, men and horses, half frozen into the ice, half trailing in the water. And in the ice were stains of blood. Last year, I remembered, it had seemed like a battle, like a victory. Had there been blood and corpses then, and I had forgotten them? The full river seemed to flow more heavily, when ice-block struck against ice-block they clanged like iron bells. (124–25)

In this passage, the ideal of Liberty precipitates out into its constituent parts: dead men, horses, and spilled blood. This second thaw makes visible the losses that constitute any victory. Here, especially, it is the flesh of horses on which the reality of these metaphors of liberty is realized. In the first spring, the river is figured as a wild horse, rearing up between its banks and finally "sweeping away its fetters, tossing its free neck under the ruined yoke." The next year, the bodies of horses, frozen into ice along with their riders, are carried inert downstream. The violent rhetoric of the first passage—the jolting and crashing, the fury, the screams and howls—is here materialized in the form of human and animal remains, victims frozen into a grisly legibility. Such an engagement with loss is modeled in Minna's story, and she insists throughout the novel on the durability of suffering.

Revolutionary consciousness in *Summer Will Show* is imagined as a desire for an impossible redemption—a total transformation of society that cannot and yet must take place.

Summer Will Show's attention to vulnerability and the inevitability of loss points toward a different form of politics. Beer writes that Warner's "works in the 1930s are imbued with the major historical events and dread of the time: the persecution of the Jews and of other groups such as gypsies and gays, the sense of betrayal and yet of the necessity for secret organizations, the willingness to be active, the dry despair in the face of overwhelming Fascist forces"[13]. Warner's antifascist politics may draw on a different political imaginary, one that is linked specifically to Judaism in the novel. Throughout her fiction, Warner is concerned with the experience of those marked visible and classified as "other" in modernity: homosexuals, Jews, the poor, gypsies, the disabled, women, people of color, colonial subjects. She considers not only the transformation of society through class revolt, but also the oppression of despised minorities. It may be more difficult to conjure up a hopeful attitude toward the future in relation to such regimes of stigmatization and denigration. Such repetitive narratives of racial hatred—grounded in "facts" of human nature such as the hatred of outsiders—are resistant to visions of social progress.

If the young Minna disavows the "wintry words of her race" when she sees Liberty in its idealized form, then the second view of the river may make these words—exile, captivity, and bondage—seem more useful. Departing from the forward-looking, progressive, and linear view of liberty that she saw in the river the first time, Minna in her second view sees the repetitive nature of the seasons: the river may burst its bounds, but come next winter, it will freeze up again; part of a cycle of inevitable repetition, spring always will come again—but it will always come bearing news of the ravages of winter.

* * *

Summer Will Show explores the paradox of how one can be a revolutionary—sustain revolutionary hope—in the light of profound losses and the despair that is the effect of such losses. Such questions have become particularly relevant in the current political context. In her article "Resisting Left Melancholy," Wendy Brown discusses the possibilities for sustaining political hope on the Left when we no longer believe in the inevitability of historical progress, when master narratives have broken down, and when our dreams for a global revolution have died—in short, when our ideal of Liberty has been smashed.[14] She diagnoses a pervasive despair on the Left, a melancholic attachment to earlier forms of politics that has proved disastrous for responding to contemporary political conditions.

Brown's diagnosis of this contemporary structure of feeling is apt; contemporary critics and activists ought, I think, attend to her suggestion that the "feelings and sentiments—including those of sorrow, rage, and anxiety about broken promises and lost compasses—that sustain our attachments to Left analyses and Left projects ought to be examined" (464). However, Brown's call for an investigation into these feelings sounds at times more like a request that such feelings should not exist. She writes,

> What emerges [in the present moment] is a Left that operates without either a deep and radical critique of the status quo or a compelling alternative to the existing order of things. But perhaps even more troubling, it is a Left that has become more attached to its impossibility than to its potential fruitfulness, a Left that is most at home dwelling not in hopefulness but in its own marginality and failure, a Left that is thus caught in a structure of melancholic attachment to a certain strain of its own dead past, whose spirit is ghostly, whose structure of desire is backward looking and punishing. (463–64)

While Brown is in a sense writing from the perspective of a Left melancholic, someone trying to think of alternative political structures of feeling given the contemporary context, her critique seems to shade into the kind of chin-up neoliberal polemics that she abhors. While her essay sets out to think about the affective consequences of historical losses, in a passage such as the one above Brown points to these bad feelings themselves as the problem. Why would this essay, so sympathetic on the one hand to melancholic politics, make a final call for the dissolution of melancholy into mourning? While I think Brown sets out to widen the range of political affects, thinking about the political usefulness of feelings such as regret and despair, in the end she returns to what is invariably invoked as the only viable political affect: hope for a better future.

In a moment late in the novel, Sophia and Minna walk along the bookstalls in Paris; Sophia's attention is drawn to the opening stanza of a poem by Marvell, "The Definition of Love." Though they are destitute at this point in the novel, Minna buys the book because she feels "an obligation toward it." The stanza reads,

> My love is of a birth as rare
> As 'tis for object strange and high:
> It was begotten by despair
> Upon Impossibility. (289)

Summer Will Show traces the narrative of a "strange and high" love—an implausible union "begotten by despair upon Impossibility." This verse aptly describes the relation between Sophia and Minna, which is begotten out of Sophia's despair, and which might seem "impossible" for any number of reasons: Sophia and Minna begin as rivals, wife and mistress to the same man; they are marked by differences in class, political allegiance, and ethnic background; and their love is marked by the historical "impossibility" of same-sex relations.

The "strange and high object" also appears as the dream of a worker's revolution and the total social transformation that it would entail. In this sense, Warner borrows the historical image of same-sex love in order to describe the women's affective relation to the desired object of revolution. Revolution in *Summer Will Show* is also begot by despair upon impossibility: it appears in the novel as an analogue for the "impossible object" of same-sex desire. She borrows from the lexicon of queer feeling: because of the longstanding link of same-sex desire with the impossible, queer experience is characterized by extremes of feeling: the vertiginous joy of an escape from social structures; and, at the same time, a despair about the impossibility of existing outside of such structures. Revolution in the novel is both that which must happen and that which cannot happen; Warner describes the mixture of hope and despair that are produced by attachment to such an impossible object.

Rather than seeing this impossibility as pure loss, Warner suggests this impossibility as a *resource*. Invoking the rhetoric of reproduction, the poem describes the speaker's "love" as the product of a union between despair and impossibility. What this rare birth does is not a consummation; despair's embrace of impossibility does not yield an assured future. And yet, the poem insists that such a rare birth is preferable—stranger, higher—than a love born out of hopefulness. In this sense, intimate experience in the novel offers a model for an alternative form of political feeling, a nonutopian form of expectancy: a kind of hope without reason, without expectation of success.[15] Such a form of political affect may be the kind of feeling we need to learn how to use in contemporary politics, when hope in its old idealizing and utopian form—of optimism—seems to have lost its hold on many of us.

It does not make sense to talk about the death of the dream of Marxist revolution in the 1930s as it does at the turn of this latest century. In *Specters of Marx*, Jacques Derrida dates the "eschatological themes of the 'end of history,' of the 'end of Marxism,' . . . and so forth"[16] to the 1950s—still twenty years after the publication of *Summer Will Show*. Sylvia Townsend Warner did not seem to be suffering from such feelings at the time; shortly after finishing the novel she joined the Communist Party and traveled to Spain with her lover Valentine Ackland. Yet the novel insistently explores the limits of revolutionary enthusiasm, opening up a range of other, darker feelings that go into the making of social change.

* * *

Gillian Beer suggests that we might read Warner's novels as "experiments in affect".[17] *Summer Will Show* offers a combination of intense joy and total devastation; it opens with hope for a better future and at the same time leaves its reader with a hollow sense of despair. I would suggest that such experiments are ways of investigating not only the range of human emotions but also the means of inciting the desire for social change. We have tended to think that such desires can only be fueled by hope, but Warner suggests that political motivation—like so many other kinds of motivation—may be opaque, irrational, and indirect. In private life, we are used to the idea that we may not want what we think we want. That much is clear in one of Warner's diary entries, written the day after she became lovers with Ackland: "My last day, and our first. It was a bridal of earth and sky, and we spent the morning lying in the hollowed tump of the Five Maries, listening to the wind blowing over our happiness, and talking about torpedoes, and starting up at footsteps. It is so natural to be hunted and intuitive. Feeling safe and respectable is much more of a strain."[18] *Summer Will Show* is remarkable in that it exposes such mixed feelings in the realm of "real" politics, suggesting that intimate experience offers a model—albeit a complicated one—for thinking the social.

The final scene in the novel gestures emphatically to the link between intimate and public politics. After searching in vain, Sophia returns to Minna's apartment, which has served throughout the novel as a revolutionary cell—a laboratory for experiments in effect. Sophia's aristocratic Aunt Léocadie is waiting for her, and she tries to recall her to her "old manner of living." Sophia is unmoved; after her aunt leaves, she turns to face the empty apartment:

> Ah, here in this empty room where she had felt such impassioned happiness, such freedom, such release, she was already feeling exactly as she had felt before she loved Minna, and wrapping herself as of old in that coward's comfort of irony, of cautious disillusionment! How soon her blood had run cold, how ready she was to slink back into ignominy of thought, ignominy of feeling! And probably only the pleasure of disagreeing, the pique of being thought shabby and deplorable, had kept her from returning to the Place Bellechasse. She looked round her, dragging her gaze over the empty, the soiled and forlorn apartment. There was the wine that Minna had left for her, the slippers she had tossed off, sprawling, one here, one there, and on the table where she had thrown it down and forgotten it, the fifth of the packets which Ingelbrecht (yes, he was dead too) had entrusted to her. She took up one of the copies, fingered the cheap paper, sniffed the heavy odor of printers' ink, began to read.
>
> *'A spectre is haunting Europe . . .'*
>
> She seated herself; and leaning her elbows on the table, and sinking her head in her hands, went on reading, obdurately attentive and by degrees absorbed. (405–6)

In one sense, it is possible to read this moment as a transition from personal to collective experience: Sophia loses her lover, but gains a party. The intensely personal nature of her final encounter with the Manifesto of the Communist Party does not support such a reading, for we find Sophia sinking down into a posture of absorbed reading that turns away from the street and the collective. Her relation to the physical text—her touching and smelling of its pages—recalls her ambivalent attraction to Minna's body early in the novel. Rather than a replacement of a bad object with a good object, the ending seems to suggest that one's relation to a collectivity might be based on a model of erotic love.

It is through loving Minna that Sophia sees her glimpse of freedom; to forsake her would only lead to coldness—ignominy of thought and ignominy of feeling. Instead, Warner suggests that waiting for Minna might serve as a model for waiting for the revolution. Rather than looking forward to a brighter future, Sophia remains in the ruined present, the signs of her loss all around her. Sinking down, Sophia allows herself to be haunted by her dead lover and by the words of the dead revolutionary Ingelbrecht.

Before her death, Minna herself serves as the exemplar of this alternate form of expectancy: attentive to the losses of the past and to the inevitable violence of the revolution, she invites ghosts rather than exorcising them. When she is asked about what good the revolution might do, she responds: "What good? None, possibly. One does not await a revolution as one awaits the grocer's van, expecting to be handed packets of sugar and tapioca" (147). Minna waits for the revolution as one waits for the beloved: with hope and with despair, but without certainty. For those of us who are still waiting, this may not be a bad model.

Notes

1. See Lisa Duggan's essay, "The Discipline Problem," in which she speculates about the reasons that history departments have failed to train historians of sexuality: "I don't think this failure is solely or even largely due to conservatism or stark prejudice (though I don't mean to underestimate the continuing importance of these sources of hostility). I would attribute the failure to hire and train historians of sexuality, and lesbian and gay historians specifically, to at least three other significant factors: (1) Sexuality, as a subject matter, is treated as trivial, as more about gossip than politics, more about psychology than history . . . (2) Lesbian and gay history, particularly, is understood as the history of a marginalized 'minority' population, as the story of a small percentage of the citizenry and their doings . . . (3) Historians of sexuality fit uneasily into existing job categories . . ." (180). Duggan, "The Discipline Problem: Queer Theory Meets Lesbian and Gay History," *GLQ* 2, no. 3 (1995): 179–91.

2. The recognition of "oneself" in the past is a complex and charged project, and queer historians have never been able to completely embrace it nor to leave it behind for good. A range of recent critics have attempted to mediate between essentialist and constructionist approaches to the past. See, for example, David M. Halperin's *How To Do the History of Homosexuality* (Chicago: University of Chicago Press, 2002). Carolyn Dinshaw's recent reflections on Foucault's fan letter to John Boswell—perhaps the historian most identified with the project of recovery—also offers a fascinating look at the conjunction between these two approaches. Dinshaw, *Getting Medieval* (Durham, NC: Duke University Press, 1999).
3. Leila Rupp, *A Desired Past: A Short History of Same-Sex Love in America* (Chicago: University of Chicago Press, 2002).
4. Sylvia Townsend Warner, *Summer Will Show*. 1936 (London: Virago, 1987). All subsequent quotations from this edition.
5. Gillian Beer, "Sylvia Townsend Warner: 'The Centrifugal Kick' " in Maroula Joannou, ed., *Women Writers of the 1930s: Gender, Politics and History* (Edinburgh: Edinburgh University Press, 2000), p. 76.
6. Beer, "Sylvia Townsend Warner," pp. 76–77. For a related account of the affective complexities of Warner's work, see Gay Wachman, *Lesbian Empire: Radical Crosswriting in the Twenties* (New Brunswick, NJ: Rutgers University Press, 2001), p. 73.
7. One crucial exception to this rule is Thomas Foster's article, which has contributed a lot to my thinking here. Taking on the trivialization of "sexual abnormality" in Lukács' *The Historical Novel*, Foster argues that "the novel . . . implies that neither Marxist nor feminist nor lesbian narratives of emancipation are sufficient to represent the totality of social life" (p. 538). He sees revolution in the novel as a challenge to the ideology of private property and to the division between the public and the private spheres. Foster makes a strong argument that in the novel "the women's story is not merely analogous to that of the revolution but instead structurally implicated in that 'other' story" (p. 550). Foster's account of the inseparability of class and sexual politics in *Summer Will Show* is crucial in understanding Warner's complex account of the relation between revolutionary, world-historical politics and the politics of everyday life. See Foster, " 'Dream Made Flesh': Sexual Difference and Narratives of Revolution in Sylvia Townsend Warner's *Summer Will Show*," *Modern Fiction Studies* 41, nos. 3–4 (1995): 531–62.
8. Georg Lukács, *The Historical Novel*, trans. Hannah and Stanley Mitchell (Harmondsworth: Penguin, 1962), p. 65.
9. Claire Harman, "Introduction" to *Summer Will Show*, p. viii. Terry Castle cites Robert L. Caserio's article "Celibate Sisters-in-Revolution: Towards Reading Sylvia Townsend Warner" as another example of the tendency to disregard same-sex desire in the novel. However, although Caserio does read the relationship between Minna and Sophia as chaste, he does not ignore it, but rather sees it as central to the novel's politics. See Castle, *The Apparitional Lesbian: Female Homosexuality and Modern Culture* (New York: Columbia University Press,

1995) and Caserio, in Joseph A. Boone and Michael Cadden, eds., *Engendering Men: The Question of Male Feminist Criticism* (New York: Routledge, 1990).

10. Castle, *The Apparitional Lesbian.*
11. Janet Montefiore, "Listening to Minna. Realism, Feminism and the Politics of Reading," *Paragraph* 14 (1991): 197–216.
12. Foster, "Dream Made Flesh," p. 548.
13. Beer, "Sylvia Townsend Warner," p. 86.
14. Wendy Brown, "Resisting Left Melancholy," in David L. Eng and David Kajanjian, eds., *The Politics of Mourning* (Berkeley, CA: University of California Press, 2003), p. 464.
15. The second stanza of the poem also seems apt:

    i. Magnanimous Despair alone
    ii. Could show me so divine a thing,
    iii. Where feeble Hope could ne'er have flown
    iv. But vainly flapt its Tinsel Wing.

16. Jacques Derrida, *Specters of Marx: The State of the Debt, the Work of Mourning, & the New International,* trans. Peggy Kamuf (New York: Routledge, 1994), p. 14.
17. Beer, "Sylvia Townsend Warner," p. 77.
18. Sylvia Townsend Warner, Diaries, October 12, 1930. See *The Diaries of Sylvia Townsend Warner*. Ed. and introduction by Claire Harman. (London: Chatto and Windus, 1994), p. 69.

Chapter 8

Virginia Woolf's Greek Lessons

Colleen Lamos

By a twist of fate, the young Virginia Woolf studied Greek from 1899 to 1900 with Clara Pater, the elderly sister of Walter Pater. This fact is dutifully recorded in her many biographies and immediately forgotten, with the exception of an obligatory footnote mentioning that Miss Pater was the model for Miss Julia Craye in Woolf's 1928 short story, "Moments of Being: 'Slater's Pins Have No Points.' "[1] The implications of this remarkable coincidence, as well as the broader and multiple effects of her lifelong study of Greek, have gone largely unnoticed. Woolf's enduring engagement with Greek language and culture influenced her views on education for women, female authorship, English literature, neopagan ethics, and homoeroticism. Unlike some of her contemporaries, such as Radclyffe Hall, Woolf's concept of "sapphism"—the word that she used for female same-sex love instead of the sexological terms "inversion" or "homosexual"—was formed in the context of late Victorian Hellenism. While Woolf plays a central role in any consideration of sapphic modernism, her affiliation with it was decidedly equivocal.

For the past thirty years, scholarship on Woolf has typically referred to her attacks on the institutional exclusion of women from the study of the classics. Like many feminist critics, Rowena Fowler argued that Woolf regarded Latin and Greek as "alien territory" belonging to men.[2] However, Fowler has recently recanted that view, admitting that she has since "learned that the relationship between women and the classical literatures and languages is often considerably more complicated."[3] Recognizing the pervasiveness and intricacy of Woolf's involvement with Greek literature, Fowler now regards her as engaged in a "dialogue" with the Greeks. Her change of mind anticipates the argument that I will advance in this essay.

Woolf's Greek lessons were both linguistic and amorous, learned from women who fired her imagination and her love. The language to which she devoted herself represented masculine scholarly authority *and* homoerotic passion, male and female, as well as other forms of nonheterosexual affection. Thus, for Woolf, Greek was both an instrument to gain a purchase on and, later, to attack that authority, *and* a means to express same-sex love, sometimes via references to Sappho. Insofar as Greece stood for a homophilic past inaccessible yet still operative in the twentieth century, she regarded it elegiacly, as a lost ideal. The association between Greece and death, reinforced by the death of her brother Thoby, is underscored by the tenuous yet powerful linkage, in *Mrs. Dalloway*, between the Greek language and madness. Moreover, despite her mastery of Greek, Woolf realized the impossibility and, indeed, bankruptcy of Hellenism in Edwardian England, including its veneration of the erotically charged though putatively chaste relationship between an older male teacher and his younger male pupil. Although subsequently derided as "the higher sodomy," these pederastic bonds were praised and cultivated in Victorian Oxford and Cambridge as inspiring and elevating.[4]

Long before Woolf became acquainted with the Cambridge Apostles, she was parsing out Greek phrases with the sister of the man who created a sensation with the publication, in 1873, of *The Renaissance: Studies in Art and Poetry*. In its "Conclusion," Walter Pater described the sources of "ecstatic" esthetic sensations as, among others, "the face of one's friend."[5] The Socratic eros embraced by Pater is enacted in Woolf's "Slater's Pins," a text that she described, in a letter to Vita Sackville-West, as "a nice little story about Sapphism."[6] Fanny Wilmot has a crush on her music teacher, Miss Craye, whose deceased brother, Julius, is modeled after Walter Pater. Fanny repeatedly thinks of Miss Craye as "queer" and "odd." "None of the Crayes had ever married," we are told three times. Reiterating yet reversing the structure of the paederastic relationship, the girl, Fanny, longs to be embraced by her teacher, "to break the pane of glass which separated them" (216). However, she displaces this desire onto Miss Craye, just as she transfers it onto a flower that, Fanny having dropped, Miss Craye picked up and "crushed" in her fingers. Fanny sees her as a heroic, happy woman "holding her flower" (like Clarissa Dalloway) in a Paterian "moment of ecstasy." The thrill, though, is surely Fanny's, when Miss Craye—now called "Julia"—"opened her arms," "kissed her," and "possessed" her (220). The story concludes with Miss Craye saying again, "Slater's pins have no points." While it is difficult to escape the metaphoric significance of the nonpenetrating, nonphallic pin, the American publisher of the story evidently did so. Writing to Vita, Woolf remarked, "The Editor has not seen the point, though he's been looking for it in the Adirondacks."[7]

The figure of the pin appears in an earlier short story, "A Society" (1921), as the object of debate among Sappho scholars. Woolf wrote it as a response to Desmond MacCarthy's claim of the intellectual inferiority of women, a charge that is given voice in the story: " 'Since Sappho there has been no female of first rate—'Eleanor began, quoting from a weekly newspaper."[8] Focusing on a group of women who form "a society for asking questions" about patriarchal civilization, the story satirizes, among other topics, the prevailing philological tradition whose major preoccupation was the protection of Sappho's virtue against accusations of lesbian vice. One of the members of the society, Castalia, is deputized to infiltrate Oxbridge "disguised as a charwoman," thereby gaining access to the office of Professor Hobkin. She reports back, "when Professor Hobkin was out I examined his life work, an edition of Sappho. It's a queer looking book. . . . Most of it is a defence of Sappho's chastity, which some German had denied, and I can assure you the passion with which these two gentlemen argued, [and] . . . the prodigious ingenuity with which they disputed the use of some implement which looked for all the world like a hairpin astounded me" (128). In fact, scholars were, in the 1920s, deliberating over Sappho's possible use of a sexual "implement." According to Margaret Williamson, "Considerable interest . . . focused upon a scrap of papyrus that may or may not be by Sappho, on which one badly damaged word can be construed to read 'receivers of the dildo.' "[9]

There were many Professor Hobkins in the early twentieth century, such as J. M. Edmonds, who were bent on proving Sappho's purity. Edmonds's *Sappho in the Added Light of the New Fragments* (1912) is, in Joan DeJean's judgment, "a perfect example of the English tradition of reading Sappho's poetry in order to show why it could not be the product of a 'bad' woman."[10] The culmination of that dominant tradition was Ulrich von Wilamowitz-Moellendorf's influential *Sappho und Simonides* (1913), in which, defending Sappho, he repeated the by then discredited story (originating in Ovid) of her doomed love for Phaon, leading to her legendary Leucadian leap. Jane Marcus cites Wilamowitz-Moellendorf as the model for Professor Hobkin, despite the fact that Woolf explicitly writes that his scholarly antagonist, who "denied" Sappho's virginity, was German—precisely the opposite of Wilamowitz-Moellendorf's position.[11] Woolf's insertion of the glaringly ahistorical detail regarding the German professor points to the significance of her critique of nationalism in the story. Disputes regarding Sappho's sexuality in England and Germany were fueled, as DeJean explains, by nationalist ardor; given the wholesale identification by philologists in both countries with the Hellenic ideal, the defense of Sappho became a defense of English or German womanhood. Writing in the wake of the Great War, Woolf took pains to resist English national prejudice and so gave the laurels for reading Sappho aright—as a sapphist—to England's despised enemy.

It is, indeed, nationalism that defeats the work of the eponymous society. Their meetings are twice interrupted—first in 1914 and, later, in 1918—by the shouts of men in the street "cry[ing] hoarsely" for "War!" or celebrating victory (133, 135). Instead of affirming a Sapphic association as a viable alternative to militant patriarchy, Woolf's satire concludes with a little girl—the fruit of Castalia's rejection of chastity—bursting into tears when she is told that she has been elected the "President of the Society of the future" (136). DeJean interprets these tears, together with the drowning out of the women's voices by those of the men, as Woolf's suggestion "that it is impossible to be Sappho's daughters."[12] Yet a better, albeit ambiguous, clue to Woolf's response to Sappho in the story is her insistent use of the word "queer." Woolf does not offer Sappho as a precursor poet, here or elsewhere, but assented, "I am altogether queer in some ways."[13] Unlike many of her contemporaries, she did not regard Sappho as a muse.

Like *A Room of One's Own*, "A Society" represents the knowledge of Greek as the prerogative of male academics. Such knowledge was a passport to what Woolf's cousin J. K. Stephen called "the intellectual aristocracy" in his *Defence of the Compulsory Study of Greek at Cambridge* (1891). Whereas Woolf excoriated the British academic system that denied women access to the classics and, especially during the early years of the Bloomsbury "Thursday evenings" (1905–1910), was angry at her exclusion from the tightly knit group of her brother Thoby's Cambridge friends, her engagement with Greek—the language, literature, and cultural ideals it represented—was far more multifaceted than some American feminist critics have allowed. In their eagerness to stress Woolf's allegiance with the "common reader," or in their hostility to an allegedly male homosexual "cultural hegemony" whose pederastic ideal supposedly exacerbated their misogyny, they overlook her profound albeit disillusioned investment in the Hellenic model and her identification with, as well as irritation by, the men that she liked to call "sods."[14] This reductive and sometimes homophobic interpretation of Woolf's understanding of Greek love ignores her long-standing interest in it as well as the intricate, manifold ways in which Greek was interwoven with her life and works. Writing in 1890 to her cousin, Emma Vaughan, she enthused, "Greek . . . is my daily bread, and a keen delight to me."[15] A glimpse of the complexity of Woolf's relation to Greek may be had by realizing that Emma's sister-in-law and Woolf's girlhood amour, Madge, was the daughter of John Addington Symonds, the famous classicist, translator of Sappho, friend of Leslie Stephen, and the first public defender, in England, of male and *female* homosexuality.

Symonds wrote two books in 1873 that proved to be pivotal to the following generation's—Woolf's—understanding of Sappho and sapphic love: *Studies of the Greek Poets* and *A Problem in Greek Ethics, Being an*

Inquiry into the Phenomenon of Sexual Inversion.[16] While arguing the case for pederasty as an ennobling, virile practice, he also insisted that it could be a physical relationship; moreover, in a groundbreaking move, he placed female same-sex love on an equal footing with the male variety and was apparently the first to use the term "homosexuality" when describing either phenomenon.[17] His translation of Sappho's "Ode to Aphrodite," included in Henry Wharton's popular and influential 1885 English edition of Sappho's works, was the first in any modern language to acknowledge the same-sex character of the passion represented in the poem.[18] In a word, he enabled an unapologetic, sapphic reading of Sappho in English.

When Woolf began her Greek lessons, she encountered not only the philologists' vigorous denial of Sappho's eroticism and Symonds's defense of a lesbian Sappho but also an emergent discourse of sapphism from the Continent. The Sappho revival underway in France was led by Natalie Clifford Barney and her lover, René Vivien, and was inspired both by Wharton's English edition of Sappho's poetry and by Pierre Louys' decadent *Songs of Bilitis*. Remote from this Parisian fashion, though, Woolf's sapphic inspiration was much closer to home in the form of her Greek tutor, Janet Case. Her love for Case was an emotionally intense romantic friendship, one of several that she enjoyed with older, maternal, or powerful women, such as Violet Dickinson, Madge Symonds, Vita Sackville-West, and Ethel Smyth. While it is easy to deride such passionate relationships as female versions of the "higher sodomy," they do conform to the Hellenic understanding of pederasty. Indeed, the affective force of Woolf's passion for Case was most likely transferred onto the Clara Pater figure in "Slater's Pins." Rather than dismissing Woolf's love for Case or Dickinson as merely an "adolescent" infatuation, as many critics do, we should recognize it as significantly sapphic *and* Sapphic. What she later called the "glamour" of Greek seems charged by the eroticism that infused her relationship with Case. Greek was the medium of their bond and the language of Woolf's love for her.

Greek was also the language of masculine affiliation and competition at this time, from roughly 1900 to 1910. When Woolf's beloved older brother, Thoby, was at Cambridge, her Greek lessons, according to Hermione Lee, "were above all a way of keeping pace with him," and, after his untimely death, Greek was a means of sustaining her "connection to Thoby."[19] With the formation of the Bloomsbury group, from 1905 onward, Woolf was compelled to match her wits and her Greek with the likes of Lytton Strachey, Saxon Sydney-Turner, and John Maynard Keynes. Her friendly combat with these men rendered Greek a bivalent mark and instrument of masculine power as well of intimate love. As we will see, Greek ultimately became, for Woolf, the language of eulogy, of disenchantment, and, finally, of an unspeakable love.

Greek is central to the unresolved struggles of Woolf's first novel, *The Voyage Out* (1915), which is laced with references to the language. The name of the ship that carries the heroine, Rachel, from London to South America, "Euphrosyne," was also the title of a volume of pseudoclassical verse written by Thoby and his Cambridge friends, which Woolf privately ridiculed. The motherless Rachel is chaperoned by her aunt and uncle, Helen and Ridley Ambrose, the latter of whom is obsessed with his editing of a volume of the Greek poet Pindar and is oblivious to all else. Resembling Woolf's father, Leslie Stephen, he is a caricature of the pedantic classicist. "What's the use of reading if you don't read Greek?" he asks (192). According to Lorna Sage, Ridley is "draped throughout [the novel] in the mystique of Greek, which patently stands for the preserve of male learning," but he offers to teach the language to Mrs. Dalloway.[20] Like Ridley, however, Woolf studied Pindar during the years in which she composed *The Voyage Out*.

In the novel, Rachel, only a girl, is surrounded by intimidating intellectuals such as William Pepper, who claims to have never married because he "never met a woman who commanded his respect. . . . [H]is ideal was a woman who could read Greek" (21–22). Two less authoritative figures—St. John Hirst and Miss Allan—represent the other side of Woolf's double-voiced attitude toward Greek. As did Strachey, Hirst argues the case for Greek love and reads A. C. Swinburne's version of Sappho's "Ode to Aphrodite" during a Sunday morning church service (267). That scandalously decadent version of Sappho, influenced by Baudelaire's lesbian "condemned poems," underscores Hirst's blasphemous behavior (during the service he also writes an "indecent" poem in which he rhymes "God" with "sod") and reinforces the queer subtext of *The Voyage Out*, which runs against the grain of its marriage plot. One of the English ladies staying at the South American resort laughingly remarks, "You men! Where would you be if it weren't for the women!" Ridley retorts, "Read the *Symposium*" (224). Less dramatically and commandingly, Miss Allan, a spinster schoolteacher with a masculine demeanor, offers an unorthodox Hellenic vision: "When I think of the Greeks, I think of them as naked black men . . . which is quite incorrect, I'm sure" (125–26). Her primitive image of the Greeks aligns them with a pagan prehistory, an affirmative vision that Woolf entertained throughout her works as an alternative to Christian civilization. Oddly, or queerly, the Greeks, in Miss Allan's dykey eyes, signify a non-Western ethos, just as the references to Sappho and Plato form a counterdiscourse to the novel's Austenian, heterosexual romance.

Woolf's relation to Greek seems paradoxical. On the one hand, she inherited it as a masculine tradition against which she fought bitterly throughout her life. On the other hand, Greek was a mode of intimacy with her teachers, lovers, friends, and brother—the means through which she formed and articulated some of her most passionate attachments. Rachel Bowlby describes this "ambiguous" relation as Woolf's "double vision" of Greek.[21] These two visions are not simply in conflict, however, for the classical heritage was a crucial medium for Woolf to express what we typically regard as authentic or sincere—that is, unmediated—affects; in some respects it was a condition of possibility for her to affirm same-sex love. Ruth Vanita argues that her "talking about the relatively more visible phenomenon of male homosexuality was the route whereby Woolf was able to express her own anxieties" and sapphic desires.[22] Very early on she came to regard Greek as a fraudulent yet still efficacious cultural ideal. In her 1921 essay, "On Not Knowing Greek" (to which I shall return below), she examined the effects of that fallen ideal. Two key texts that mark the process of her disillusionment are the short story "A Dialogue upon Mount Pentelicus" and *Jacob's Room*. Both of these fictions were written about and for Thoby and manifest the aforementioned structure of desire in which Greek—an alienating, patriarchal inheritance—is also, through its deliquescence, a means of expressing an untranslatable intimacy.

"A Dialogue" was composed in 1906, immediately after Woolf's trip to Greece with Thoby, Adrian, and Vanessa, a trip that proved fatal to Thoby, who died shortly thereafter of typhoid fever contracted during their journey. The story mocks the conventional English adulation of ancient Greece. For instance, the English tourists "condescend" to speak to the peasant boys who guide them up Mount Pentelicus, addressing them "in their own tongue as Plato would have spoken had Plato learned Greek at Harrow."[23] When the boys fail to understand them, they are dismissed as "barbarians." Two aspects of this story transcend satire, though. Arguing against the "worship" of Greece, the Thoby character observes that we moderns have created an idol that we call the Greeks. In contrast to the debunked, Arnoldian Hellenic vision, Woolf offers, at the end of the story, a prehistoric image of Greece in the form of a monk toiling up the mountainside with a bundle of wood on his back. He seems like "one of those original figures which . . . have resisted time, and recall the first days and the unobliterated type" of "Man" (67). The immortality intimated by the monk (in his imagined eye, "the world swam in its girdle of eternity") is likely motivated by Woolf's grief in the wake of Thoby's death, and it also evokes a pre-Hellenic, primitive, even barbaric Greece.

Jacob's Room (1922) gives a more ample narrative of the eponymous hero's disenchantment with Greece. As a student, Jacob Flanders is thrilled by his knowledge of Greek, and with a fellow undergraduate he converses until dawn. The skeptical narrator remarks, however, that the "love of Greek" is a "strange thing," for, in truth, "Jacob knew no more Greek than served him to stumble through a play."[24] Greek is also the medium of his male friendships. The homosociality—and homosexuality—implied by the language is reinforced later when Jacob, ensconced in his room late at night, continues to read the *Phaedrus* while a drunken woman in the street below bangs at the door, shouting, "Let me in! Let me in!" (109). The scene is typically read as an allegory of women's exclusion from Greek learning and points to Woolf's insistence that outsiders be admitted to the privileged sanctum of classical scholarship. (However, in "On Not Knowing Greek," Woolf reverses the positions of insiders and outsiders, turning the tables, as Angeliki Spiropoulou observes, "by questioning the extent to which the heirs of the classical tradition really know Greek.")[25] When Jacob subsequently travels to Greece, the reality of the modern country shatters his fantasies. Imagining Jacob's thoughts, the narrator notes: "we have been brought up in an illusion" (138).

While writing *Jacob's Room*, in 1921, Woolf was also composing "On Not Knowing Greek," which similarly analyzes the modern fascination with ancient Greece. Although we may be able to read the language, she claims, "it is vain and foolish to talk of Knowing Greek" literature because there is so much of which we are ignorant regarding the culture and language of ancient Greece.[26] Her primary argument is, as in "A Dialogue," that we moderns project upon the ancient Greeks our own dreams and desires. We are "forever drawn back to Greek" and speculate upon its "meaning" (24), but, she asks, "are we really reading Greek as it was written," or are we merely imputing to the Greeks what we "lack"? (36). The Greeks are our supplement, she asserts, the prop upon which we rest to cover our inability to face the fact that "truth is various" (34), an acknowledgment that Woolf, in a quick resort to the Greek supplement, claims is an invariant truth recognized by the Greeks, in their proto-Nietzschean knowledge of (the untruth of) absolute truth. In short, we can never "know Greek" because, however good we are at translation, its inner import is inaccessible to us. Indeed, Greek signifies an endlessly alluring yet impossible epistemological desire—"we wish to know Greek"—so that "we" (the ambiguous third person in which the essay is written) are all ultimately in the position of the aforementioned drunken woman who shouts at the door, "Let me in!" Greek is also the language of love in this essay. Woolf observes that the Greeks were able to write about their emotions "directly," whereas modern poets have had to do so in a "sidelong" manner. She places the blame on the traumas of modernity: "In the vast catastrophe of the European war our emotions had to be . . . put at an angle from us before we could allow ourselves to feel them" (35). Wilfred Owen and Siegfried Sassoon, gay poets of that war, could not "be direct without being clumsy"; indeed, they could not be direct at all about their emotions, as Woolf knew, for fear of homophobic censorship. Tacit in her comparison of Owen and Sassoon to the Greeks is the latter's freedom to eulogize the deaths of their beloved friends; thus, Simonides was able to write openly and without embarrassment of his fallen comrades. The modern difficulty of mourning, both for soldiers and for Woolf, stems in part from the difficulty of representing an unspeakable same-sex love. The intimate relationship between Greek love and Greek loss in Woolf's writing suggests, rather, the equivocalness of Hellenism as a "symbolic resource."

In "On Not Knowing Greek," Woolf suppresses the homoerotic aspect of Sappho's poetry. The poet is mentioned three times, twice in passing and once in reference to her alleged leap from the cliff of Leucas, after having been abandoned by her supposed male lover, Phaon. Woolf was well aware that this was a discredited legend but nevertheless says, "Sappho leapt from a cliff" (25). In an essay that challenges the claims of classical scholarship, Woolf may have wished to avoid a dispute over Sappho's homosexuality; indeed, her oblique allusion to Owen and Sassoon's self-censorship implicitly refers to her own. Her deliberate obfuscation of Sappho's notorious sapphism in an essay that dwells upon the impossibility of understanding ancient Greece effectively buries female same-sex love in obscurity while pointing toward its epistemological allure. Greece offers a vision, however deceitful, of "the earth unravaged, the sea unpolluted" (36)—in short, of an idyllic place before or beyond history and, hence, as a locus of mourning.

In 1921, Woolf was also writing her reminiscence of "Old Bloomsbury," including her nervous breakdown in 1904 when she lay in bed, "thinking that the birds were singing Greek choruses."[27] Those birds singing in Greek, as Lee notes, not only repeat a phrase from "On Not Knowing Greek" but also echo a passage that appears in *Mrs. Dalloway* describing Septimus Smith's hallucinations.[28] She persuasively argues that Woolf conflated her 1904 auditory hallucination with her subsequent 1921 essay and 1925 novel. The birds that sing in Greek to Septimus speak a language familiar to other shell-shocked gay soldiers, a language of love and death: "A sparrow . . . chirped . . . in Greek words how there is no crime and, joined by another sparrow, they sang in voices prolonged and piercing in Greek words, from trees in the meadow of life beyond a river where the dead walk, how there is no death."[29] Greek is, thus, the thread that links Septimus's madness, his elegiac love for Evans, homoeroticism, Thoby, Woolf's experience of madness, and, finally, Clarissa Dalloway's passion for Sally Seton.

Her passion is recounted in words that reverberate with Sappho's fragment 31, sometimes referred to as "Peer of the Gods." Anne Carson translates its first two lines as follows: "He seems to me equal to gods that man/whoever he is who is opposite you."[30] This well-known poem describes a triangular relationship in which the female speaker burns with desire for a woman who is occupied by the attention of a man. Similarly, at the party in *Mrs. Dalloway* where Clarissa first caught sight of Sally, she "could not take her eyes off Sally" and asked "the man she was with, Who is *that?*" (32–33; emphasis Woolf's). Later, at "the most exquisite moment of her life," when Sally kisses her, they are immediately and "horribl[y]" interrupted by Peter Walsh (35–36). Molly Hoff observes that Clarissa's feelings for Sally "run the gamut of Sappho's desire" in fragment 31.[31] Clarissa's exhilaration has a biographical basis in Woolf's love for Madge, who was the model for Sally as well as the daughter of J. A. Symonds—all the more reason that Clarissa and Sally should "read Plato in bed" together (33).

Ought we to suppose that the homoeroticism in *Mrs. Dalloway* is a Sapphic version of Symonds's notion of Greek love? Pondering "this question of love, . . . this falling in love with women," Clarissa initially recalls "yielding to the charm of a woman" in which "she did undoubtedly feel what men felt": a clitoral tumescence, the "pressure of rapture, which splits its thin skin and gushed and poured" into a climactic "illumination: a match burning in a crocus" (32). This striking figure combines the floral and fiery figures common in Sappho's poetry. A bit later, Woolf describes such a passion in ways that align it with the Hellenic homoerotic ideal: "The strange thing . . . was the purity, the integrity, of her feeling for Sally. It was not like one's feeling for a man. It was completely disinterested, and besides, it had a quality which could only exist between women, between women just grown up" (34). Unlike relationships with men, those with women are not compromised by material interests, such as those concerning marriage, or by competitive striving for power, but they are characterized by sheer "radiance." This impossibly ecstatic language of love is, figuratively, "Greek" inasmuch as it attempts to describe "the religious feeling" of a "revelation" (36). It is the language of a transcendent epiphany, of an ineffable desire whose "inner meaning [is] *almost* expressed" (32; emphasis mine), but which lies beyond one's grasp.

Mrs. Dalloway is the high-water mark of Woolf's engagement with Sappho. With minor exceptions in *The Waves*, references to Sappho and to the Greeks in general dropped out of her published fiction after 1925, although she continued to comment on sapphism in her letters and diaries. Two motives were at work: first, she became less interested in Greek as a trope for love and death; second, and more importantly, she became much more sensitive to homophobic censorship. After Hall's *Well of Loneliness* was banned for obscenity in 1928, she deleted actionable references to female same-sex love in her public work. For instance, she canceled sexually suggestive passages from early drafts of *A Room of One's Own* (1929); nonetheless, she expressed the fear that "I shall be . . . hinted at for a sapphist."[32] In the final version of *Orlando* (1928), she excised "dangerous details," such as "references to

Sappho, to Orlando's 'lusts,' and [to] her love affairs with women," according to Lee.[33] Practicing what Lee calls "an aesthetics of inhibition," she obscured sapphic implications in *The Waves* (1931) and *The Years* (1937).

Instead, in her last novel, *Between the Acts* (1941), Woolf describes the playwright Miss LaTrobe, who sinks into a reverie of a prehistoric England in which she imagines rhododendrons growing wild in the place that would become Piccadilly Square. Woolf's representation of primeval England as a place of freedom parallels the vision of the ancient monk at the end of "A Dialogue" as well as Miss Allan's image of the Greeks as "naked black men" in *The Voyage Out*. Indeed, her fictions often conclude with an evocation of primitive origins. This vision was significantly informed by the work of Jane Ellen Harrison, the classical anthropologist whose inquiry into pre-Hellenic rituals and myths stressed what Nietzsche, in *The Birth of Tragedy*, described as the dark, Dionysian side of Greek religion. Harrison argued that the Homeric pantheon of patriarchal gods was preceded by a chthonic, matriarchal religion centered upon the worship of the great mother.

Both in person and in her work, Harrison was an appealing figure to Woolf; she was, as it were, the last of her Greek tutors. They were on friendly terms. Harrison gave her a copy of *Ancient Art and Ritual* in 1923, and Woolf described her in respectful and admiring terms. The Hogarth Press published her *Reminiscences* (1925), and Woolf cited Harrison's scholarly stature as evidence of the "immense" "advance in [the] intellectual power of women" since they gained a measure of "education and liberty."[34] Equally important to her was Harrison's sapphic status. From her private correspondence, it is evident that Woolf regarded Harrison and Hope Mirrlees as lovers. For instance, writing to Molly McCarthy regarding a forthcoming trip to Paris, she mentions that she plans to "meet Jane Harrison & Hope Mirrlees who have a Sapphic flat."[35] Recounting to Jacques Raverat a party that she had attended, she remarks how she "like[d] to see [Hope] and Jane billing and cooing together."[36]

Harrison's vision of an archaic matriarchy served as the basis for an influential body of feminist scholarship in the 1980s and 1990s that regarded Woolf as endorsing such a vision and, thus, that read her novels as written under Harrison's signature. Sandra Shattuck argues that Harrison's fingerprints are all over *Between the Acts*, for instance, in Lucy Swithin's interest in the primal origins of civilization, in the novel's concluding description of Giles and Isa as cave dwellers, and, especially, in Woolf's use of a quasi-Greek chorus in Miss LaTrobe's play: "It is as if Woolf were staging Harrison's" *Ancient Art and Ritual*.[37] Mary Carpentier goes further, arguing that Woolf and Harrison "both sought in their work to resurrect the primacy of the mother over the father, of mysticism over rationalism, of merger over separation, of collectivity over individuality."[38] By her account,

Mrs. Ramsey, in *To The Lighthouse*, is Harrison's "Themis," "the very spirit of the assembly incarnate."[39] In a more measured assessment, Annabel Robinson claims that Woolf's sense of "the common life" and of the continuity of the past and the present in *A Room of One's Own* is indebted to Harrison's anthropology, although Woolf did not share Harrison's belief that she had "discovered afresh a real religion."[40] Finally, Rowena Fowler demonstrates that "Woolf absorbed from Harrison insights about the way Greek ritual conventions embody archetypal emotions and states of mind," especially in Woolf's use of the Greek chorus in *The Waves*.[41] Woolf was drawn to the chorus for technical as well as conceptual reasons; its undifferentiated voices enabled her to achieve certain dramatic effects in her prose as well as to foreground the alienation of modern spectators, as in *Between the Acts*.

Did Woolf regard Harrison's work as, in Carpentier's words, the "imaginative recreation of a female-dominated past, almost a feminist utopia"? How do Harrison's "Greek lessons" square with Woolf's previous engagement with Greek language and culture? Why is it that references to Sappho and to the Greeks largely disappear from her novels at about the same time—the late 1920s—when Harrison's influence becomes visible? Harrison's evocation of a pre-Hellenic, Dionysian world challenged contemporary Hellenism and, in Woolf's works, seems to supplant the latter. While she was intrigued by Harrison's speculations regarding a primitive matriarchy, Woolf did not, however, equate it with modern feminism, much less with female same-sex desire. Who can forget her scathing depiction of Doris Kilman in *Mrs. Dalloway*? In Woolf's novels, passion between women does not in itself result in female solidarity and as often as not issues in jealousy and isolation. For instance, the image of archaic England at the conclusion of *Between the Acts* coincides with Miss LaTrobe drinking alone in a pub. Rather than offering a plausible alternative to modernity, Harrison's vision of a primitive matriarchy is, for Woolf, a site of bereavement and mourning, akin to her representation of dead mothers. Even Harrison did not regard her work as a blueprint for modern women, observing that "Matriarchy gave to women a false because magical prestige."[42] Her vanished matriarchy renders sapphism impossibly distant, a lost ideal like that of Greek love.

Given Woolf's mastery of Greek as well as her sometimes hostile attitude toward the desire to which Sappho's Lesbos gave its modern name, where should we place her in the spectrum of "sapphic modernism"? The landmark text for reading the works of many Anglo-American modernist women authors as sapphic is Susan Gubar's 1984 essay, "Sapphistries." In keeping with her effort, together with Sandra Gilbert, to recast the modernist canon, Gubar argues that "Sappho's status as a female precursor empowered a number of female modernists," such as Vivien, H. D., Woolf, and Amy Lowell. Although she does not use the term "sapphic modernism," Gubar presents Sappho as the presiding muse for twentieth-century women writers.[43] Like Gubar, Shari Benstock's aim is to reshape the modernist canon in gynocentric terms, but her claims are grander. Benstock argues for a conception of sapphism that goes beyond the confines of lesbian sexuality to embrace female same-sex love as both a disruptive psychic desire and a deconstructive textual energy. Her essay is frequently cited as the authoritative source for the definition of sapphic modernism, yet little attention is paid to the critical distinctions in her argument, the most important of which is that between conventional literary texts with a lesbian content and avant-garde texts with an ambiguously queer content. She differentiates "those women . . . whose writings followed traditional models of form and style, but whose subject matter was Sapphism," such as Hall, from "those writers who filtered the lesbian content of their writing through the screen of presumably heterosexual subject matter or behind experimental literary styles," such as Woolf, Gertrude Stein, and H. D.[44] In short, Benstock's poststructuralist "sapphic modernism" is very different from Gubar's conventional understanding of Sappho as a literary influence in the form of a mythic, feminine figure. Like other defenders of the concept of sapphic modernism, Diana Collecott argues that "Sapphic modernism" has "emerged as the term for manifestations (however obscure or disruptive) that privilege the *Sapphic.* This word has multiple meanings embracing aesthetic and intersubjectivity as well as sexual practice."[45] Collecott does not want to restrict the term to precise sexual practices for the laudable reason that one never knows what goes on in bed between women.

To sum up this brief survey of the scholarship on "sapphic modernism," the concept moves in two, opposite trajectories, what I shall call, crudely and unoriginally, "the pure and the impure." Those who regard Sappho as a model for the authentic expression of female same-sex desire and friendship, one that is recoverable from the lengthy and checkered history of Sappho's representation, fall into the first camp. H. D.'s representation of Sappho is the locus of the "pure" version. She undertook a pilgrimage to Lesbos and devoted much of her early work to rewriting Sappho's poems. In her later epic poems, she elevated Sappho to a mythic, deific status. A similarly uplifting image of Sappho is apparent in the works of American lesbian-feminists from the 1970s and 1980s.

The opposing, "impure" tradition is, needless to say, French. Baudelaire's decadent poems about lesbians, *les femmes damnées*, were the inspiration for Louys' 1894 *Songs of Bilitis*, a quasi-pornographic set of prose poems that represent Sappho as the madam of a salon catering to both women and men. Vivien learned Greek in order to translate Sappho's poems in a daringly original, lesbian fashion, against the tide of contemporary philology, and understood sapphism as characteristic of artistic abnormality. Her appropriation of the sadistic Sappho, according to Gubar, gave her access to "the unholy excess and implacable cruelty of lesbian desire," enabling her to "uncover the demonic power that drew Baudelaire and Swinburne to the lesbian femme fatale. Indeed, Vivien suggests that the 'unnatural' longing of the decadent's Sappho turns the lesbian into a prototypical artist."[46] The image of a Sappho who is doomed by her exorbitant, deviant passion has a long literary history that has largely been forgotten but which had a powerful impact on modernist writers.

Woolf appears to have been unmoved by either school of sapphic modernism. She did not embrace either the pure or the impure versions of Sappho, neither idealizing her as an icon of female same-sex desire or as a literary muse, nor regarding her as a model for avant-garde literary or sexual practices. She understood Sappho as the leader of a community of women and as a lover of women but refused rendering sapphism as the defining characteristic of a category of persons, namely, lesbians. However, it is appropriate to enlist her works in Benstock's broad conception of sapphic modernism as instances of literature that "redefines genres" (193). Woolf's *A Room of One's Own* and *Three Guineas* certainly reconfigure the genre of nonfiction, while her narratives have been read as seductive gestures toward women. Her evocation of the force of unconscious desires fits squarely within Benstock's definition of sapphic modernism, while no reader can doubt the disruptive psychic and textual energies at work in her writings.

Although Woolf frequently alluded to Sappho in her works, she was far too modest, not to mention too scrupulously aware of our ignorance of Sappho, to posit her as the precursor of a literary tradition. Her skepticism of lesbianism as an ontological category (of which she did not consider herself a member) should caution us against reducing sapphic modernism to "lesbian modernism," that is, to a body of work produced by self-identified lesbian writers. One of Woolf's "Greek" lessons for her readers is to resist the modern bifurcation of same- and other-sex desires. Moreover, the articulation of same-sex desire in Woolf's work, even the most personal and genuine, is thoroughly mediated by the Hellenic literary tradition. By drawing upon the discourse of Greek love to express erotic longing and loss as well as correlated epistemological yearnings and lacks, Woolf suggests that intimate desires may be written—indeed, may only be written—through an inevitably alienating language. Greek is, as it were, a catachresis, the enigmatic mark of the untranslatability of love.

Notes

1. Quentin Bell, *Virginia Woolf*, vol. 1 (New York: Harcourt Brace Jovanovich, 1972), p. 68. Woolf's story was published in *Forum* (1928) and was subsequently

reprinted in *The Complete Shorter Fiction of Virginia Woolf*, ed. Susan Dick, 2nd ed. (New York: Harcourt, 1989). Further references cited in text.

2. Rowena Fowler, " 'On Not Knowing Greek': The Classics and the Women of Letters." *Classical Journal* 78 (1983): 337.
3. Rowena Fowler, "Moments and Metamorphoses: Virginia Woolf's Greece," *Comparative Literature* 51, no. 3 (Summer 1999): 218–19.
4. For "the higher sodomy," see Linda Dowling, *Hellenism and Homosexuality in Victorian Oxford* (Ithaca: Cornell University Press, 1994), pp. 116, 135.
5. Walter Pater, *The Renaissance: Studies in Art and Poetry*, Donald Hill, ed. (1873; rpt. Berkeley: University of California Press, 1980), p. 189.
6. *The Letters of Virginia Woolf*, Nigel Nicolson and Joanne Trautmann, eds., 6 vols. (New York: Harcourt Brace Jovanovich, 1975–80), 3: 432.
7. Ibid., 431.
8. "A Society," *The Complete Shorter Fiction*, p. 132. Further references cited in text.
9. Margaret Williamson, *Sappho's Immortal Daughters* (Cambridge: Cambridge University Press, 1995), p. 91.
10. Joan DeJean, "Sex and Philology: Sappho and the Rise of German Nationalism," in Ellen Greene, ed., *Re-Reading Sappho: Reception and Transmission* (Berkeley: University of California Press, 1996), p. 144.
11. Jane Marcus, *Virginia Woolf and the Languages of Patriarchy* (Bloomington: Indiana University Press, 1987).
12. Joan DeJean, *Fictions of Sappho: 1546–1937* (Chicago: University of Chicago Press, 1989), p. 136.
13. *The Diary of Virginia Woolf*, Anne Olivier Bell, ed., 5 vols. (New York: Harcourt Brace Jovanovich, 1977–84), 3: 53 (December 21, 1925).
14. Marcus, in *Virginia Woolf and the Languages of Patriarchy*, rails against male "homosexual hegemony," p. 177 *passim*.
15. Quoted in Lyndall Gordon, *Virginia Woolf: A Writer's Life* (New York: W. W. Norton, 1984), p. 84.
16. J. A. Symonds, *Studies of the Greek Poets* (London: Smith, Elder, 1873) and *A Problem in Greek Ethics*, printed for private publication (London: 1901).
17. DeJean, *Fictions of Sappho*, p. 223.
18. Ibid., p. 248.
19. Hermione Lee, *Virginia Woolf* (New York: Knopf, 1998), p. 142.
20. Lorna Sage, "Introduction," *The Voyage Out* (London: Oxford University Press, 1992), p. xix. Further references cited in text.
21. Rachel Bowlby, *Feminist Destinations and Further Essays on Virginia Woolf* (Edinburgh: Edinburgh University Press, 1997), p. 231.
22. Ruth Vanita, "Bringing Buried Things to Light: Homoerotic Alliances in *To The Lighthouse*," in Eileen Barrett and Patricia Cramer, eds., *Virginia Woolf: Lesbian Readings* (New York: New York University Press, 1997), pp. 165, 167.
23. "[A Dialogue upon Mount Pentelicus]" in *The Complete Shorter Fiction*, p. 64. Further references cited in text.
24. *Jacob's Room* (1922; rpt. New York: Harcourt, Brace, and Company, 1950), p. 76. Further references cited in text.
25. Angeliki Spiropoulou, " 'On Not Knowing Greek': Virginia Woolf's Spatial Critique of Authority," *Interdisciplinary Literary Studies* 4: 1 (Fall 2002): 4, 15–16.

26. Virginia Woolf, "On Not Knowing Greek," *The Common Reader*, first series (New York: Harcourt, Brace, and Company, 1925), p. 24. Further references cited in text.
27. Quoted in Lee, *Virginia Woolf*, p. 190.
28. Ibid., pp. 191–92.
29. *Mrs. Dalloway* (New York: Harcourt Brace Jovanovich, 1981), pp. 24–25. Further references cited in text.
30. Anne Carson, *If Not, Winter: Fragments of Sappho* (New York: Random House, 2002), p. 63.
31. Molly Hoff, "Woolf's *Mrs. Dalloway*," *The Explicator* 55, no. 4 (Summer 1997): 215.
32. *Diary*, 3: 262 (October 23, 1929).
33. Lee, *Virginia Woolf*, p. 517.
34. "The Intellectual Status of Women" in Michele Barrett, ed., *Virginia Woolf: Women and Writing* (New York: Harcourt Brace Jovanovich, 1979), p. 56.
35. *Letters* 3: 30 (April 22, 1923). The published edition of Woolf's letter omits the reference to a "Sapphic flat." Citing this letter, Beard reproduces the manuscript, held by the Lilly Library of Indiana University at Bloomington.
36. *Letters* 3: 163 (February 1, 1925).
37. Sandra D. Shattouck, "The Stage of Scholarship: Crossing the Bridge from Harrison to Woolf," in Jane Marcus, ed., *Virginia Woolf and Bloomsbury: A Centenary Celebration* (Bloomington: Indiana University Press, 1987), p. 178.
38. Mary Carpentier, *Ritual, Myth, and the Modernist Text: The Influence of Jane Ellen Harrison on Joyce, Eliot, and Woolf* (Amsterdam: Gordon and Breach, 1998), p. 173.
39. Ibid., pp. 176, 183.
40. Annabel Robinson, "Something Odd at Work: The Influence of Jane Harrison on *A Room of One's Own*," *Wascana Review* 22, no. 1 (Spring 1987): 86.
41. Fowler, "Moments and Metamorphoses," p. 230.
42. Harrison, quoted in Marcus, *Virginia Woolf and Bloomsbury*, p. 195.
43. Susan Guber, "Sapphistries," *Signs* 10 (1984): 42–72; rpt in *Re-Reading Sappho*, ed., Greene, p. 202.
44. Shari Benstock, "Expatriate Sapphic Modernism: Entering Literary History," in Karla Jay and Joanne Glasgow, eds., *Lesbian Texts and Contexts* (New York: New York University Press, 1990), p. 185. Further references cited in text.
45. Diana Collecott, *H. D. and Sapphic Modernism* (Cambridge: Cambridge University Press, 1999).
46. Gubar, "Sapphistries," p. 204.

Chapter 9

"A Sudden Orgy of Decadence": Writing about Sex between Women in the Interwar Popular Press

Alison Oram

In two successive issues in 1924, *The People*, a mass market Sunday newspaper, warned its readers of an insidious new moral danger. In the first article, "The Smear Across London," feature writer Hannen Swaffer wrote of a "definite cult" of "decadent" people (of both sexes), addicted to "perversion" and "the unnatural" who congregated around the theater and literary world whenever plays such as "Salome" or "Dorian Gray" were performed. The "slime" of certain types of art and literature and the neurotic people associated with them were "poisoning London . . . and menacing our future."[1]

The following week Leonora Eyles, a journalist who wrote mainly for the middle-class magazine market, fleshed out these allusions a little further and applied them specifically to women. The difficulty of writing about sexual relationships between women in the popular press in this period is emphasized by the awkward grammar and vocabulary of her title: "Another Phase of 'The Smear': Women Friendships that People Talk About."[2] Adopting Swaffer's glutinous and sexually loaded phrase "smear" in her title and throughout her article, Eyles also repeats the term "decadence" several times. She spliced together a number of concerns, including the growing awareness that this practice was also found among women: "the 'smear across London' is on the women as much as the men" and had effects on innocent female friendships. "It is so open a smear that today two women journalists, often seen together at first nights in the course of their work, and two other women, both artists sharing a flat, have been gossiped about." She suggested that readers should be as concerned about raves in girls' boarding schools as about morality in boys', and quoted the views of a psychoanalyst who blamed this "sudden orgy of decadence" on the war and sex antagonism. She also implied that the vice was most likely to be found "among artists, theatrical and society people" and connected it to the Russian Ballet, which "attracts in the audience many undesirable decadents."[3] The pretext for these articles was to name a new threat of perversion, now found among both women and men in a kind of modern gender equality, sensationalize it by pointing to the diversity of forms it might take, and, in doing so, introduce some middle-class anxieties to a popular readership.

Modern Papers, Modern Readers

The popular press is a significant vector for these new ideas about sexual deviance. Late nineteenth-century sexual science and its influence on relatively elite groups (the medical profession and the judiciary, writers, and artists) has been seen as central to the subsequent development of lesbian culture and identity between the wars.[4] But sexual modernity was also about the democratization of specialist understandings. This chapter, which is based on a systematic study of the two largest circulation Sunday newspapers (*The News of the World* and *The People*),[5] addresses what Sally Alexander argues was a watershed in the transmission of sexual knowledge among a wider population. The limits of what could be said about sexuality were tested in a variety of public and private arenas, while "one of the driving forces of modernity" was young women's break with tradition to take up new vocabularies of sexual desire and femininity.[6] What little is known about how sexual love between women (and eventually lesbian identity) was acknowledged and represented in popular culture and in texts available to ordinary people, and this changed between the 1910s and World War II. The mass market Sunday press is an important means of access to the popular representation of same-sex desire because it reached such a large proportion of working-class and lower-middle-class people and because its main subject matter—gathered up from the dailies and local papers of the previous week—was crime, disaster, and gossip, much of which was sexually prurient.

Fuelled by widespread literacy and the growth of advertising, Sunday newspapers had been reaching mass markets since the 1890s. Between the wars the popular daily papers increasingly adopted the sensational content of the Sundays, which was presented in more attractive layouts and greater informality of writing style to broaden their appeal and gain larger circulations. This intense commercialization was copied in turn by the Sundays, which used more photography, bigger headlines, and shorter stories and took up the selling techniques of the dailies.[7] The popular Sunday press was an interesting mixture of the self-consciously "modern" in its technology, layout, and advertising, while retaining much that was traditional in its content—scandal, popular amusements, and homemade fun as well as reviewing the new mass commercial entertainment.

The News of the World and *The People* were the top-selling Sunday newspapers by some way in this period, with a readership more truly national (despite some regional variations) than any other Sundays. *The News of the World* claimed a circulation of over 2 million in 1912, rising to 4 million in 1939, while *The People* was not far behind, selling over 3 million copies in 1937.[8] These two newspapers found the bulk of their sales among the lower middle class and the working class, that is to say, the majority of the population. By 1938 the market for Sunday papers was considered to have nearly reached saturation point, almost every home taking at least one title.[9] The readership of both *The People* and *The News of the World* was split fairly evenly between men and women[10]; indeed they were presented as family newspapers, with different sections aimed at men, women, and children. The popular press helped to produce the shared mass culture of modernity, in the process tending to homogenize a diverse range of working-class and lower-middle-class views (as well as gender and age differences) into a commercial product, while providing a shared lexicon for the public discussion of sex and scandal. Newspaper stories both contributed to and appropriated meanings from the culture within which they were produced and were part of the process by which lesbian identities gradually became intelligible.[11]

Readers of both *The News of the World* and *The People* were not ashamed to admit that they read these papers for their sensational reporting of sex crimes, murders, disasters, and the marital delinquency of the wealthy and famous.[12] But the semantics of sexuality were far from transparent in their pages. To maintain respectability as family reading while providing sexual titillation, these newspapers used a faux-genteel or ambiguous vocabulary to report sexual wrong-doing in the divorce and criminal courts, with terms such as "intimacy," "molested," or "grave crime" (which might mean abortion, sexual abuse, or gross indecency between men). During the 1920s and 1930s, both papers became slightly more straightforward and less ambiguous in reporting sexual transgression—indeed this was part of their claim to be modern. *The News of the World* in particular trod a thin line between respectability and salaciousness in its long-standing interest in the seedy and sexual underside of British society. Representing itself as a moral newspaper, on the grounds that it reported the punishment as well as the crime, *The News of the World* stressed its accurate and detailed reporting.[13] *The People*, more inclined to assert opinion through editorial and feature articles (being a little less sensational than *The News of the World* it was seen as slightly more respectable), offered, for example, more suitable reading for young people.[14] Working-class respectability, however thin a veneer, allowed these two papers to publish lubricious upper-class scandals under the guise of moral outrage, a highly entertaining form of class antagonism.

Given its greater emphasis on features and opinion pieces, it is not surprising that it was *The People* that first revealed middle-class ideas about lesbianism to a working-class and lower-middle-class readership. The types of women Eyles describes are all middle-class or elite, and as professional workers and divorcees they are undoubtedly also modern. She lays out here some of the key images of same-sex female desire from the middle-class imagination. In the years that follow we can trace those ideas about the lesbian that leaked from middlebrow nonfiction to the working-class press. Yet female homosexuality was rarely directly named in the popular press until after World War II. How was female same-sex desire represented to a working-class readership in major "lesbian" cases involving the cultural elite such as the 1918 Maud Allan libel case, or the censorship of *The Well of Loneliness* in 1928 as well as in more "everyday" stories?

Reporting Lesbians

There was no coherent idea of love between the women in British popular culture during the interwar period. In the British press the lesbian is an elusive figure who has a submerged as well as at times more overt presence in diverse stories including divorce cases, female husband narratives, and crime reports. Images of lesbianism, such as they are, take shape from earlier periods of modernity as well as from developing new discourses. Judith Walkowitz has argued that the 1920s concerns about dangerous female sexualities, associated with cosmopolitanism and the commercialization of culture, had their roots in London in the years spanning 1890 to 1920, and that therefore the conventional division between post–World War I cultural history and prewar developments must be reconsidered.[15] Historians have used the term modernity to designate a variety of time periods, but some agreed features are the expansion of mass communications, the consciousness of moving into a new pace of life (with attendant challenges and threats), and the deployment of new modes of understanding and expertise.[16] Here

I am concerned with the overlapping of old and new ideas within interwar modernity, as the popular Sunday press initially invoked ideas from the late nineteenth century in projecting lesbian desire rather than mobilizing newer sexological models. The femme fatale of fin-de-siècle decadence, the sexually powerful, often predatory woman, is a figure that also begins to represent same-sex desire. She embodies a feminine parallel to male homosexuality, a modern form of gender equality in an era of anxiety about women's greater sexual and social freedom. The longevity of these representations challenges assumptions that modern lesbian identity was formed in the first place in response to the sexological category of gender inversion, the mannish woman, developed in Britain by Havelock Ellis.[17] The particular traditions of the British press and its notional adherence to respectability led to diffuse images of same-sex desire, and the masculine lesbian only begins to appear in the 1930s.

These shifting, often opaque images of lesbian desire are inflected with class-specific meanings. Throughout most of the interwar period, same-sex female desire is located in the worlds of the wealthy and upper class, or alternatively in the bohemian milieu of the arts and theater, long coded as sexually permissive. The moral failure of these groups of "others" provides the popular press with opportunities for a traditional interest—titillating scandals about the new vices of the elite. Working-class communities are not represented as hosts to this new phenomenon and are not directly threatened by it. Sexual meanings that might be attached to the figure of the cross-dressed "female husband" (the woman who dresses and passes as a man and has a wife or girlfriend) are dissembled through humor and her traditional place in working-class culture. Female masculinity did not automatically signal same-sex desire even in the 1930s, and when it did begin to, it was linked to the "rough" and threateningly cosmopolitan areas of the city, rather than the respectable spaces of working-class life. Nevertheless, these Sunday newspapers were co-opting their readers into some middle-brow fears about lesbianism, and thereby enrolling them in a cross-class abjection of same-sex desire.

Decadent Women

The significant term used by Eyles in her 1924 article to indicate female homosexuality was "decadence," and this, together with her reference back to the 1890s "wave of hedonism," shows how the modern recognition of love between women depended upon the reworking of fin-de-siècle anxieties about sexuality, degeneracy, and the arts. The earliest popular press representations of lesbianism had already begun to take shape in the reporting of the sensational 1918 court case in which the dancer Maud Allan sued the right-wing MP Noel Pemberton Billing for the libel that she was a lesbian. One area of evidence explored in the trial, reported at length by *The News of the World*, was the planned appearance of Maud Allan in the play "Salome," written by "the moral and sexual pervert" Oscar Wilde and originally published in 1895, just as public consciousness of male homosexuality was being raised by Wilde's trial. The play was alleged to be "full of homosexual inclinations" and its producer, according to one witness, "employed the language of sodomy."[18] While Allan's counsel attempted to emphasize that the play depicted heterosexual passion, the mass of evidence reported included the questioning of Lord Alfred Douglas, Wilde's lover in the 1890s.

Through her dance performance, especially her interpretation of Salome, and the trial, Maud Allan became "the bearer of the Wildean decadent legacy," embodying disease and sexual perversion, Walkowitz has argued.[19] I want to suggest that among the diverse sexual practices alluded to in the reporting of the trial, one interpretation (and indeed the one that Billing was asserting) was that there was a female parallel to Wildean vice. The staging of "Salome" had attracted notoriety and accusations of lasciviousness elsewhere in Europe, and Maud Allan was not the first performer in the title role to be associated with lesbianism.[20] While the play itself has been read for its subtext of male homosexual desire,[21] I suggest that the idea of active female sexuality, combined with the name of Oscar Wilde, also begins to signal desire between women in some contexts. Wilde's name was to resurface as a sign of lesbian decadence ten years later, when the *Sunday Express* condemned Radclyffe Hall's novel *The Well of Loneliness* through a comparison with "the Oscar Wilde scandal."[22] By the 1920s, "decadence" was a derogatory catch-all term for sexual vice, especially that linked to the avant-garde. While it referred back to sexual science, eugenics, and the debates about national degeneration, it did not necessarily imply any specific theories (though sexology made an appearance in the Allan trial),[23] but was used rather to indicate pathology and perversion in general. Historians have emphasized the role of experts in creating the new knowledge of female homosexuality. But the decadent woman with lesbian desires has other origins too: through the connection with Wilde's work she also evokes the late nineteenth-century cosmopolitan world of the Baudelarian lesbian, diluted and translated to a British context.

Reflecting fears about female sexual subjectivity, the decadent woman figure was invested with considerable power to disrupt society, especially as a femme fatale, a predatory woman seducing men and, now, women. As a lesbian she had a strong presence in anxious British middlebrow writing on sexuality between the wars. The best-selling 1917 novel *Regiment of Women* was frequently cited as an example of the malign corrupting influence of an older woman teacher who preyed on young women and girls, endangering marriage and family life.[24] Apart from the concerns raised by Eyles in 1924, the popular press was not interested in the dangers of schoolgirl crushes or relationships between pupils and teachers. This was a theme of lesbian panic that did not translate across class boundaries, perhaps because the danger was perceived to be most acute in boarding schools. The voluminous professional literature on this problem, in which the influence of *Regiment of Women* was demonstrated by a number of citations, was largely a middle-class concern.[25] But across both middlebrow journalism and (though less strongly) the popular press, anxiety about the lesbian seductress was transposed onto two related figures, the wife-snatcher, threatening the private home, and the powerful older woman, making advances to the more innocent in the public spaces of the modern woman's life. The lesbian seducer was represented as a threat by Eyles, who wrote that professional women were at risk from same-sex erotic approaches, not just actresses but social workers, artists, and writers, including the author herself, who had received "frankly erotic" letters from women decadents.[26] The seducer trope was used in the attack on Maud Allan's sexual character in the 1918 case wherein it was suggested that she had a dubious friendship with a married woman, Margot Asquith, wife of the prime minister. Other evidence from witnesses alleged that Mrs Asquith, like Allan, was one of the list of 47,000 "moral perverts" collected by German secret agents. It was an article about this list, published by Billing, that had triggered Allan's attempt to sue for libel.

> Did you go to Downing-street?—I did.—Did you dance?—No.—Did you see Mrs. Asquith there?—Naturally, when I was her guest.—Have you met her anywhere else?—Yes.—Has she ever been in your dressing-room at the Palace?—Never.—You would recognise her, of course?—I have eyes. . . .[27]

How clearly were these different ideas suggesting female same-sex love reported in the Sunday newspapers? The censored reporting and complexity of the evidence brought up in the Maud Allan case meant that the nature of the central allegation remained obscure in many press accounts.[28] *The News of the World*, independent of the popular Sunday newspapers, did publish in full the explicit language of the indictment for libel, including the accusation that Maud Allan's "private performances of an obscene and indecent character, [were] so designed as to foster and encourage unnatural practices among women, and that the said Maud Allan associated herself with persons addicted to unnatural practices."[29] The report in *The People* was so abridged as to make the proceedings tantalizing but unintelligible,[30] a vagueness that Swaffer and Eyles promised to rectify in their 1924 articles. For many readers, no doubt, the Allan case was another story about the titillating sexual misdemeanors of the elite, with little connection to everyday life. Allan's own position in the upper middle-class, particularly her profession as a dancer, rendered her a high profile figure who was also on the moral margins. But both the Allan case and the Eyles article suggested that modern sexual equality might produce a new female version of an older vice.

The Wife Stealer

Apart from the somewhat opaque reference in the Maud Allan case, the threat to married life posed by the predatory lesbian was first set out in the popular press in the reporting of the 1921 Parliamentary debates on criminalizing sex between women. This was a rare example of direct discussion of female homosexuality in the press. *The News of the World* did not report all the details of the debate in the House of Commons and omitted the more explicit language used by some MPs, simply reporting the terminology of the proposed clause to punish "any act of gross indecency between female persons." It reported parts of those speeches that emphasized that it was "a matter for medical science and for neurologists" and that this "dreadful degradation" was familiar to divorce and criminal lawyers.[31] While some of the contributions to the debate might have been informed by European sexology,[32] these did not appear in *The News of the World* story; the most vivid images of the lesbian embedded in its report were those of asylum inmate or marriage wrecker. One MP was acquainted with a man who "told . . . how his home had been ruined by the wiles of one abandoned female who had pursued his wife." Another speaker (Sir Ernest Wild, later to preside over the Colonel Barker trial) told a remarkably similar story that earned the subheading "Married Life Was Ruined," of a man whose "wife had been taken from him by a young woman."[33]

Middlebrow advice books were much bolder than the popular press in developing the theme of the lesbian marriage breaker. In one advice book published in 1922, the young husband was warned to protect his wife from the "many strange types of women abroad to-day who may desire her, and who are just as great pests to society as the male degenerates who consort only with their fellows."[34] The author, actor-manager Seymour Hicks, presented himself as having greater sexual sophistication and knowledge than the average innocent Englishman. This kind of woman was "more dangerous than all the men who attack your household put together" since she was difficult to identify: "her caresses may have as an excuse 'sympathetic femininity,' and you may hesitate to label her a Lesbian."[35] While the home and private space of companionate marriage were important sites of modernity for women,[36] they were also vulnerable to the newly recognized dangers of the city. "[T]hese wretches have multiplied immoderately of late," Hicks warned, and their sexual power was considerable: they "will wreck your home more thoroughly than you can imagine."[37]

Readers of the mass circulation Sunday press were offered a diluted version of these fears in some divorce court reports. These were a staple feature of the Sunday press, offering the sexual misconduct of the upper and middle classes as prurient entertainment to readers who could not themselves afford the cost of divorce either in respectability or financial terms. Divorce court proceedings may sometimes have been abridged in the press, but not sufficiently to avoid the passing of the 1926 Act that restricted the reporting of divorce cases to protect public morality and class hierarchies.[38] Among the cases known to "all lawyers who have had criminal and divorce practice"[39] there may have been one of 1915, reported in the *News of the World* with the judge's eugenicist comment as the headline: "Not Fit to Marry." The wife, an actress, held that her artist husband had agreed to her request before marriage that theirs "should be a platonic union" and that her friend, another actress, should continue to live with them after the marriage. On the wedding night the wife "slept in a room with her lady friend, petitioner sleeping at his wife's cottage, as had been previously arranged." Sometime later, after a violent quarrel about the terms of their marriage, the wife asked her husband to leave, though he maintained that "he never threatened to 'ruin' her by going to all her friends." The judge strongly condemned the wife's "perfectly scandalous" and "immoral" conduct, which may be understood as both her refusal to have sex with her husband, and her preference for intimacy with her woman friend.[40] The bohemian world of the theater and the arts occupied by the protagonists may also have alerted knowing readers to the possibility of sexual transgression.

A wounding case of 1927 included some similar features, but it took place in a more proletarian class context. A printer had stabbed his wife of two months after she asked for a separation. His wife had "stayed away from time to time. When she returned it was with a girl friend, who was to stay with them against his wish." Indeed, as in the 1915 case, she usurped his place in the marital bed. Cross-examined by the magistrate, the old school friend, a bank clerk, "mentioned that she slept with Mrs. Willis, and the husband slept in the kitchen."[41] These husbands appear defenseless against their assertive wives and their women friends. They cannot command their marital rights and are banished to marginal domestic spaces or excluded from the home altogether. Now that active female desire was beginning to be acknowledged in modern courtship and marriage,[42] women's sexual choices could also be diverted or corrupted away from heterosexuality and motherhood.

The Mannish Woman and Lesbian Desire

In none of the examples discussed above from the 1910s and 1920s are the women represented as particularly mannish in appearance. Maud Allan's stage persona drew upon long-established conventions of seductive femininity as well as on modern dance styles. Although Eyles quoted a psychoanalyst who appeared to draw on the British sexologists in linking female decadence to feminist politics, he did not cite their ideas of gender inversion. The same-sex seducers of the 1921 Parliamentary debate and related stories of broken marriages were dangerous precisely because they were not distinguishable from normal women, according to most commentators, though their assertive sexuality and power to lure wives away may be read as masculine.

This is not to say that mannish women were absent from the popular press. Stories and cartoons about women wearing trousers, taking up masculine sports and professions, even growing facial hair (allegedly as a consequence of the bob) appeared frequently in the newspapers. This was a means of generating controversy and sales in the 1920s when the implications of the modern woman's greater political and economic freedom were the subject of debate.[43] While these reports reflect anxiety about a possible breakdown of sexual difference, they were normally lighthearted in tone and not freighted with transgressive sexuality.

Nor were stories of cross-dressing women, a well-established genre in the popular press. Some lesbian historians have read the female husband as a historical expression of same-sex desire.[44] But the Sunday press presented the dozens of cross-dressing stories they published throughout the 1920s and 1930s as light entertainment. They followed a fairly standard dramatic narrative, recounting the disclosure of "true" gender, and giving a detailed description of the cross-dresser's appearance and achievement in passing as the opposite sex and a pragmatic economic or social explanation for the masquerade. Elements of comedy might turn on sexual ignorance or mistaken identity, as seen in reports of William Holton, a forty-two-year-old "Man-woman" from the Midlands, whose biological sex was revealed after he was admitted to hospital in 1929: "So completely did the latest man-woman adopt masculine guise that she worked as a timber haulier, a coal heaver, a cow-man, a road mender, and a navvy, drank heavily and smoked black twist, and, most astonishingly of all, claimed paternity of a child born to a woman with whom she had lived for over four years."[45] Holton's wife was reportedly "bewildered by the startling turn of events. 'I believed him to be a man,' she declares, 'and our life together was perfectly normal.' "[46] While Holton's marriage was referred to as a "strange association," this and the other female husband stories generally remained free of any explicit discussion of sexual misbehavior well into the 1940s.

With no cross-reading available within these newspapers to suggest that female masculinity might denote homosexuality, the preferred reading of passing women stories was as family entertainment, akin to the male impersonator of the music hall or variety theater, whose acts were reviewed in the entertainment pages of the same papers.[47] *The News of the World* had particularly strong connections to music hall tradition, printing a popular song every Sunday until 1942 for readers to play at home or at the pub.[48] On the other hand, the culture of "knowingness"—the innuendo and suggestiveness—established in the music hall between performer and audience might have been carried over for some readers into allusions of same-sex hanky-panky.[49]

One exception to this obliviousness occurred briefly in the reporting of the prominent 1929 trial of "Colonel Barker" (Valerie Arkell-Smith) for bankruptcy and perjury regarding her marriage to another woman. The judge referred to Barker's "perverted conduct," which had "outraged the decencies of nature,"[50] but this suggestion of sexual transgression was largely ignored by the press and not repeated in subsequent similar cases until after World War II. Colonel Barker was atypical, however, both in this direct reference to sexual vice and in her class position: originally from the affluent middle class, she had successfully masqueraded as an ex-army officer for several years. Most cross-dressers were from working-class backgrounds and their capacity for masculine manual labor or skilled work was part of the "well I never" tone of the story. The press was unwilling to represent female husbands as sexual deviants, and continued to reflect the fact that gender impersonation had an accepted place in working-class culture, albeit as an entertaining spectacle.[51] Where greater sexual frisson was suggested, it was associated with the degenerate leisured classes, not found in working-class communities, and can be read as another expression of cross-class animosity.[52]

Historians have recently argued that it is only after the *Well of Loneliness* trial in 1928 that female masculinity begins to signify lesbianism in culture.[53] In the popular press specifically, the stories I have surveyed show that this association develops slowly and is not automatically made, even in the late 1930s. A language to indicate same-sex female desire had already been established, and *The Well of Loneliness* trial did not initiate an immediate discursive shift. Women passing as men, even if they had girlfriends, continued to be reported sympathetically, as family entertainment, in the 1930s and 1940s.[54] The masculine woman was not necessarily lesbian and the lesbian figure was not always masculine. Even the treatment of *The Well of Loneliness* trial did not link lesbianism to mannishness across all of the Sunday press. *The News of the World* reported that the book was found obscene because it dealt favorably with the subject of "unnatural practices between women."[55] Stephen, the protagonist, was "depicted as a child with unnatural tendencies" who goes on to have three friendships with women.[56] In contrast, *The People* intervened with editorial judgment from the beginning and emphasized gender inversion. The initially unnamed "secret" novel "treats with astounding frankness a revolting aspect of modern life," it asserted, expanding on the "sexual aspects" of the book with a comment from the publishers: "It is concerned with the phenomenon of the masculine woman in all its implications."[57] The paper's description of the plot continued this theme. The parents hoped for a son, and their daughter "began with a boy's instincts, a boy's thoughts which later developed into the instincts and thoughts of a man. . . . Miss Hall seeks not only to explain her pervert 'heroine,' but also to justify her."[58] *The People*, always inclined to offer more extended commentary than *The News of the World*, highlighted the association between lesbianism and the mannish woman as had the original attack by *The Sunday Express*.[59]

In the late 1930s the mannish lesbian begins to take up a place in the modern cityscape alongside the decadent woman and (in middlebrow journalism) the predatory older woman "on the prowl for the young and innocent," who "may have a mannish suggestion about [her] dress, or . . . be feminine and fluffy in appearance."[60] Her fleeting appearance in these Sunday newspapers was usually in less respectable West End nightclubs. Some of the threats of the cosmopolitan city resounded across both the middle-class and the working-class imagination, to judge by press reports, including miscegenation (unwise marriages of white girls to black or Chinese men were frequently noted by the Sunday press), the existence of ethnic minority communities, and the connections between racial mixing, drug-taking, and the criminal underworld.[61] Long coded as effeminacy, more could be said in the popular press about crimes associated with male homosexuality by the 1930s and, as with the Oscar Wilde allusion a decade earlier, a female parallel of gender inversion signifying same-sex desire occasionally appeared in these stories and locations. In the 1934 Caravan Club trial, in which over 100 men and women were charged with corrupting public morals, it was alleged that: "Some of the women sat on men's knees and embraced each other. One of the women smoked a pipe, and the behaviour generally was of a grossly improper character."[62] The Eton crop, which in the 1920s was represented simply as modernist high fashion for society ladies and women writers alike,[63] starts to become a code for female homosexuality during the 1930s. A *People* journalist wrote of Soho in London, in 1939, "I could take you to three different dens almost next door to one another in the same alley that should be closed immediately. One caters for blond and rouged young men and Eton-cropped women; the second for coloured men and women of low repute; and the third for a gang of criminals . . . ."[64] The initial appearance of the mannish lesbian in the 1930s was in the seedy criminal hangouts of the city rather than in the more glamorous nightclubs. Nor did she yet appear in ordinary working-class communities; the popular press remained generally tolerant of the masculine woman as female husband.

Conclusions

Before World War II, the figure of the lesbian which emerges in these mass market Sunday newspapers is given shape by reference to 1890s decadence, male homosexuality and her power to seduce, in both private domestic space and in certain bohemian milieux of the modern city. The idea of the mannish lesbian is of secondary importance, appearing intermittently from the late 1920s, and she, too, is connected with urban danger. This puts into question the reach of sexological discourses of inversion in this period and demonstrates the need to track multiple origins for the ways lesbianism was imagined in modern popular culture.

These lesbian "types" borrowed extensively from middlebrow writing, though they were less clearly drawn in the pages of *The People* and *The News of the World.* Yet a number of anxieties developed by middle-class commentators and informed by the concerns of educational and medical professionals simply did not translate to the popular press. These newspapers were not interested in the potential same-sex dangers to the adolescent girl, nor in psychological analyses of lesbianism until the 1950s. Indeed female homosexuality was largely represented as another aspect of elite sexual vice, rather than having much to do with everyday working- or lower-middle-class life. Foreshadowed by the fleeting interwar appearance of the mannish lesbian, only from the late 1940s does the press begin to associate love between women with female masculinity and criminality and directly name it as female 'perversion' or 'unnatural passion'.

Notes

I would like to thank Reina Lewis and the editors of this book for their helpful comments on earlier drafts of this essay.

1. Hannen Swaffer, "The Smear Across London," *The People*, November 23, 1924, p. 8.
2. *The People*, November 30, 1924, p. 8.
3. Ibid.
4. Lucy Bland and Laura Doan, eds., *Sexology in Culture: Labelling Bodies and Desires* (Cambridge: Polity Press, 1998). Laura Doan, *Fashioning Sapphism: The Origins of a Modern English Lesbian Culture* (New York: Columbia University Press, 2001).
5. I would like to thank Chris Willis and Marie-Claire Balaam for assisting with this research with the aid of a British Academy small grant no. 29750.
6. Sally Alexander, "The Mysteries and Secrets of Women's Bodies: Sexual Knowledge in the First Half of the Twentieth Century," in Mica Nava and Alan O'Shea, eds., *Modern Times: Reflections on a Century of English Modernity* (London: Routledge, 1996), p. 163.
7. Martin Conboy, *The Press and Popular Culture* (London: Sage, 2002), pp. 113–14. James Curran and Jean Seaton, *Power Without Responsibility: The Press and Broadcasting in Britain* (London: Routledge, 1991), pp. 56–57, 66–68. Matthew Engel, *Tickle the Public: One Hundred Years of the Popular Press* (London: Victor Gollancz, 1996), p. 227.
8. Between 60–75% of people in the south and the Midlands read *The News of the World* and/or *The People* in 1937. Engel, *Tickle the Public*, pp. 221, 228. Political and Economic Planning [PEP], *Report on the British Press* (London: PEP, 1938), pp. 84, 243, 247.
9. PEP, *British Press*, pp. 86, 235.
10. Mass Observation, *The Press and Its Readers* (London: Art and Technics Ltd, 1949), p. 17.
11. See Margaret Beetham, *A Magazine of Her Own?: Domesticity and Desire in the Woman's Magazine, 1800–1914* (London: Routledge, 1996), pp. 1–14 and Stuart Hall, "Encoding/Decoding," in Stuart Hall et al, eds., *Culture, Media, Language: Working Papers in Cultural Studies* (London: Hutchinson, 1980).
12. Mass Observation, *The Press*, pp. 28–30, 44–46, 108, 114.
13. Cyril Bainbridge and Roy Stockdill, *The News of the World Story* (London: Harper Collins, 1993), pp. 90–93.
14. B. Seebohm Rowntree and G. R. Lavers, *English Life and Leisure: A Social Study* (London: Longmans, Green and Co., 1951), pp. 290–91.
15. Judith Walkowitz, "The 'Vision of Salome': Cosmopolitanism and Erotic Dancing in Central London, 1908–1918," *American Historical Review* 108, no. 2 (April 2003): 337–76.
16. Nava and O'Shea, eds., *Modern Times*. Becky Conekin, Frank Mort and Chris Waters, eds., *Moments of Modernity: Reconstructing Britain 1945–1964* (London: Rivers Oram, 1999).

17. This contrasts with the USA where the scare figure of the mannish lesbian with violent tendencies appeared in the sensationalist press from the 1890s. Lisa Duggan, *Sapphic Slashers: Sex, Violence, and American Modernity* (Durham and London: Duke University Press, 2000).
18. *The News of the World*, June 2, 1918, p. 3. Elaine Showalter, *Sexual Anarchy: Gender and Culture at the Fin de Siécle* (London: Virago Press, 1992), pp. 149–50, 171.
19. Walkowitz, "Vision of Salome," pp. 345, 373.
20. Showalter, *Sexual Anarchy*, pp. 159–62.
21. Ibid., chapter 8. Peter Horne, "Sodomy to Salome: Camp Revisions of Modernism, Modernity and Masquerade," in Nava and O'Shea, eds., *Modern Times*.
22. *The Sunday Express*, August 19, 1928.
23. Lucy Bland, "Trial by Sexology?: Maud Allan, *Salome* and the 'Cult of the Clitoris' Case," in Bland and Doan, eds., *Sexology in Culture*.
24. Clemence Dane [Winifred Ashton], *Regiment of Women*. 1917 (London: Virago Press, 1995).
25. See Alison Oram and Annmarie Turnbull, *The Lesbian History Sourcebook: Love and Sex between Women in Britain from 1780 to 1970* (London: Routledge, 2001), chapter 4.
26. *The People*, November 30, 1924, p. 8.
27. *The News of the World*, June 2, 1918, p. 3.
28. Bland, "Trial by Sexology?"
29. *The News of the World*, June 2, 1918, p. 3.
30. *The People*, June 2, 1918, pp. 1 & 5.
31. *The News of the World*, August 7, 1921, p. 4.
32. Laura Doan, " 'Acts of Female Indecency': Sexology's Intervention in Legislating Lesbianism" in Bland and Doan, eds., *Sexology in Culture*.
33. *The News of the World*, August 7, 1921, p. 4.
34. Seymour Hicks, *Difficulties: [An Attempt to Help]* (London: Duckworth and Co., 1922), p. 260.
35. Ibid., p. 261.
36. Judy Giles, "Narratives of Gender, Class, and Modernity in Women's Memories of Mid-Twentieth Century Britain," *Signs: Journal of Women in Culture and Society* 28, no. 1 (2002): 21–41. Alexander, "The Mysteries and Secrets of Women's Bodies." Alison Light, *Forever England: Femininity, Literature and Conservatism between the Wars* (London: Routledge, 1991).
37. Hicks, *Difficulties*, pp. 260–61.
38. Gail Savage, "Erotic Stories and Public Decency: Newspaper Reporting of Divorce Proceedings in England," *The Historical Journal* 41, no. 2 (1998): 511–28.
39. *The News of the World*, August 7, 1921, p. 4.
40. Ibid., January 24, 1915, p. 5.
41. Ibid., January 9, 1927, p. 15.
42. At least in middle-class marriage, following Marie Stopes' books. Lesley Hall, *Sex, Gender and Social Change in Britain since 1880* (London: Macmillan, 2000), pp. 107–8.

43. Adrian Bingham, "Debating Gender: Approaches to Femininity and Masculinity in the Popular National Press in Inter-war Britain" (unpublished D.Phil thesis, University of Oxford, 2002), pp. 59–62, 82–85.
44. See Oram and Turnbull, *Lesbian History Sourcebook*, pp. 11–15.
45. *The News of the World*, May 12, 1929, p. 3.
46. Ibid.
47. See, for example, *The News of the World*, September 27, 1925, p. 12; *The People*, March 28, 1937, p. 13.
48. Bainbridge and Stockdill, *The News of the World Story*, p. 81–82.
49. Peter Bailey, *Popular Culture and Performance in the Victorian City* (Cambridge: Cambridge University Press, 1998), chapter 6. For the debate on whether male impersonators were seen as lesbians see Martha Vicinus, "Turn of the Century Male Impersonation: Rewriting the Romance Plot," in Andrew H. Miller and John Eli Adams, eds., *Sexualities in Victorian Britain* (Bloomington and Indianapolis: Indiana University Press, 1996) and Jacky Bratton, "Irrational Dress," in Vivien Gardner and Susan Rutherford, eds., *The New Woman and Her Sisters: Feminism and Theatre 1850–1914* (Hemel Hempstead: Harvester Wheatsheaf, 1992).
50. *The News of the World*, April 28, 1929, p. 6. See James Vernon, " 'For Some Queer Reason . . .' The Trials and Tribulations of Colonel Barker's Masquerade in Interwar Britain," *Signs* 26, no. 1 (2000): 37–62, for further discussion.
51. Working-class acceptance and middle-class persecution worked differently for effeminate men, however. See Matt Houlbrook, " 'Lady Austin's Camp Boys': Constituting the Queer Subject in 1930s London," *Gender and History* 14, no. 1 (2002): 31–61.
52. See, for example, *The People*, July 24, 1932, p. 2.
53. Doan, *Fashioning Sapphism.*
54. See, for example, *The News of the World*, July 31, 1932, p. 4; February 8, 1942, p. 3.
55. *The News of the World*, November 18, 1928, p. 3.
56. Ibid., December 16, 1928, p. 8.
57. *The People*, August 19, 1928, p. 2.
58. Ibid., August 26, 1928, p. 14.
59. Doan, *Fashioning Sapphism*, chapter 6.
60. Mrs Cecil Chesterton, *Women of the London Underworld* (London: Readers Library Publishing Co. Ltd., 1938), pp. 72–73.
61. Lucy Bland, "White Women and Men of Color: Miscegenation Fears in Britain after the Great War," *Gender and History* 17, no. 1 (2005). Marek Kohn, *Dope Girls: The Birth of the British Underground* (London: Lawrence and Wishart, 1992).
62. *The News of the World*, September 2, 1934, p. 13.
63. Laura Doan, "Passing Fashions: Reading Female Masculinities in the 1920s," *Feminist Studies* 24, no. 3 (1998): 663–700.
64. *The People*, July 9, 1939.

Part 4

Embracing Discursive Space: Re-Imagining Psychoanalysis and Spirituality

Chapter 10

Edith Ellis, Sapphic Idealism, and *The Lover's Calendar* (1912)

Jo-Ann Wallace

Passion, when it mates with true love, is lost in its own exquisiteness . . . . It must for the hour dwell in a world given over to those things which are profoundly deep, profoundly real and profoundly simple. From such hours youth is renewed, life is consecrated and the world gains through the joyfulness of two made utterly one.[1]

For on the Ideal hangs the whole question.[2]

Suzanne Raitt's 1998 article on "Sex, Love and the Homosexual Body in Early Sexology" makes several important interventions in recent discussions about the ways in which English sexologists such as Havelock Ellis and sexual utopians such as Edward Carpenter represented homosexuality at the turn of the nineteenth and twentieth centuries.[3] Among Raitt's significant contributions are, first, to emphasize the centrality of a discourse of love in turn-of-the-century sexology; second, to trace its continuing effects in lesbian self-understanding and writing of the 1920s; and, third, to note how Freud's somewhat later work, like that of Otto Weininger, "pathologized" the experience of love. To probe the effects of these developments, Raitt examines the ways in which Vita Sackville-West uses her 1920 autobiography, unpublished in her lifetime, to try to understand the guilt and shame she feels as a consequence of her "perversion." As Raitt points out, "The 'perversion' she describes is a moral, emotional and sexual dereliction," one that Vita Sackville-West ascribes to weakness and self-indulgence.[4] The contents of the autobiography, together with the elaborate and unnecessary lengths she went to in order to hide the manuscript, point to a pronounced and "symptomatic performance of her own shame."[5]

In marked contradistinction to the performance of shame that attends the writing and the concealing of Sackville-West's autobiography is the passage quoted as the first epigraph to this chapter. It is from a short prose poem written by Edith Ellis, an English lesbian (or, as she would have called herself, an "invert" or "abnormal") of one generation earlier and included in her 1912 edited anthology, *The Lover's Calendar*. The passage is remarkable for what might strike twenty-first century readers as its etherealized and sentimental style, but also for its complete *lack* of shame and the claims it makes for the transformative nature of passionate love. The evidence suggests that Edith Ellis frequently felt *fear*—hers was, after all, the generation that was in its adult prime during the trial of Oscar Wilde—but never shame. *The Lover's Calendar* (like much of Vita Sackville-West's writing) is a minor text within the oeuvre of an admittedly minor writer. In effect, it comprises just one of the many lost, abandoned, destroyed, or discarded texts of very early English modernism. For that very reason, however, it offers a kind of snapshot of a moment in the formation of English modernism, a moment of enormous promise and hopefulness, and a legacy the later modernists would disavow.

My use of the term "early English modernism" here is a generous one: I intend it to mean cultural practices in England from about the mid-1880s to World War I. The term "cultural practices" should also be generously understood to mean everything from experiments in living (including experiments in marriage, in simple living, in communal households, and so on) to new religious movements to literary and other artistic activities. This kind of wide-ranging experimentation was characteristic of a generation of English thinkers, activists, and writers whose lives and work have mostly been lost to literary and cultural history. Among them was a loose affiliation of men and women who are perhaps best described as *progressive idealists*. Influenced in part by the debates of English philosophical idealists, their own form of idealism, as I shall discuss in greater detail below, drew from a wide variety of sources and traditions and had as its goal progressive social transformation.

Foremost among the progressive idealists was the Fellowship of the New Life, a group with which Edith Ellis was closely associated from about 1887 until her marriage in 1891. The fellowship was founded in 1883 by Percival Chubb and several others who, under the influence of the Scottish philosopher Thomas Davidson, got together "in united effort to establish their lives upon a basis of love, truth, and freedom" and in pursuit of the "ideal . . . of a perfect life—a life lived resolutely in the Whole, the Good, the Beautiful."[6] Shortly after the fellowship began meeting, several of its members broke off to form the Fabian Society, feeling, in the words of George Bernard Shaw, that "the revolution would have to wait an unreasonably long time if postponed until [the members] personally had attained perfection . . ."[7] In spite of Shaw's representation of the fellowship as hopelessly and naively idealistic, several people, including Ramsay MacDonald, remained members of both organizations. During its fifteen-year lifetime, from 1883 to 1898, the fellowship published a quarterly magazine, established a school, and conducted a printing press, among other activities. As Vivian Zenari has argued, the fellowship also articulated significant idealist arguments about "the relationship between self-reform and social change," notions that elaborated an ethics of love, ethical responsibility, and service that continued to resonate for Edith Ellis in spite of her later reservations about some of the fellowship's members and accomplishments.[8]

As was typical of the progressive idealists, members of the fellowship were recognizably "modernist" in their emphasis on newness, on social experimentation, and new forms of community. However, they were nothing like the later modernists in their use of traditional literary and subliterary genres to further social change—genres such as hymns, ballads, regional novels, the pastoral, sprawling book-length odes, and, as in the case of Edith Ellis, the calendar or commonplace book. They were also nothing like the later high modernists in the highly local quality of their engagements. Although some members of the fellowship traveled—Edward Carpenter to India, Percival Chubb to the United States—and although their influences ranged from American transcendentalism to Sufism, they were a mostly English, not an international, phenomenon. The highly personal quality of their political and cultural engagements meant that their influence was muted, though it has persisted in contemporary new age and simplicity movements.

When Edith Ellis left the fellowship in 1891 she was disillusioned by its inability to live up to its ideals. However, she remained committed to the fellowship's ideal of progressive personal relationships as the true foundation of social change. Before examining the ways in which *The Lover's Calendar* enacts a vision of a socially transformative sapphism, I will briefly rehearse some salient details of Edith Ellis's life.

* * *

Edith Mary Oldham Ellis (1861–1916), born Lees, was better known then and now as Mrs. Havelock Ellis, her married name and the name under which she chose to publish and lecture. Although she was a well-published novelist, short-story writer, playwright, and journalist, as well as a successful lecturer with two extensive lecture tours of the United States in 1914 and 1915, her primary claim to cultural memory today is as the lesbian wife of the famous sexologist. What we know about Edith Ellis we know mostly from Havelock Ellis's 1939 autobiography *My Life*, fully two-thirds of which is devoted to his life with Edith although she died more than twenty years prior to its writing.[9]

She was born prematurely in 1861 in Cheshire, her mother dying shortly afterward. She appears to have been educated partly at a convent school in Manchester, and then at a school near London run by a "Madame Thesmar," a German freethinker. Following a short period in which she worked as a daily governess, Edith briefly ran a girls' school of her own in Sydenham. Something, perhaps the bankruptcy of the school, caused a nervous breakdown and she was taken in by the family of the Rev. Stopford Brooke with whom she became involved in helping to run a philanthropic "fresh air" organization for children from London's East End slums. Her association with the Brooke family brought her into contact with Percival Chubb who is likely the source of her introduction to the Fellowship of the New Life. She first met Havelock Ellis, with whom she was initially unimpressed, at a New Life country excursion in 1887. Two years later she became secretary of the fellowship, a voluntary position that consisted primarily of managing the fellowship's experiment in communal living at 29 Doughty Street in Bloomsbury. While on holiday in Cornwall she again encountered Havelock at the home of a mutual friend. They had opportunities to talk and discovered that their highly progressive views on marriage were compatible. They married in December 1891 and Edith resigned her position as secretary of the fellowship shortly thereafter.

It was also very shortly after her marriage—a marriage based on principles of mutual economic independence and mostly separate living—that Edith seems to have had her first sexual relationship with a woman identified, in Havelock's autobiography, only as "Claire." This would be the first of a series of relationships with women, the most serious of which was with a St. Ives-based artist, Lily Kirkpatrick. Edith's relationship with Lily began in approximately 1899 or 1900. They had a briefly passionate relationship, blocked to some degree by Lily's older sister, necessitating secret meetings (Havelock helping to accommodate some of these); however, Lily's feelings for Edith seem to have cooled even before Lily's death of Bright's disease in 1902. This remained, in many ways, the defining relationship of Edith's life, a relationship she sought to perpetuate through the services of a well-known medium.

By 1906 Edith had given up her large house in Carbis Bay, near St. Ives, where she had lived for large parts of the year since 1894, for a smaller cottage and a room in London and devoted herself more and more to writing, including playwriting. One of her one-act plays, *The Subjection of*

Kezia, achieved success as a curtain opener in various London and regional theaters; she published a second novel, *Attainment*, a *roman à clef* about her time managing the fellowship house, and she began to place some of her short stories in newspapers and magazines.[10] She became a very active member of the Lyceum Club in London, the first women's club to break into the men's club enclave of Piccadilly Street. Among her publications of this period was the 1912 *The Lover's Calendar*. The connections Edith established at the Lyceum Club, which catered to women writers and artists and which counted among its founding members many American women, probably helped underwrite her first American lecture tour in 1914. She died of pneumonia in 1916 shortly after returning from her second tour, a tour that seemed also to have precipitated a serious nervous collapse.

This is what remains, the brief public text of her life, relayed largely through the memories of a husband from whom she was estranged (for reasons I discuss briefly below) at the time of her death. While Havelock Ellis's autobiography appears to be remarkably open and candid, and while he quotes generously from Edith's letters—letters he later destroyed—it is clearly impossible for us to fully reconstruct the meaning of these events for Edith. It is also difficult for us to reconstruct the *social* meaning of a text such as *The Lover's Calendar*, a text that to high modernist and postmodernist sensibilities seems sentimental and peculiar. In what follows, I will describe the book in some detail before moving to a consideration of the ways in which it borrows from several traditions to elaborate a narrative of sapphic idealism.

* * *

Edith Ellis published *The Lover's Calendar*, an anthology of love poetry arranged in accordance with the 365 days of the calendar year, in 1912, a decade after the death of Lily Kirkpatrick. Her married name, as always, appears on the title page. Each day of the calendar year in Edith's collection is allotted an entire book page, each containing a love poem or, more often, a carefully chosen excerpt from one. There is plenty of white space on each page, presumably to allow the reader to add personal notes or reflections. The poets whose work is anthologized in the volume are as diverse as Dante, Conventry Patmore, Spenser, Shelley, Tennyson, Emily Dickinson, Matthew Arnold, and many more. The book also includes two prose poems by Edith Ellis (both ascribed to E.M.O.E.)—"Love as a Fine Art" for January 29 (from which I quote in the first epigraph to this essay) and "To the Beloved" for August 28—as well as four translations from Spanish folk songs by her husband, Havelock Ellis, and twelve excerpts from *Towards Democracy* by her friend Edward Carpenter. There is a brief, one-paragraph preface, two pages of acknowledgements and permissions, and an index of poems.

My copy, purchased from an antiquarian bookstore, includes an autographed inscription on its flyleaf. The inscription reads "E. Leeming. Just a Calendar to cheer when shadows fall. EMO Ellis. March 1915." Someone, presumably E. Leeming, has recorded names on several pages of the book, likely the birth or death dates of friends and loved ones. Certainly Edith Ellis's preface, which I quote in its entirety below, anticipates such uses and identifications by the reader while also gesturing to a specific narrative and a specific relationship:

> In this Anthology I have tried to represent the whole course of Love in its birth, its slow growth, its inevitable sorrow and its joyous fruition. The history of love, with its changing seasons, corresponds to the course of the year, and I have sought to work out the sequences as closely as possible. Death also, and the union of spirits after death, may make a claim on the reader's desire for romance and adventure as powerful as the passionate love of those who are still on earth; and these two facts must enter into the calendar if the cycle of Love is to be complete. This epitome of a love history has been compiled during the last twelve years, in the hope that it may help all lovers, those who are together, and those who are divided, either by Life or by Death.[11]

The emphasis here on the lovers' union after death is striking. At the time *The Lover's Calendar* was published, Edith Ellis's husband, her formally acknowledged "lover" and a well-known figure, was very much alive and in the public eye. In fact, he would outlive Edith by almost a quarter century. The love story of which *The Lover's Calendar* is an "epitome" is that of Edith and Lily Kirkpatrick. As I have already indicated, their relationship was well known to Havelock—who later described *The Lover's Calendar* as Edith's "monument to Lily, an exquisite shrine at which she could carry on a kind of worship"[12]—and it is safe to presume that it was also well known to her close friends.

What ordinary readers of the time, who were unacquainted with the details of Edith Ellis's private life, made of the volume and its preface we cannot know. Unlike most of her other books, which received at least some critical attention when they were published, *The Lover's Calendar* was not reviewed, in spite of the fact that it was published simultaneously in London and New York by two well-known publishing firms. We cannot read too much into the lack of reviews. Unlike anthologies that offered broad and representative surveys (of the poetry of a nation or historical period, for example), individualist or idiosyncratic poetry anthologies were not widely reviewed. Nor can we read too much into the fact that of the 151 poets listed in the index, a small handful—Edward Carpenter, Michael Field, George [Cecil] Ives, John Addington Symonds, Walt Whitman, and Oscar Wilde—would be recognized by readers today as poets of same-sex love and desire. The great majority of the poets included in *The Lover's Calendar* are poets of heterosexual or divine or other (more vaguely) spiritual love.

Regardless, *The Lover's Calendar* is a remarkably public confession and celebration of Edith's relationship with Lily. It is all the more remarkable because, while some English women of a slightly later generation and higher-class background, such as the writer Radclyffe Hall (born 1880) or the artist Gluck (born 1895), were able to live more or less openly as lesbians, Edith Ellis appears to have been terrified of being publicly exposed as an "invert" or "abnormal." Again, because of the destruction of most of her private papers, we can only infer both the degree and cause of her fear. Although she discusses inversion or abnormality in some of her public lectures, lectures in which she advocates policies of positive eugenics and sublimation of same sex-desire, she always lectured under her married name and never admitted to a personal interest in the issue.[13] Elsewhere, in other lectures and some short stories, she discusses inversion almost metonymically, by referring to some other "abnormality." She does this, for example, in her short story "The Idealist," which explores a Cornish fisherman's persecution for his nonsexual love of the drowned bodies he recovers from the sea, a love that the story represents as spiritual or, as the title indicates, idealistic.[14]

There is only one remaining private document in which Edith Ellis openly and explicitly refers to her own inversion, an undated and very moving letter to Edward Carpenter: "my inversion is the talk of [the] Higher Thought.[15] How it has got out heaven knows or whether they only *think* it or know it I don't quite realise but when I went to your sister the other day with trembling lips and hands she questioned me about what she had heard . . . . I said *if* it is true it would be sheer purity & sweetness to me & so for *me* the best the world cd have for me."[16] Edith's response exhibits a striking combination of fear and self-respect, quite different from the performance of shame that Suzanne Raitt notes in Vita Sackville-West. Her courageous insistence that "it would be sheer purity & sweetness to me" is highly reminiscent of the position attributed to "Miss H," case history 36 of Havelock Ellis's *Sexual Inversion* and widely believed to be a case history of Edith. The concluding paragraph of the case history reads, in part, "She believes that homosexual love is morally right when it is really part of a person's nature, and provided that the nature of homosexual love is always made plain to the object of such affection . . . . The effect on her of loving women is distinctly good, she asserts, both spiritually and physically, while repression leads to morbidity and hysteria."[17]

Given Edith's unwavering belief in the moral rightness of "loving women"—her *shamelessness*—the source of her equally deep-seated fear is important. It is possible that her fear of exposure, her "trembling lips and hands," may have stemmed from her inadvertent involvement in the Bedborough Case, the 1898 prosecution of George Bedborough for selling copies of Havelock Ellis's *Sexual Inversion*.[18] Although she was stalwart in her support of Havelock throughout that period, she must have suffered in two respects: first, the appearance of her own sexual history in a book on public trial must have caused her enormous anxiety; and second, *Seaweed: A Cornish Idyll*, her first novel (which itself made a bold statement about women's sexual needs), was also seized during the raid on Bedborough's office.

However, her fear of exposure likely had two additional sources, one of which I have already mentioned, the 1895 trial of Oscar Wilde. Wilde remained for Edith Ellis an ambivalent and troubling figure. Unable to approve entirely of his work and his lifestyle—his "cultured gluttony in pleasure"—she nonetheless understood him to have been a scapegoat, and his persecution represented, for her, "the knowledge . . . that society itself often creates what it ultimately sacrifices."[19] The second source of her fear was her long-standing dread of being committed to an insane asylum, a fear that is evident in one of her unpublished lectures, "Insanity: Its Cause & Cure," and one that also occasioned her legal separation from Havelock shortly before her death.[20]

Clearly one function of Edith Ellis's *The Lover's Calendar* is to allow the compiler, and later the reader, to acknowledge, remember, and memorialize the life and death of a loved one. Given her fear of exposure, what was it that was available to her as a potential vehicle for commemorating her love affair with Lily? In putting together *The Lover's Calendar*, Edith Ellis drew from several well-established literary genres and traditions, including the devotional calendar, the commonplace book, the almanac, and the pastoral. These highly traditional forms provided a structuring narrative, while the poets on whose work she drew provided a language and a set of symbols through which she could express her love for Lily and its impact on her life. They also provided a language through which she could explore the social meaning of her inversion. For example, the entry for March 9, Edith Ellis's own birthday, is an excerpt from Robert Browning's closet drama *In a Balcony*. The first six lines of the excerpt identify her inversion and her love for Lily as foundational to the meaning of Edith's life:

One made to love you, let the world take note!
Have I done worthy work? be love's the praise,
Though hampered by restrictions, barred against

By set forms, blinded by forced secrecies!
Set free my love and see what love can do
Shown in my life—what work will spring from that!

This sentiment is completely reflective of Edith Ellis's progressive idealist politics and worldview that, like Edward Carpenter's, understood love and sexuality to be at the heart of social change. As Carpenter argued in his essay on "The Place of the Uranian in Society," love and sexuality have the capacity to eradicate class and other differences and establish "true Democracy." In his words, "Eros is a great leveller."[21]

There are few correlations between calendar dates and the poems attached to them, correlations as direct as that between Edith's birthday and Browning's description of a love "hampered by restrictions, barred against / by set forms." For example, Lily died on June 16 but, in keeping with the seasonal nature of the calendar, the death of the loved one in *The Lover's Calendar* takes place at the beginning of November. The remainder of that month is given over to poems of despair, while the poems of December affect a kind of reconciliation: with the idea of death, but also with the loved one in a life beyond death. The seasonal nature of the narrative—what Ellis in her preface calls "the cycle of Love"—is enacted (by choice of excerpts) throughout, from the uncertain birth of love through its full flowering to the eventual death of the loved one.

Many of the selections are highly erotic, as in the June 3 entry, an excerpt from Arthur Symons's *London Nights*:

And this in a pout I snatch, and capture
That in the ecstasy of rapture,
When the odorous red-rose petals part
That my lips may find their way to the heart
Of the rose of the world, your lips.

The rapturous poems of high summer—June, July, and August—contain numerous references not only to roses but also to lilies: "Her breast, like lilies ere their leaves be shed; / her nipples, like young blossomed jessamines" (June 30, from Edmund Spenser) and "Lilies twain are her breasts, / Her body a bed of lilies" (August 31, from Percy Osborne) are only two of many examples. Significantly, the lily references do nothing to further the narrative; the pleasure is clearly in "saying" the name of the loved one. And so Edith Ellis found a way, within the very public conventions of the calendar and the pastoral, to name her very private love and to argue, implicitly, for the naturalness of their relationship. Significantly, too, many of the excerpts are very explicit about the poet's, and by implication the compiler's, love *for a woman*, as with the January 15 entry, an excerpt from Maeterlinck's

Treasure of the Humble: "When Fate sends forth the woman it has chosen for us . . . we are warned at first glance." Others complicate gender, as in the following entry for April 26, ascribed only as "From the Persian": "Four eyes met. There were changes in two souls. And now I cannot remember whether he is a man and I a woman, or he a woman and I a man. All I know is, there were two. Love came, and there is one."

To readers "in the know" *The Lover's Calendar* must have been astonishingly transparent in its celebration and commemoration of Edith's passionate love for Lily. However, as I have described above, there were also sufficient clues scattered throughout the Calendar to signal the nature of the relationship to almost any alert reader. It may seem surprising that so public and seemingly conservative a literary form was put to so radical a use; however, Brian Maidmont, in his recent article on "the almanac, the day book, and the year book as popular [nineteenth century] literary forms," reminds us of the existence of an earlier "radical almanac tradition" in Britain.[22] This was a tradition that understood the calendar as both a literary and an ideological form and that recast traditional calendars "in ways which reflected, subverted or even tried to reconstruct the experience of cyclical time as a form of social practice."[23] Certainly there is something of this in Edith Ellis's use of pastoral and calendar conventions to represent the "naturalness" of her love for Lily.

While the radical almanac or calendar tradition went into decline by the end of the nineteenth century, it did not altogether die out. Edith Ellis would almost certainly have been familiar with *The Woman's Calendar* compiled and published in 1906 by her friend Dora Montefiore, who twelve years later brought out *The People's Calendar* to commemorate the sacrifices made by the working class in World War I.[24] In 1928 Djuna Barnes's *Ladies Almanack* revived the radical calendar or almanac form in its erotic burlesque of life within the circles associated with Natalie Barney's lesbian salon in 1920s Paris.[25] It is tempting to speculate that Barnes may have been familiar with Edith Ellis's much tamer calendar. Barnes's entry for July opens with the following sentence: "The Time has come, when, with unwilling Hand, I must set down what a woman says to a Woman and she be up to her Ears in Love's Acre." *Love Acre*, intended quite differently, was the title of Edith Ellis's last novel.[26]

However, while *The Lover's Calendar* is indebted to radical almanac traditions, it is also rooted in some of the more esoteric preoccupations of late nineteenth-century progressive idealism, preoccupations that continued to find expression in early English modernism.

* * *

In his autobiography, Havelock Ellis is concerned to play down Edith's involvement with various forms of spiritualism, insisting that she was "without any taste for spiritualism in general," that she was "never the adept of any methodological system of Spiritism," and that she always retained her "shrewd powers of estimating human nature."[27] His insistence—scattered as it is throughout the pages recounting Edith's visits to a medium (who conveyed messages and advice from Lily), her "occasional visitations from Lily's spirit apart from intermediary aid," and her visit from Swedenborg (also through the medium)—is ultimately unpersuasive. So is his argument that Edith's interest in what we might today call "alternative spirituality" or mysticism was occasioned only by Lily's death and remained bound up only with "a kind of worship of Lily."[28] Nowhere in his autobiography does Havelock Ellis mention, for example, that Edith was initiated into Sufism shortly before her death, noting only, without comment, that Inayat Khan (founder of "The Sufi Order in the West") attended her cremation at Golder's Green Crematorium.[29] However, her attraction to Sufism, like her after-death communications with Lily, was only the final stage of a long engagement with mysticism. As her obituary notice in *The Sufi* indicates, her interest in mysticism began "with her association with Edward Carpenter, the well-known mystic writer."[30] It is certainly no accident that *The Lover's Calendar* contains so many excerpts from Carpenter's magnum opus, the book-length Whitmanesque *Towards Democracy*, including its final December 31 entry: "Ah! who but the lover at last should know what Death is? . . . / To love without sorrow, and to send love forth to bathe the world, healing it from its wounds! / Ah! who at last but the lover should know what Death is?"

This is an extraordinary passage with which to end her calendar, claiming as it does a redemptive Christlike capacity and function for Edith's sapphic love for Lily. It is in large part owing to the work of Carpenter that Edith Ellis was able to conceptualize her inversion in this way; in fact, it is likely that Carpenter had a much greater impact on her self-understanding than did Havelock Ellis. This is especially true with regard to her ability, or at least her attempts, to locate her inversion not only within a broad social context but also within a broader evolutionary and spiritual context. Indeed, for Carpenter the evolutionary, the spiritual, and the sexual were not easily distinguished and this seems to have been what Edith Ellis most valued about his work. Characterizing him as one of "three modern seers" in a 1910 collection of the same name (the other two are James Hinton and Nietzsche), Edith Ellis describes Carpenter as "a forerunner, not only of a robust and sane democracy, but of a sincere spirituality, a spirituality which cannot be content to preach or to merely be preached to, but must manifest itself in love."[31] That this love is physical as well as spiritual and emotional is key: "Edward Carpenter is a prophet of the soul and of the body. He proclaims the emancipation of the soul through the completion of its relation to the body."[32]

Scholars have begun to recover Edward Carpenter's influence on fin-de-siècle and modernist lesbian writers together with the distinctive character of modernist women's involvement in various mystic and spiritualist movements.[33] However, the specific nature of Carpenter's "mysticism" and the degree to which it informed his social vision and sexual utopianism remains underexamined. The focus of contemporary scholars primarily has been on those of Carpenter's texts that deal explicitly with sexual issues (especially *The Intermediate Sex*), with some secondary interest in his writing on socialism. Little attention has been paid to his more metaphysical books, such as *The Art of Creation*, and yet an understanding of his philosophical principles and influences is crucial to understanding the claims he makes for the "heroic uses" of "homogenic love," claims that Edith Ellis took very much to heart.[34]

It is not difficult to understand the relative lack of interest today in Carpenter's metaphysics. Contemporary readers find it difficult to reconcile his altogether admirable advocacy of homosexual rights with passages that describe "a continual ebullition and birth going on within us, and an evolution out of the Mind-stuff of forms which are the expression and images of underlying feeling."[35] However, while passages such as these can appear vague or even obscure, this kind of writing was not atypical of progressive idealists of the period and it emerged from a coherent worldview that would have been apparent to sympathetic readers. The many influences upon Carpenter's specific form of idealism included Lamarckian evolutionism (which argued that acquired characters could be inherited), Eastern mysticism (especially through his Ceylonese guru, the Gñani Ramaswamy), American transcendentalism (especially that of Emerson and Thoreau), and the poetry of Walt Whitman.[36] These influences combined to produce an almost classical idealism that insisted on the *generative* capacity of ideas (or, in Carpenter's locution, Ideas). Thus, in his discussion of "Platonic Ideas and Heredity" in *The Art of Creation*, Carpenter points to "the great formative ideas lying even behind the evolution of races, and largely guiding these evolutions" and argues that "Plato was justified in saying that the Ideas were the real thing and the mundane objects only illusive forms."[37]

Understanding the nature of Carpenter's idealism is crucial to understanding his vision of the role of the "intermediate" (or "urning" or invert or homosexual) in helping to create progressive social change. Briefly, Carpenter argues that homogenic love can "supply the force and liberate the energies required for social and mental activities" that will model "new forms of society, new orders of thought, and new institutions of human solidarity."[38] While heterosexual relationships are necessarily devoted to establishing households and families, homogenic relationships "may be turned to social and heroic uses, such as can hardly be demanded or expected from the ordinary marriage."[39] Carpenter leaves room for non-physical "comrade love" as a positive generative force, but it is also clear that the physical, erotic expression of homogenic love is an important "binding and directing force" that has the capacity to displace "the Cash-nexus," which defines most current human relationships. While it is in part the specific and innate nature of the "superior types of Uranians" that equips them for this important work (the greater sensitivity of the men, the greater intellectual acumen of the women), their experience of suffering (at the hands of an intolerant society) and capacity to remain outside of the marriage market are also important factors.[40] Carpenter makes it clear that all individuals have the capacity (and the obligation) to manifest true democracy; however, those whose experiences and natures are "unconventional" may have a special duty to live out their "ineradicable desires": "If they underlie [one] man's life, and are nearest to himself—they will underlie humanity."[41]

When Carpenter says that "on the Ideal hangs the whole question" (quoted as the second epigraph to this chapter), he means to emphasize what I have described as the *generative* capacity of ideas. It is because ideas have the capacity to generate new social—and even biological—forms that individuals have a duty to model or manifest new and better relationships. By virtue of their innate characteristics, coupled with their social experience, intermediates have a special ability and responsibility to give physical and social form to new and better ideals. "Creation," in Carpenter's terms, "is a process . . . which we can see at any time going on within our own minds and bodies, by which forms are continually being generated from feeling and desire; and, gradually acquiring more and more definition, pass outward from the subtle and invisible into the concrete and tangible."[42]

This is the tradition of thought that forms an important context for reading Edith Ellis's *The Lover's Calendar* and which helps to explain the "shamelessness" of her love for Lily. When Ellis describes the calendar as an "epitome of a love history," we must understand "epitome" to mean not only a "summary" or "condensed record" (*OED*) but also the potentially generative representation—in a way, the *emblem*—of an idealist sapphic love that survives both social opprobrium and death. The discourse of love that Suzanne Raitt identifies as central to nineteenth-century sexology, especially in its English formation, was only in part a discourse of romantic and sexual love. It is difficult now to reconstruct the *weltanschauung* that would understand sexuality not as a science or as an identity but as one aspect of the larger spiritual evolution of human society. The difficulty in recreating this milieu has two sources: the first is simply how alien these habits of thought are to most twenty-first century subjects; the second is the slenderness, the contingent politics, of the archive associated with English progressive idealism. It is important, then, that we look to other sources and consider books such as *The Lover's Calendar* both as an archive of the literary influences that motivated the progressive idealists as and an example of the enabling narratives they spun for themselves.

* * *

Overt forms of homogenic and sapphic idealism did not survive the displacement of sexology by psychoanalysis. Nor did they survive the profound political and social ruptures of World War I. Nonetheless, we can trace the intellectual and literary legacies of sapphic idealism in the work of later modernist writers such as Virginia Woolf. Jeffrey Weeks briefly notes the continuing impact of Edward Carpenter's thought and lifestyle in Bloomsbury's emphasis on personal relationships.[43] Whatever one might think of Bloomsbury's class politics, it is correct, I think, to understand Bloomsbury as inhabiting some of the same conflicts and questions as those facing members of the Fellowship of the New Life and the newly formed Fabian Society. What is the best way to ensure progressive social change? Is it by modeling new forms of relationship or by pursuing policy change at the government level? While some members of the Bloomsbury Group, such as Virginia Woolf, Vanessa Bell, and E. M. Forster chose the former, others, such as Leonard Woolf and Maynard Keynes, chose the latter. The progressive idealist commitment to ameliorating class divisions through personal, and especially erotic, relationships is also clear in Forster's novels, most notably *Howard's End* and the posthumously published *Maurice*.

The question of influence, however, is always a complicated one and it is important to recognize that many core members of the Bloomsbury Group, including Virginia Woolf, disavowed the kind of influence I am describing here. The progressive idealists, after all, were of their parents' generation. It is certainly the case that Virginia Woolf's father, Leslie Stephen, took up similar questions in his philosophical work (especially in his 1882 *The Science of Ethics*, which examines the ethical consequences of evolutionary theory). Woolf's response was, in part, to distrust the philosophical, especially the idealist, enterprise and spoof it in novels such as *To the Lighthouse* where Lily Briscoe can understand Mr. Ramsay's work on "subject and object and the nature of reality" only as a free-floating "phantom kitchen table."[44] Lily's choice of the esthetic over the philosophical—in effect, the high modernist choice of the esthetic as a superior ethic—corresponds to Woolf's own choice.

Nonetheless, it is possible to trace the continuing, if muted, influence of homogenic and sapphic idealism in Woolf's representations of same-sex desire. The following passage—Clarissa Dalloway's shameless recollection of her attraction to Sally Seton and the spiritually healing effect of Sally's kiss—is highly reminiscent of the Carpenter excerpt with which Edith Ellis concludes *The Lover's Calendar* ("To love without sorrow, and to send love forth to bathe the world, healing it from its wounds!"):

> It was a sudden revelation, a tinge like a blush which one tried to check and then, as it spread, one yielded to its expansion, and rushed to the farthest verge and there quivered and felt the world come closer, swollen with some astonishing significance, some pressure and rapture which split its thin skin and gushed and poured with an extraordinary alleviation over the cracks and sores! Then, for that moment, she had seen an illumination; a match burning in a crocus; an inner meaning almost expressed. But the close withdrew; the hard softened. It was over—the moment.[45]

Edith Ellis, who died in September 1916, from complications arising from the pneumonia she contracted while watching a Zeppelin attack upon London, did not live to read any of Virginia Woolf's novels. At the time of her death she was dispirited by Europe's march to war, worrying her friends with her frenetic activities (holding frequent and rambling lectures in her flat, setting up a cinema company, arranging to have her works translated into French) and fearing that she would be committed to an asylum by Havelock Ellis, from who she was now legally separated. I read the freneticism of her last months as, in part, an attempt to secure her legacy, a legacy that seemed to evaporate almost from the moment of her death. Nonetheless, she was part of a small and mostly informal coterie whose influence went underground but never fully disappeared. I like to think that she might have passed the very young Virginia Stephen on the streets of St. Ives sometime during her own years in that community, and that they might have exchanged glances.

Notes

This paper, part of a larger research project on Edith Ellis, is enabled by a grant from the Social Sciences and Humanities Research Council of Canada.

1. E. M. O. E. [Edith Ellis], entry for January 29, *The Lover's Calendar*, compiled and edited by Mrs. Havelock Ellis (London: Kegan Paul, Trench, Trübner and Co. Ltd; New York: E. P. Dutton & C., [1912]), p. 33.
2. Edward Carpenter, "England's Ideal" in *England's Ideal and Other Papers on Social Subjects* (London: Swann Sonnenschein, Lowrey and Co., 1887), p. 4.
3. Suzanne Raitt, "Sex, Love and the Homosexual Body in Early Sexology," in Lucy Bland and Laura Doan, eds., *Sexology in Culture: Labelling Bodies and Desires* (Chicago: University of Chicago Press, 1998), pp. 150–64.
4. Ibid., p. 152.

5. Ibid., p. 153.
6. These phrases are from one of the few surviving documents associated with the fellowship, a "manifesto" published in *The Pioneer* in 1886. See CHUBB 2/5/7, Percival Chubb Papers, British Library of Political and Economic Science.
7. George Bernard Shaw, *The Fabian Society: Its Early History*, Fabian Tract No. 41. 1892. (Reprint, London: The Fabian Society, 1899), p. 3.
8. Vivian Zenari, "The Care of the Self and the Fellowship of the New Life," unpublished 2002 paper.
9. Havelock Ellis, *My Life*, with a Foreword by Françoise Delise and an Introduction and detailed Bibliography by Alan Hull Walton. 1940. (Reprint, London: Neville Spearman, 1967).
10. Mrs. Havelock Ellis, *The Subjection of Kezia: A Play in One Act* (Stratford-on-Avon: Shakespeare Head Press, 1908); Mrs. Havelock Ellis, *Attainment* (London: Alston Rivers, 1909). Her first novel was Edith Ellis, *Seaweed: A Cornish Idyll* (London: Henry J. Glaisher, 1898).
11. Mrs. Havelock Ellis, *The Lover's Calendar*, [n. p.].
12. Ellis, *My Life*, p. 328.
13. See, for example, "Eugenics and the Mystical Outlook" and "Eugenics and Spiritual Parenthood," collected in Mrs. Havelock Ellis, *The New Horizon in Love and Life* (London: A. & C. Black Ltd., 1921).
14. See Mrs. Havelock Ellis, "The Idealist" in *The Imperishable Wing* (London: Stanley Paul & Co., [1911]). For a more detailed discussion of this story see Jo Ann Wallace, "The Case of Edith Ellis" in Hugh Stevens and Caroline Howlett, eds., *Modernist Sexualities* (Manchester: Manchester University Press, 2000), pp. 13–40.
15. This is presumably a reference to the Higher Thought Centre that was established in London in March 1900, under the secretaryship of Alice Callow, as a branch of the "Metaphysical Movement" in England.
16. See *Fabian Economic and Social Thought, Series One: The Papers of Edward Carpenter 1844–1929 from Sheffield City Libraries* (microfilm), Reel Five, MSS.358–15 (1–4).
17. Havelock Ellis, *Sexual Inversion* in *Studies in the Psychology of Sex*, vol. I, 3rd ed. (New York: Random House, 1942), p. 226.
18. For background on the Bedborough Case see Phyllis Grosskurth, chapter 13, "The Bedborough Trial," in *Havelock Ellis: A Biography* (Toronto: McClelland and Stewart, 1980).
19. E. M. O. Ellis, "A Note on Oscar Wilde," *The Fortnightly Review* (1917): 759–60.
20. See undated 10 pp. manuscript essay, "Insanity: Its Cause & Cure," in Havelock Ellis Papers, British Library, GB 0058 ADD MS 70537.
21. Edward Carpenter, "The Place of the Uranian in Society" in *The Intermediate Sex* (New York: Mitchell Kennerley, 1912), p. 107. First published London: S. Sonnenschein, 1908.
22. Brian Maidmont, "Re-Arranging the Year: the Almanac, the Day Book and the Year Book as Popular Literary Forms, 1789–1860," in Juliet John and

Alice Jenkins, eds., *Rethinking Victorian Culture* (Houndmills: Macmillan Press Ltd., 2000), p. 92.

23. Ibid., p. 91.
24. *The Woman's Calendar*, selected by Dora B. Montefiore (London: A. C. Fifield, [1906]); *The People's Calendar*, compiled by Dora B. Montefiore (London: British Socialist Party, [1918]).
25. [Djuna Barnes], *Ladies Almanack.* Written and illustrated by a lady of fashion (Paris: printed for the author, and sold by E. W. Titus, 1928).
26. Mrs. Havelock Ellis, *Love-Acre: An Idyl in Two Worlds* (New York: Mitchell Kennerley, 1914; London: Grant Richards, 1915).
27. Ellis, *My Life*, pp. 329–30.
28. Ibid., p. 328.
29. Ibid., p. 509. Evidence of her initiation to Sufism appears in "Mrs. Havelock Ellis," *The Sufi: A Quarterly Magazine* II, 2 (November 1916): 3.
30. "Mrs. Havelock Ellis," *The Sufi*, p. 3.
31. Mrs. Havelock Ellis, "Edward Carpenter's Message to His Age" in *Three Modern Seers* (London: Stanley Paul & Co., 1910), p. 225.
32. Ibid., p. 205.
33. See Laura Doan, " 'The Outcast of One Age Is the Hero of Another': Radclyffe Hall, Edward Carpenter and the Intermediate Sex," in Laura Doan and Jay Prosser, eds., *Palatable Poison: Critical Perspectives on The Well of Loneliness* (New York: Columbia University Press, 2001), pp. 162–78; Suzanne Raitt, *Vita and Virginia: The Work and Friendship of V. Sackville-West and Virginia Woolf* (Oxford: Clarendon Press, 1993), pp. 117–45; Joy Dixon, *Divine Feminine: Theosophy and Feminism in England* (Baltimore: Johns Hopkins University Press, 2001).
34. Edward Carpenter, *The Art of Creation: Essays on the Self and Its Powers* (London: George Allen, 1904); Edward Carpenter, "The Homogenic Attachment" in *The Intermediate Sex*, p. 76.
35. Carpenter, *The Art of Creation*, pp. 21–22.
36. Jeffrey Weeks, *Sex, Politics and Society: The Regulation of Sexuality Since 1800*, 2nd ed. (London and New York: Longman, 1989), p. 172.
37. Carpenter, *The Art of Creation*, pp. 119–20.
38. Carpenter, "The Homogenic Attachment" in *The Intermediate Sex*, pp. 68–69.
39. Ibid., p. 76.
40. Carpenter, "The Place of the Uranian in Society" in *The Intermediate Sex*, pp. 114–15.
41. Carpenter, "Social Progress and Individual Effort" in *England's Ideal*, pp. 60–61.
42. Carpenter, *The Art of Creation*, p. 31.
43. Weeks, *Sex, Politics and Society*, p. 74.
44. Virginia Woolf, *To the Lighthouse*. 1927. (Reprint, New York: Harvest/Harcourt, 1981), p. 23.
45. Virginia Woolf, *Mrs. Dalloway*. 1925. (Reprint, London: Penguin Books, 2000), pp. 34–35.

Chapter 11

Séances and Slander: Radclyffe Hall in 1920

Jodie Medd

Although the 1928 obscenity trial against *The Well of Loneliness* may be the legal event for which Radclyffe Hall is best remembered, her scandalous homosexual trials began long before the publication of her lesbian Bildungsroman. In fact, her dedication of *The Well of Loneliness* to "Our Three Selves" gestures to the complicated triangle of relationships that brought Hall—and accusations of lesbianism—into the courtroom before she had even penned her first novel. In Hall's cosmology, her identity and destiny were mystically intertwined with two other "selves": Mabel Batten, who died in 1916, and Una Troubridge, who lived with Hall from Batten's death until Hall's own death in 1943. It was Hall's passionate attachment to the dead Batten, and Troubridge's equally ardent devotion to her bereaved lover that brought the ghostly communications of this lesbian threesome to the headlines in 1920, when Hall charged St. George Lane Fox-Pitt, a member of the Society for Psychical Research (SPR), with slandering her as a "grossly immoral woman." Though brief, the trial made front-page news as a "society scandal" and was considered "of unusual general interest" by the press.[1] Attending to the details and implications of the trial, I want to argue for the significance of this rich and telling event within the juridical history and cultural functions of sapphic modernity.

Hall's 1928 obscenity trial has been thoroughly documented as a formative moment in the juridico-discursive representation of lesbianism; recently, two other legal events in early twentieth-century Britain have received critical attention for their representation of female homosexuality: Maud Allan's 1918 "Cult of the Clitoris" libel trial against Noel Pemberton Billing for his suggestion that she was a lesbian involved in a wartime conspiracy of homosexual espionage, and the 1921 parliamentary debates over criminalizing female homosexuality.[2] In the former case, a newspaper headed by a radical right-wing ideologue alleged that Maud Allan's performance in Oscar Wilde's *Salome* was part of a German plot to invade England through homosexual seduction and blackmail. Pemberton Billing deployed the suggestion of Allan's lesbianism as an occasion for publicizing his theories of government corruption and England's vulnerability to internal moral invasion. In my reading, it was precisely lesbianism's resistance to determinate cultural representation and legal definition that allowed it to focalize a range of anxieties about national security within the fraught wartime climate.[3]

In the latter case of 1921, the House of Commons and House of Lords debated the proposal to add "acts of gross indecency" between women to the Criminal Law Amendment Act, in effect extending the law that condemned Wilde for his "acts of gross indecency between men," to include women. While the bill passed through the Commons, it was defeated by the Lords, ostensibly out of concern that it would inadvertently "advertise" exactly that which it wanted to prohibit, by suggesting lesbianism to an otherwise innocent and ignorant female population.[4] The Lords even referred to the potential danger of scandalous trials that could result from the legislation, an anxiety that both recalls Pemberton Billing's trial and anticipates *The Well of Loneliness* trial.[5]

I want to consider Hall's 1920 slander case against Fox-Pitt as another link in the juridical history of Sapphic modernity, one that connects the events of 1918 and 1921 with Radclyffe Hall. Whereas Gay Wachman dismisses the trial as "reflect[ing] the naïveté of [Hall's] identification with the patriarchy,"[6] because Hall enlisted the law to defend herself and the honor of Mabel Batten, I think the dynamics of the trial have much to teach us about the definitional crises and unlikely deployments of lesbian suggestion in early twentieth-century Britain. Lesbianism's historically fraught relationship to representation is particularly demonstrated and exploited in the trial, where lesbianism functions ever only as a matter of (mistaken) interpretation. The very undefinability of lesbian allegation then leaves it open to appropriation and redeployment within the courtroom. For while Fox-Pitt seems to have intended to damage Hall's reputation with an unmistakable lesbian suggestion, when he was called to trial for slander his defense rested on rendering his allegation a hermeneutic puzzle. With strange contortions of logic and rhetoric, Fox-Pitt attempted to elide his lesbian suggestion with a campaign against scientific malpractices configured as dangerous to the vulnerable postwar population. Although Fox-Pitt may not have expected his allegations to make headlines, once they were brought into court and the public domain, they focalized such postwar concerns as the precarious state of marriage and the dissolution of rational culture, while the unusual ghostly narrative subtending the trial emerged as particularly relevant to and representative of the national climate.

Laura Doan connects this trial with Pemberton Billing's to signal "the beginning of an important shift in the visibility of lesbianism in English legal discourse and in the public arena."[7] She points out, however, that in both cases "the accusation of lesbianism was not an end in itself but a means to another end, political or personal in nature," and claims that the two men's ultimate detraction of their alleged lesbian accusation "provides further proof that 'sexual immorality' was only distantly related to their larger stratagems."[8] I am interested in precisely that slippage: the ways in which the undefinable *suggestion* of lesbianism—which can be strategically evoked as a means to a political or personal end, only to be retracted after a crisis of interpretation—becomes a figure for and diffuses into wartime and postwar concerns. If one can suggest lesbianism only to claim to be talking *really* about something else, then what does that tell us about the historical emergence of lesbianism as an identity category and the cultural function of that category? What does it mean to say that lesbianism comes into the public arena as a provocative suggestion whose meaning is always foreclosed by/as "something else"? How is it that lesbianism becomes "visible" as a ghostly invisibility?

Psychic Maze

Unlike Pemberton Billing's plot, which linked lesbianism with international espionage, Fox-Pitt's allegations pertained to a specific domestic drama. To begin with the personal, as Fox-Pitt did, we must begin with a narrative of love, betrayal, and loss. In 1907, twenty-seven year old Radclyffe Hall fell in love with Mabel Batten, who was fifty.[9] They traveled together extensively and shared a home after the death of Batten's husband in 1910. During their relationship, Hall published poetry, converted to Catholicism, adopted the nomination "John," had an affair with a banker's wife, wrote recruitment leaflets for the Great War, and began to write fiction, embarking on the path that would eventually lead to a career as a novelist. In the course of all of this activity, Batten suffered deteriorating health until an automobile accident in 1914 rendered her a virtual invalid. Hall grew restless, and in 1915, when she met Batten's cousin, Una Troubridge, she began another affair. Unhappily married to an admiral who was twice her age and posted overseas for the war, Troubridge was passionate and artistic but wholly unfulfilled. As Hall and Troubridge's intimacy deepened, Hall neglected Batten, whose health steadily declined. One evening in 1916 Hall returned home late from an outing with Troubridge and was scolded by Batten for her inconsideration. Hall lost her temper and in the middle of the row Batten collapsed from a cerebral hemorrhage. After ten days of speechless paralysis Batten died, leaving Hall wracked with guilt and grief and desperate for consolation. Consequently, at the very moment when Hall was longing for atonement, her personal amorous history intersected with her country's martial history: both England and Hall were desperate to converse with the dead.

The Great War had rendered mourning a national activity, reviving the spiritualist movement that had taken root in the late nineteenth century.[10] As Jay Winter writes, "During and after the Great War, interest in the paranormal and the after-life naturally deepened. It was inevitably and inextricably tied up with the need to communicate with the fallen . . . . The period of 1914–1918 was the apogee of spiritualism in Europe."[11] David Cannadine concurs that the war transformed the public opinion of spiritualism: "Instead of being regarded as an inaccessible elite intellectual activity, or as a popular pastime of cranks and crooks, spiritualism suddenly assumed a widespread and urgent relevance for those seeking to come to terms with their bereavement brought about by the First World War."[12] Una Troubridge, anxious to help Hall make peace with the past, consulted the medium Gladys Leonard, whose self-declared purpose was "to prove to those whose dear ones had been killed [in the war] that they were not lost to them and the dead had never died."[13] Consequently, Hall and Troubridge began what would become an all-absorbing "investigation" into psychical research and soon formed a passionate lesbian triangle that encompassed both the quick and the dead.

Under a trance, Mrs. Leonard would be possessed by her "control" in the spirit world, a girl named Feda, who communicated with those on the Astral Plane. In Hall's first sitting with Mrs. Leonard, Feda encounters a soldier, whom Hall immediately dismisses with "I do not know him. Is there no one else?" When Feda mentions "a lady of about sixty years old, perhaps," Hall's interest is piqued, but the persistent soldier intervenes: "The soldier knows you. Feda had to describe him, he insisted on it . . . . Now he has put his hand on your arm." Hall firmly rebuffs him, "Please leave him as I do not know him, I am afraid I cannot help, though I would do anything I could. Will you describe the lady of about sixty?"[14] This exchange is telling: As Hall determinedly seeks her lover, she abandons the pleading soldier, the primary object of spiritual communication during the war and the basis of Mrs. Leonard's livelihood. While spiritualism may have become a national obsession during the Great War, Hall appropriated its mechanisms and proponents for her own private psychic campaign.

Troubridge began attending the sittings, recording detailed notes, and keeping a jealous eye on Hall's paranormal passion for Batten. Soon Batten's spirit was communicating freely and Hall was able to express her unfailing devotion and secure forgiveness for the disagreement that had brought Batten to her deathbed. These exchanges, in which Hall assures Batten, "that I am devoting my life to her as though she were here," and Batten replies, "there is more in our love than there has ever been between two women before," were inevitably painful for Troubridge.[15] Soon, however, Batten entrusted Troubridge with the responsibility of taking care of Hall in the mortal realm and the three women negotiated an amicable relationship, with Hall devoted to Batten and Troubridge devoted to Hall, determined to secure her love and confidence even if it meant condoning Hall's otherworldly romance.[16]

Pamela Thurschwell has argued that the late nineteenth-century obsession with spiritualism indicated a contemporary interest in alternative modes of forging unconventional human intimacies.[17] Certainly paranormal communications provided Hall with not only a means of maintaining, even deepening, her relationship with her dead beloved, but also the "medium" for Hall and Troubridge to develop their own relationship. The occult offered these lesbian relationships a remarkable form of courtship and affiliation that escaped the heterosexual matrix—the prevailing structure of earthly intimacy—to achieve paranormal allegiances that resisted cultural constraints on ways of loving. Such a ghostly sapphic alliance adds a different, and less repressive, dimension to Terry Castle's notion of the "apparitional lesbian." Here, the literal "ghosting" of Batten sustains and multiplies Hall's same-sex intimacies, while constituting a fascinating lesbian threesome.

Regarding their sittings as serious psychical research, Hall and Troubridge joined the SPR and became obsessed with scrupulously recording their sittings and verifying obscure details. Encouraged to present their findings to the SPR, they prepared such an impressive document that its presentation extended over two meetings. Proposing "to deal exclusively with the purporting attempt of discarnate intelligences to communicate *evidential* matter," the paper suppressed the more passionate and affective exchanges with Batten.[18] Inevitably, however, it conveyed the intimacy and intensity of Hall's relationship with Batten, while intimating Troubridge and Hall's present partnership. Cataloguing the domestic details and personal ties among the three women, the paper in effect attested to an emotional lesbian alliance that exceeded the physical world while flouting compulsory heterosexuality.

By the time Hall delivered her paper, she had established a home with Troubridge and declared themselves married.[19] Their attachment was consolidated by their shared obsession with psychical research, and they were quite open to the SPR about the status of their relationship.[20] Meanwhile, Admiral Troubridge, absented by the war, disapproved of his estranged wife's occult enthusiasms and her plans to abandon him and make a life with Hall. In early 1919, Troubridge returned to England, confronted his wife and Hall, and eventually demanded a legal separation. This same year, Hall and Troubridge's research paper was published in the SPR's journal, providing an official testament to a complicated lesbian triangle constituted under the sign of psychical research. One of the SPR's members, St. George Fox-Pitt, disapproved of both the paper and Hall and Troubridge's relationship, and he met with Admiral Troubridge to discuss Hall's pernicious influence and paranormal preoccupations. Troubridge, resentful of losing his wife to a mannish woman obsessed with her dead lover—he also considered Batten "an objectionable woman"—told Fox-Pitt that he held Hall and her spiritualism responsible for the failure of his marriage and for Una's mental instability.[21]

Fox-Pitt, the son-in-law of Wilde's notorious libeller, the Marquess of Queensberry,[22] brought Troubridge's accusations to the attention of Isabel Newton, the secretary of the SPR, and Helen Salter, the editor of the SPR's journal, in order to protest Hall's election to the SPR's council. Radclyffe Hall, he purportedly told them, was a "grossly immoral woman" who has "a great influence over Lady Troubridge and has come between her and her husband and wrecked the Admiral's home."[23] Hall, independently wealthy and apparently not shy of publicity, was not one to suffer assaults upon her or Batten's honor, and upon hearing of the accusations she promptly charged Fox-Pitt with slander. Just two and a half years after Pemberton Billing's libel trial, the suggestion of lesbianism was once again debated in court and circulated in the press, this time coupled with sensational headlines about communications with the dead. Indeed, the proceedings of the case were uncannily similar to Pemberton Billing's trial. They condensed new, volatile, and ineffable social anxieties onto the suggestability of lesbianism, while the courtroom debates over how to interpret the lesbian meaning of the allegations were simultaneously debates over how to read and respond to Britain's postwar cultural concerns.

Since Fox-Pitt had only intended to damage Hall's reputation in the SPR, not cause a public scandal, once he found himself accused of slander he quickly reneged. Acting in his own defense, he insisted that Hall's charge misinterpreted his statements; reading and locating lesbian meaning once again became a question for the law. Ellis Hume-Williams, the same lawyer who represented Maud Allan against Pemberton Billing, acted as Hall's lawyer and deployed exactly the same rhetoric as he had in 1918. According to the London *Times*, Hume-Williams argued that Fox-Pitt had made "as horrible an accusation as could be made against any woman in this country. The words used by the defendant could only mean that the plaintiff was an unchaste and immoral woman who was addicted to unnatural vice and was consequently unfit to be a member of the council."[24] The *Daily Chronicle* similarly reported, "Sir Ellis Hume-Williams submitted that the suggestion made in the slanders could only bear one interpretation."[25] As in the Pemberton Billing case, Hume-Williams insisted that Fox-Pitt's alleged assertion that Hall was "grossly immoral, in every way" and that her influence over Troubridge had destroyed her marriage could only be interpreted as an accusation that Hall was a lesbian, or, in the language of the court, that Hall was "unchaste" and "addicted to unnatural vice." Indeed, the term "lesbianism" never appeared in press reports, but as we will see, it was present in the very prohibition of its utterance. In his defense, Fox-Pitt insisted that he did not use such terms as "immoral" in any sexual sense, nor had he *intended* to suggest that Hall was guilty of "unnatural vice." Once again, a baffled jury was set the task of determining where lesbian meaning resides.

Like Pemberton Billing's insinuations about Maud Allan, Fox-Pitt's initial suggestion and later denial of lesbian meaning constituted an interpretive dilemma that allowed for the combination and confusion of seemingly unrelated issues. While Hall's lawyer insisted that Fox-Pitt's words could only be interpreted as allegations of lesbianism, Fox-Pitt contended that in claiming that Hall had exercised over Una Troubridge a pernicious "influence," leading to the failure of her marriage, he was not referring to a sexual influence, but to Hall's unscientific psychical research. As recounted by the *Express*, "Mr. Fox-Pitt . . . insisted that he was not using the word 'immoral' in its sexual sense in reference to her, but in connection with her work or paper."[26] Similarly, the *Daily News* reports that Fox-Pitt "explained that he did not attack the plaintiff's chastity or sexual morality, but was finding fault with the paper she wrote and read to the society."[27] With Fox-Pitt's repeated insistence that his words "were not spoken of the plaintiff or her character, or of her sexual morality or chastity, but were merely spoken of the papers which she had read and her method or treatment of investigation," the allegation of lesbian immorality was not erased, but *displaced* onto the irrational practice of psychical research.[28] He denies the lesbian allegation by shifting attention from Hall's personal character to the contents of her research paper. Of course, the paper was as much a thinly veiled account of lesbian relationships as it was a document of psychical research; however, it is precisely the obscuring veil of lesbian inconceivability that Fox-Pitt tries to drape back over the allegation in order to protect himself.

Fox-Pitt's semantic equivocations and disavowals demonstrate the problematic of lesbian representation. In a manner that I consider characteristic of this period in lesbian legal and cultural history, lesbian meaning proved to be no more, and no less, than a matter of interpretation. The provocative but elusive lesbian suggestion could be constantly generated and borne along by a metonymic chain of cultural associations, but it never came to rest as a stable unit of referential meaning. As D. A. Miller writes of the operations of connotation, which he considers to be the "dominant signifying practice of homophobia,"[29] "on the one hand, connotation enjoys or suffers from, an abiding deniability,"[30] while on the other hand, connotation exercises a "limitless mobility" that "tend[s] to raise the ghost [of homosexuality] all over the place."[31] Subsequently, as much as Fox-Pitt retroactively tried to pry the homosexual implications away from his accusations about Hall's "immorality" and substitute accusations about her unscientific psychical activities, the terms inevitably slid back together again; lesbianism, once invoked, travels freely and Fox-Pitt's confused displacements only reinforced the connection between Hall's lesbianism and her foray into the spiritual realm. Indeed, not only was Hall engaging in psychical research in order to communicate with her former lover (as implied in her paper), but according to Fox-Pitt's charge, this activity had lured Una Troubridge away from her husband. For example, the *Times* reports that Fox-Pitt maintained that "Admiral Troubridge had told him that Lady Troubridge had said to him that this 'spirit' business was now her life and that she had henceforth no further concern in his views, interests, or occupations."[32] Lesbian seduction was *enabled*—not excluded—by the "immorality" of psychical research. As a floating possibility, the deniable but irrepressible lesbian suggestion attaches to a range of situations, from the failure of a marriage to the impropriety of a psychical research paper. It was precisely this infectious and inosculating power of lesbian suggestion that Fox-Pitt had intended to mobilize in his attempt to block Hall's election to the SPR's council; however, once it slipped beyond his control, he struggled to subvert and disavow its damaging presence, by retroactively trying to foreclose its possibility.

As in the Pemberton Billing trial, the case turned on the interpretation of Fox-Pitt's suggestive words; however, the court avoided a lesbian exegesis of the slander. For example, cross-examining Isabel Newton on her testimony that he had accused Hall of "unnatural vice," Fox-Pitt's request that she explain "what she meant by unnatural vice" is interrupted by the judge's anxious desire to keep lesbianism in the realm of the always already known but never yet spoken of. "Now! now!" the judge interjects, "The jury are men of the world and know. You cannot put such an indelicate question to the lady. I will not allow it."[33] Even though it is precisely the lesbian meaning that is under debate, the legal authorities refuse its articulation, and divide lesbian knowledge and its unspeakability along gender lines: the men of the jury *know* what the female witness of the slander must not *speak*. While Fox-Pitt insists that "the meaning of such language never entered his mind," Newton explains that she "put the sexual interpretation on his words in this action because that seemed the only possible interpretation, the words being 'a grossly immoral woman in every way.' "[34] Not only does "a grossly immoral woman in every way" gesture to the criminal prohibition against male "gross indecency," but Newton's lesbian interpretation also partakes of the cultural notion that whatever lesbianism might be, it constitutes the defining limit of female immorality—lesbianism is the ultimate "way" in which a woman could manifest her moral bankruptcy.

Disavowing the lesbian meaning he had once tried to convey, Fox-Pitt insists that the witnesses misinterpreted his utterance; their misprision, not his intention, was responsible for the lesbian interpretation. Since the " 'sexual interpretation' turns on the word 'immoral,' " Fox-Pitt points out in his cross-examination of Helen Salter that the dictionary devotes "many columns" to defining "immoral" but, "there is no sexual association throughout."[35] Salter responds to this lexicographic lesson with, "I did not take the dictionary meaning, but the context."[36] Her insistence on the contextual determination of meaning corroborates Newton's inference that Fox-Pitt was suggesting "some perversion" between Hall and Batten given "the *context* of 'gross immorality' and 'objectionable woman.' "[37] In another tactic (which contradicts his recourse to the dictionary), Fox-Pitt contended that "he had not used the word 'immoral' in a popular, but in a very special sense," a sense specific to his "scientific" occupation: "I am a special student of moral science; it is my special theme, and we do not use the word 'immoral' in a sexual or erotic sense."[38] According to both witnesses, the associations between such phrases as "gross immorality" and "objectionable woman" constituted a hermeneutic context, associations that enforce an inevitable lesbian interpretation; meanwhile, Fox-Pitt exploited the indeterminacy of these phrases and relied upon the cultural illegibility of female homosexuality to evade the charges against him.[39]

Fox-Pitt's very attempt to retrovert the lesbian accusation into a crusade against "immoral" psychical research effectively aligned lesbianism with the dissolution of rational culture, such that lesbian danger ghosts the threat posed by spiritualist malpractices to the vulnerable postwar population. The *Times* reports Fox-Pitt's claim:

> that the subject of psychical research . . . was of the utmost importance at the present time [and] that they should preserve the scientific spirit. For many years there had been what was called a cult of spiritualism, and to his mind it

> was a most mischievous and dangerous movement. . . . this recrudescence of ancient superstition was a source of great danger to the public.[40]

Other papers recount Fox-Pitt's insistence that he is "fighting a good cause, because spiritualism had become a real danger to society"[41] and that "the cult of spiritualism, as it was now professionally practiced in particular . . . was a matter of grave danger to the public health and sanity."[42] This transformation of lesbian accusations into a campaign for protecting "public health and sanity" from the danger of spiritual superstition evinces the remarkable (re)tractability of lesbian suggestion—the moral injunction against lesbianism can transferentially apply to nearly any other social concern, while lesbianism's ontological coherence is so unstable that it can always be denied. Indeed, in all of the above press citations, one could substitute "lesbianism" for "spiritualism," and both the sense and the moral imperative would remain intact. In this way, the suggestion of lesbianism functions as a productive placeholder that is both entirely empty of determinate reference and inexhaustibly rich in scandalous possibilities. Indeed, after maintaining in his cross-examination of the witnesses that his purported accusations about Hall's immortality held anything *but* a lesbian meaning, when Fox-Pitt took the stand, he denied that he had *even uttered* the description of Hall as "grossly immoral in every way."

Baffled by Fox-Pitt's interpretive contortions, the jury returned a verdict that "the words were uttered, but that the words were not intended to apply to the plaintiff's personal character, but were intended to apply to the research work of the plaintiff, as calculated to influence the character of the Psychical Society."[43] As the grammar and semantic repetitions indicate, Hall's lesbian "character" and its influence on Troubridge are directly displaced onto her immoral influence on the "character" of the SPR. The judge pointed out that such a decision constituted a decision in favor of Fox-Pitt. Asserting that the jury "had used an awkward word in saying intended,"[44] he advised that according to legal precedent "the question of intent was immaterial,"[45] and "further directed the jury that they must say not what they thought the defendant intended the words to mean, but what in their ordinary and natural meaning the words would convey to an ordinary man."[46] After further deliberation, the jury ruled in Hall's favor, awarding her 500 pounds for damages. In effect, then, the jury decided that while Fox-Pitt may have claimed that he did not intend a lesbian meaning, his words, "in their ordinary and natural meaning," carried enough of the extraordinary and unnatural meaning of lesbian vice to have damaged Hall's character to the sum of 500 pounds.

Hall was certainly fortunate that Fox-Pitt backed down from his initial accusations and fumbled into such an awkward defense, for if he had pursued the lesbian charges, he may have succeeded in exposing Hall's relationship with both Batten and Troubridge, thereby putting Hall's sexuality on trial rather than her psychical research. Why did Hall take this risk? Or, we might ask, why did she deny a sexual identity that she would openly claim several years later in print and in court? The answer, I think, turns again on Fox-Pitt's accusations of Hall's "gross immorality." Perhaps it was not so much his suggestion of her lesbianism, but the immoral web in which he situated it that fueled Hall's case against him. In denying Fox-Pitt's accusations, Hall was not necessarily denying her lesbianism, but denying the imputation of lesbianism as "immoral" or "grossly indecent." In fact, Hall's legal action may be read as a public moral defense of her relationships with Troubridge and Batten that she held so dear.[47]

Domestic Unhappiness in Time of Peace

In spite of Fox-Pitt's disavowal of the lesbian charges, his emphasis on Hall's responsibility for ruining Admiral Troubridge's marriage was particularly highlighted by the press and resonated with the postwar national epidemic of failed marriages. As divorce historian Lawrence Stone notes, "The divorce rate per 1000 married couples . . . jumped sixfold between the last pre-war year, 1913, and the post-war peak in 1921. This striking increase in divorces must have reflected a real and massive increase in marital breakdowns in the years immediately following the war."[48] Certainly both literary and historical accounts of the Great War fixate on how the war finally cracked the bourgeois ideal of heterosexual marriage that had been under pressure since the late nineteenth century, while idealizations of domesticity looked to marriage as a means of "restoring social harmony in postwar Britain."[49] Accordingly, the newspaper accounts of Hall's court battle appeared alongside reports of divorce proceedings and pleas for restitution of "conjugal rights," reports that savored the intimate details of marital dramas.[50] The popular press particularly enjoyed publicizing the conjugal troubles of high ranking officials, with such headlines as "Generals in Court: Domestic Unhappiness in Time of Peace,"[51] and "Suits Against Two Generals: Dramatic Discovery in a Hotel Register."[52] The sensational narrative of the Fox-Pitt trial, with its spiritual communications and lesbian intrigue, was heightened by the added interest of an admiral's marriage in ruins. Many of the reports foregrounded the Troubridges' troubled marriage, with such headings as "Admiral's Wife and the Unseen: Psychic Factor in the 'Wrecking' of a Home?"[53] (where the "unseen" is not only a ghost, but in fact an apparitional lesbian), "Case of Admiral and Lady Troubridge,"[54]

"Admiral Has a Scene With his Wife,"[55] and "Features of Society Slander Suit: Domestic Differences of an Admiral."[56] With Hall's influence over Una Troubridge blamed for "wreck[ing] the Admiral's home," a failed marriage formed the human-interest center of the case and was made all the more intriguing by Admiral Troubridge's absence from the trial. His marriage and its failure then lent itself to speculation based on suggestive and salient details from the witnesses. The press noted, for example, that Hall's "means were considerably larger than those of Admiral Troubridge," allowing her to pay Una's medical expenses and take her abroad for her health.[57] This financial observation configures Hall and Admiral Troubridge in a rivalry as masculine providers for Una's tremulous femininity. Recounting the decline of the Troubridges' marriage, the reports emphasized the "serious differences between the Admiral and Lady Troubridge"[58] that led to "a most violent scene" when Admiral Troubridge confronted his wife and Hall, a confrontation that in turn resulted in a deed of separation.[59] Both Hall and Una Troubridge insisted that "the row . . . between Admiral Troubridge and his wife did not concern" Hall, but this disavowal only drew attention to Hall's role in yet another threesome.[60]

As much as the trial was a crisis in reading lesbianism, then, it was mapped onto a marital crisis and served as a metonym for the larger postwar concern for the ailing institution of the married couple. The Great War was attributed with depriving a generation of women of their potential husbands, alienating the sexes from each other, dissolving sexual morality, and encouraging women's independence from men. Hall's trial brought such social narratives to a new pitch within a drama of high society scandal, adding the possibility that while military leaders were protecting the nation, wealthy lesbians had been stealing their wives. Hall's active support of the war, particularly her energetic recruitment efforts, only augments the intriguing construction of lesbianism as an internal threat to home front stability. The paranoid fantasy of the lesbian as a figure of international espionage, as intimated in the Maud Allan case, was transformed into the paranoid fantasy of the lesbian as a figure of domestic sabotage, a figure that was then reinvoked in the 1921 parliamentary debates over the criminalization of female homosexuality.

I am arguing, then, for the inclusion of this inconclusive trial within understandings of sapphic modernity for several reasons. For one, it would expand and nuance Radclyffe Hall's significance within lesbian legal history beyond *The Well of Loneliness* trial, while providing a meaningful link between the "Cult of the Clitoris" trial of 1918 and the parliamentary debates of 1921. More importantly, it might help reconfigure the terms of lesbian history and analysis, where perhaps instead of charting lesbianism's "visibility" or lamenting its invisibility, we might consider hermeneutic, epistemological, and functional questions about lesbianism's (mis)interpretability and cultural deployment. For while this trial did not elucidate a lesbian signified and even disavowed any lesbian signifiers, the elusive *suggestion* of lesbianism came to figure in postwar cultural concerns ranging from scientific rationalism to the crisis of marriage. Furthermore, the dynamics of the trial certainly inspire a rethinking of Castle's repressive notion of the "apparitional lesbian," where Castle uses "ghost" and "phantom" as tropes for how the ontological "reality" of lesbianism (which Castle takes as a transhistorical phenomenon) has been effaced, "made to seem invisible,"[61] and derealized.[62] If we resignify and historicize lesbian "ghosting," we might consider how the very cultural notion of *lesbianism comes into being* as a mode of provocative suggestion and through a kind of conjuring up of possibility, even by those who work retroactively to disavow or "derealize" the suggestive lesbian stories they tell. Like someone who confesses to encountering a ghost, only to insist they must have been seeing "something else," it is the initial ghostly possibility that takes hold of the imagination. Rather than thinking of lesbian "ghosting" as the effacing or "murdering" of lesbian authenticity,[63] I'd propose that it is the very discursive *conjuring* up of lesbianism as a ghostly possibility—incoherent, undefinable, diffuse, mobile, evasive, shaped by its invisibility—that performatively begins to *bring lesbianism into being*, historically as a cultural category of identity. And, as Radclyffe Hall and Una Troubridge seemed to have believed: once the possibility of a ghost is conjured up, its haunting presence becomes increasingly more convincing and harder to deny.

Notes

My eassy title and all sub-headings come from the headlines of the newspaper reports of the trial.

1. *Daily Telegraph*, November 20, 1920, p. 7
2. See Lucy Bland, "Trial by Sexology?: Maud Allan, *Salome*, and the 'Cult of the Clitoris' Case," in Lucy Bland and Laura Doan, eds., *Sexology in Culture: Labelling Bodies and Desires* (Chicago: University of Chicago Press, 1998), pp. 183–98; Laura Doan, "Act of Female Indecency: Sexology's Intervention in Legislating Lesbianism," in Bland and Doan, eds., *Sexology in Culture*, pp. 199–213; Laura Doan, *Fashioning Sapphism: The Origins of a Modern English Lesbian Culture* (New York: Columbia University Press, 2001), chapter 2; Philip Hoare, *Oscar Wilde's Last Stand* (New York: Arcade Publishing, 1998); Jodie Medd, "The Cult of the Clitoris: Anatomy of a National Scandal," *Modernism/Modernity* 9, no. 1 (January 2002): 21–49; Jennifer Travis, "Clits in Court: *Salome*, Sodomy, and the Lesbian 'Sadist,' " in Karla Jay, ed., *Lesbian*

Erotics (New York: New York University Press, 1995), pp. 147–63; and Gay Wachman, *Lesbian Empire: Radical Crosswriting in the Twenties* (New Brunswick, NJ: Rutgers University Press, 2001), chapter 1.

3. See Medd, "The Cult of the Clitoris."
4. On the debate in the House of Commons, see *Hansard* (1921) Official Reports, 5th Series, Parliamentary Debates, House of Commons, vol. 46, August 4, 1921, 1799–1806. On the debate in the House of Lords, see *Hansard* (1921) Official Reports, 5th Series, Parliamentary Debates, House of Lords, vol. 14, August 15, 1921, 565–77.
5. See *Hansard* (1921) Official Reports, 5th Series, Parliamentary Debates, House of Lords, vol. 14. (August 15, 1921): 569–74.
6. Wachman, *Lesbian Empire*, p. 30.
7. Doan, *Fashioning Sapphism*, p. 32.
8. Ibid., pp. 32, 33.
9. My account of the narrative leading up to the trial is indebted to the biographies of Hall and Troubridge: Michael Baker, *Our Three Selves: A Life of Radclyffe Hall* (New York: William Morrow and Company, 1985); Sally Cline, *A Woman Called John* (London: John Murray, 1997); Diana Souhami, *The Trials of Radclyffe Hall* (London: Virago, 1999); and Richard Ormrod, *Una Troubridge: The Friend of Radclyffe Hall* (New York: Carroll and Graf Publishers, Inc., 1985).
10. On the history of spiritualism, see Ruth Bradon, *The Spiritualists: The Passion for the Occult in the Nineteenth and Twentieth Centuries* (New York: Alfred A. Knopf, 1983), and Janet Oppenheim, *The Other World: Spiritualism and Psychical Research in England, 1850–1914* (Cambridge: Cambridge University Press, 1989).
11. Jay Winter, *Sites of Memory, Sites of Mourning: The Great War in European Cultural History* (Cambridge: Cambridge University Press, 1995), pp. 58, 76.
12. David Cannadine "Death and Grief in Modern Britain," in Joachim Whaley, ed., *Mirrors of Mortality: Studies in the Social History of Death* (New York: St. Martin's Press, 1981), p. 228.
13. Gladys Leonard, *My Life in Two Worlds* (London: Cassell, 1931), p. 54.
14. Radcylffe Hall and (Una) Lady Una Troubridge, "On a Series of Sittings with Mrs. Osborne Leonard" *Proceedings of the Society for Psychical Research* Part 78 (December 1919): 348.
15. Baker, *Our Three Selves*, p. 90. The records of the sittings are available in the archives of the SPR, at the Cambridge Library.
16. The dynamics of this paranormal triangle are delineated in the notes for the sitting of March 27, 1918: "MRH [Hall] took up Psychical Research to obtain hope of MVB's [Batten's] survival. UVT [Troubridge] took it up in order to help MRH." Ormrod, *Una Troubridge*, p. 97.
17. See Pamela Thurschwell, *Literature, Technology and Magical Thinking, 1880–1920* (Cambridge: Cambridge University Press, 2001). In *Noël Coward and Radclyffe Hall: Kindred Spirits* (New York: Columbia University Press, 1996), Terry Castle argues that Coward's 1941 comedy, *Blithe Spirit*, not only takes an occult inspiration from the Hall-Troubridge-Batten communications,

but also invokes spiritualism as a means of undermining heterosexual marriage in favor of homosocial relations and homoerotic possibilities.

18. Hall and Troubridge "On a Series of Sittings," p. 345. Emphasis in the original.
19. Troubridge records in her diary on January 30, 1918, "John said I've married Ladye and I've married you." Cline, *A Woman Called John*, p. 137. Given that Batten's death has not ended her relationship with Hall, Hall seems to be declaring a sort of lesbian polygamy.
20. Ormrod, *Una Troubridge*, p. 103.
21. *Pall Mall Gazette*, November 19, 1920, p. 7.
22. The Marquess of Queensberry was the father of Lord Alfred Douglas; his libel against Wilde resulted in Wilde's sensational trials and eventual imprisonment.
23. *Times*, November 19, 1920, p. 4.
24. Ibid., p. 7.
25. *Daily Chronicle*, November 19, 1920, p. 8.
26. *Daily Express*, November 19, 1920, p. 1.
27. *Daily News*, November 19, 1920, p. 1.
28. *Times*, November 20, 1920, p. 4.
29. D. A. Miller, "Anal Rope," in Diana Fuss, ed., *Inside/Out* (New York: Routledge, 1991), p. 125.
30. Ibid., p. 124.
31. Ibid., p. 125.
32. *Times*, November 20, 1920, p. 4.
33. *Daily Telegraph*, November 20, 1920, p. 7. The *Pall Mall Gazette*'s report highlights this exchange with the byline "An Indelicate Question" *Pall Mall Gazette* November 19, 1920, p. 7.
34. *Daily Telegraph*, November 20, 1920, p. 7.
35. Ibid. In a curious aside, the judge calls into question the usefulness of a dictionary in addressing lesbian meaning. When Fox-Pitt asks permission to quote from a dictionary, the judge responds, "Certainly, if you think a dictionary is going to help us to understand what the words 'grossly immoral' mean as applied to a lady in the circumstances in which it was used here. Certainly; not only one, but a number of dictionaries. (Laughter)." His ironic comment seems to be an expression of exasperation with the absurdity of the case, while implying that a dictionary is the last place one should look for elucidating a lesbian suggestion.
36. Ibid.
37. *Times*, November 20, 1920, p. 4. Emphasis mine.
38. Ibid.
39. To support his claim that "immorality" referred to the spiritualist practices, and not the lesbian alliances such practices facilitated, Fox-Pitt recounted his exchange with Admiral Troubridge: "The Admiral used to be amused when Lady Troubridge first took up spiritism, but when he (the defendant) showed him the joint paper last January he was very angry . . . in defending the society he (the defendant) said that it was engaged in doing a high moral work. That was the first time that the word 'moral' was used. The Admiral said, 'Call it moral; I call it immoral.' " See *Times*, November 20, 1920, p. 4. Although Fox-Pitt

cites this exchange to defend against a (homo)sexual interpretation of "immoral," Troubridge's comment actually does not separate "sexual" immorality from scientific immorality, rather it completely maps them onto one another.

40. *Times*, November 20, 1920, p. 4.
41. *Daily Telegraph*, November 20, 1920, p. 7.
42. *Daily News*, November 20, 1920, p. 3.
43. *Times*, November 20, 1920, p. 4.
44. *Daily Chronicle*, November 20, 1920, p. 1.
45. *Times*, November 20, 1920, p. 4.
46. *Daily Telegraph*, November 20, 1920, p. 7.
47. Here my speculation directly contrasts Gay Wachman's reading of Hall's decision to pursue legal action. See *Lesbian Empire*, pp. 29–30.
48. Lawrence Stone, *The Road to Divorce: England 1530–1987* (Oxford: Oxford University Press, 1990), p. 394. Colin Gibson, *Dissolving Wedlock* (London: Routledge, 1994), George Behlmer, *Friends of the Family* (Stanford: Stanford University Press, 1998), and Jay Winter, *The Great War and the British People* (Cambridge, MA: Harvard University Press, 1986) all similarly observe the massive increase of divorce during and after the war.
49. Susan Kingsley Kent, *Making Peace: The Reconstruction of Gender in Interwar Britain* (Princeton: Princeton University Press, 1993), p. 109.
50. For example, beside the *Times* report of the trial on November 19, appears a report of a "Restitution Order Against an Army Officer," in which Dame Leach "prayed for a decree of restitution of conjugal rights" against her Brigadier-General husband, whose "conduct toward her had altered" since his return from the war. Alongside the November 20 *Times* report of Hall's case appears a report of a Lieutenant-Colonel's divorce from his wife on the grounds of her adultery with a Captain. Throughout the month of November alone, there are multiple cases of divorce or restitution orders that situate marital troubles within the context of the war.
51. *Daily News*, November 19, 1920, p. 5.
52. *Daily Express*, November 19, 1920, p. 5.
53. Ibid., p. 1.
54. *Daily Chronicle*, November 19, 1920, p. 1.
55. *Daily Herald*, November 19, 1920, p. 2.
56. *Daily News*, November 19, 1920, p. 1.
57. Ibid. See also *Daily Express*, November 19, 1920, p. 1.
58. *Daily Herald*, November 19, 1920, p. 2.
59. *Daily Telegraph*, November 19, 1920, p. 7.
60. Ibid.
61. Castle, *The Apparitional Lesbian*, p. 4.
62. Ibid., pp. 6–7.
63. Castle refers to the "murderous allegorizing" involved in cultural and literary attempts to "exorcize" the lesbian ghost. See *The Apparitional Lesbian*, pp. 6–7.

Chapter 12

Telling It Straight: The Rhetorics of Conversion in Elizabeth Bowen's *The Hotel* and Freud's *Psychogenesis*

Petra Rau

After a long Victorian slumber of romantic sublimation and odd spinsterhood, lesbian desire seemed to become de rigueur in the novels of the 1920s. Once relegated to nonrealist forms of representation—sentimental metaphors, sensational embraces, and gothic encounters—it now seemed to merge with a modernist esthetic as a sign of the real and a signifier of modernity: the representation of lesbian desire, in other words, continued to bypass realist modes. A number of women writers imagined their modernist epiphanies as sapphic experiences of *jouissance*: there is, for instance, the pear tree that blissfully if allegorically unites Bertha Young with her husband's mistress Pearl Fulton in Katherine Mansfield's "Bliss" (1922); Virginia Woolf's famous orgasmic metaphor of the "match burning in a crocus" that captures Mrs. Dalloway's feelings for other women; and Rosamond Lehmann's dizzy moments in Judith Earle's devotion to fellow student Jennifer Baird in *Dusty Answer* (1927).[1] Here lesbian desire erodes or at least undermines the conventional heterosexual teleology of the realist novel and yet this is done with considerable ambivalence about the rules of engagement with sapphism. In all these texts lesbian desire is either framed or superseded by heterosexual romance and marriage. In other words, lesbian desire can become supremely real as a moment of *jouissance* only if it is subsequently rendered episodic in the course of a conversion narrative. While this sapphic epiphany functions repeatedly as a nostalgic disruption of straight romance, often interpreting heterosexual practice as a result of disappointed homosexual desire, it also ensures that this desire is temporary and that it does not *prevent* heterosexual teleologies, but merely makes them look desperate, bland, or implausible. The result of this technique is a curious tension within the text in which lesbian desire is marginalized by the plot but can remain for that very reason its epistemological and pleasurable center.

What interests me about sapphism in the 1920s is how much it relies on this narrative strategy of heterosexual conversion (which ostensibly renders lesbian desire less real) in order to have a greater claim than before on subjective and objective reality through its use of epiphanies. Elizabeth Bowen's first novel, *The Hotel* (1927), in which she struggles with realist and Edwardian legacies and strives for a modernist focus on subjectivity, particularly pushes conversion to its limits. Conflating an esthetic and a sexual agenda, its difficult coming out into sapphism and modernism alike is still couched as a conversion, but Bowen is also reluctant to tell the (lesbian's) story "straight." Furthermore, *The Hotel* shows striking similarities to Freud's last case study, "The Psychogenesis of a Case of Homosexuality in a Woman" (1920): both texts grapple with the story of a young woman who feels irresistibly attracted to an older one of slightly dubious reputation within a heterosexual narrative teleology that must result in a form of conversion and, therefore, will risk excising the very desire it seeks to represent or explain. In both texts, lesbian desire can no longer be accommodated through conversion, but this failure makes all the more visible the rhetorics and strategies of conversion the texts strain to employ to obfuscate lesbian desire as a sign of the real.

Conversion, in the widest sense, as a form of "turning" to heterosexuality rests on the assumption that this turning is normative and corrective.[2] By the 1920s, psychoanalysis had established itself as the scientific discourse that would implicitly consolidate an oedipally motivated heterosexual norm by exploring and explaining deviations from it. While Freud never formally extrapolated the Oedipus complex it is nonetheless the matrix upon which all other desires are grafted. Yet by 1920 Freud himself began having difficulties recognizing in his patients' lives and symptoms the results of oedipal vicissitudes. Nowhere is his growing doubt more palpable than in the contradictory rhetorics of his last case study.[3] In it Freud describes the analysis of an eighteen-year-old girl who "was not in any way ill" (375) but had developed a passion for a *demi mondaine* that publicly embarrassed her family. While Freud emphasized that he could not comply with the father's wish to convert his daughter "to a normal state of mind" (373), his explanation of her etiology into homosexuality suggests otherwise: it is remarkable how much of the dynamics of Freud's rhetorics in this case are devoted to heterosexualizing the young woman. Talking about female homosexuality therefore results in a perfectly straight story, albeit not a straightforward one. In this case lesbian desire actually functions as a catalyst in revealing the oedipal narrative as a *discours manqué*, insufficient in representing the reality and variety of sexual desire. Perhaps this is the reason why Freud cannot take his patient's desire at face value: her desire as a sign of the real cannot be accommodated in his oedipal concept without automatically turning her straight.

"Psychogenesis": Setting the Record Straight

"Psychogenesis" also documents a similar tension between core and margin in the narrativisation of lesbian desire that we find in sapphic texts: it is a real blind spot in Freud's sexual taxonomy. In the famous analytical failure of "Dora" (1900), Freud had overlooked that the "homosexual (gynaecophilic) love for Frau K. was the strongest unconscious current in Dora's mental life."[4] So while this desire is central to her erotic life, its reality is initially ignored by her analyst and reaches only the margins of retrospective footnotes in 1923. In "Psychogenesis" he meant to come to terms with this inconspicuous lesbian desire, "much less glaring" than its male equivalent (371), by centering a whole case history on the "mystery of homosexuality" (398). Yet "Psychogenesis" itself has become famous for being a rather glaring effort at continuing to obscure this mystery with straight rhetoric.

Freud describes the anonymous lesbian patient, whose father had delivered her over to Freud in an act of middle-European melancholy, as beautiful and clever, from a good family, cunning ("raffiniert"), and "in fact a feminist. She felt it to be unjust that girls should not enjoy the same freedom as boys, and rebelled against the lot of women in general" (397). This affair had not been her only passion; previously she had fallen in love with an actress and a schoolteacher, and had had proposals from a school-friend, but so far her "genital chastity [. . .] had remained intact" (378). The problem for Freud is to conduct an analysis and construct a case in the absence of psychopathological symptoms. As he had argued in the *Three Essays*, sexual perversion did not necessarily point to mental abnormalities.[5] Homosexuality as a libidinal vicissitude could therefore not necessarily be a "case." What, then, is he making a case for? The title's double genitive "The Psychogenesis of a Case of Homosexuality in a Woman" ("Über die Psychogenese eines Falles von weiblicher Homosexualität") suggests that what we are reading is an account of the psychogenesis of a case, rather than the psychogenesis of homosexuality. This awkward phrase in fact draws attention to the rhetorics of the genre of the case history rather than the etiology of the specific phenomenon under discussion: Freud's case makes a case *of* homosexuality, rather than *for* it, by inverting the radical ideas of the *Three Essays*.

The sheer number of illogical turns, gaps in coherence, and contradictions in this text have attracted considerable attention from feminist scholars, queer readers, and psychoanalysts alike,[6] but it is worth dwelling a little on Freud's major train of thought in this case history in order to appreciate the metamorphoses to which the patient's identity and desire are subjected. Freud argues that the girl's lesbian desire emerged as a consequence of the revival of her infantile Oedipus complex in puberty:

> She became keenly conscious of the wish to have a child, and a male one; that what she desired was her *father's* child and an image of *him*, her consciousness was not allowed to know. And what happened next? It was not *she* who bore the child, but her unconsciously hated rival, her mother. Furiously resentful and embittered, she turned away from her father and from men altogether. After this first great reverse she foreswore her womanhood and sought another goal for her libido. (383)

The style of this passage is remarkably rhetorical, although James Strachey's translation dramatises this frustrated oedipality even more than the original German. Strachey presents the patient's development like a series of surprises ("And what happened next?") that gloss over the implausibility of the return to heterosexuality with which this passage begins. Freud's own style (devoid of such a rhetorical flourish) nonetheless offers us the oedipal narrative like the plot summary of a cheap novella:

> Hell bewußt wurde ihr der Wunsch, ein Kind zu haben, und zwar ein männliches; daß es ein Kind vom Vater und dessen Ebenbild sein sollte, durfte ihr Bewußtsein nicht erfahren. Aber da geschah es, daß nicht sie das Kind bekam, sondern die im Unbewußten gehaßte Konkurrentin, die Mutter. Empört und erbittert wendete sie sich vom Vater, ja vom Manne überhaupt ab. Nach diesem ersten großen Mißerfolgt verwarf sie ihre Weiblichkeit und strebte nach einer anderen Unterbringung ihrer Libido. (234)

Stylistically this is probably the oddest passage in the case history, mixing portentous quasi-biblical phrases ("Aber da geschah es") with stage tragedy. The choice of the emotive adjectives "empört" and "erbittert," which Strachey further intensifies into "furiously resentful and embittered," underlines the full force of unconscious tornados. And the dynamic verbs "abwenden," "verwerfen," "zustreben" (turn away; repudiate/foreswear; seek/strive) translate the oedipal story of paternal rejection into a grand Victorian melodrama of jilted love. The next act offers an astonishing transformation, for which the reader is carefully prepared by an opening up and then a narrowing down of developmental options in extremity:

> It is evident that at this point a number of things could have happened. What actually happened was the most extreme case. She changed into a man and took her mother in place of her father as the object of her love. [. . .] Since there was little to be done with the real mother, there arose from this transformation of feeling the search for a substitute mother to whom she could become passionately attached. (384)

The "extreme" solution to jilted love, in Freud's oedipal tragedy, involves a sexual metamorphoses and a corresponding change of objects of desire: the girl who is now a man loves a woman who is not her mother but ultimately stands in for her father. Yet we are still within the heterosexual oedipal matrix. As a "man," the girl can only love a woman; in order to love a woman, the girl must have turned into a man. And what happened next?

> Henceforth she remained homosexual out of defiance against her father. [. . .] The girl's inversion, however, received its final reinforcement when she found in her 'lady' an object which promised to satisfy not only her homosexual trends, but also that part of her heterosexual libido which was still attached to her brother. (386)

So while the invert appears to be loving women, her object choice actually incorporates a bisexual disposition; in his oedipal archaeology, Freud never allows her not to love men *as well*, no matter how "furiously resentful and embittered" that first experience may have made her; no matter how much her lesbian affair intensifies into "a consuming passion of elemental strength" (394). On the contrary, a lot of energy is expended in diminishing the girl's agency in her choice of object. Not only is homosexuality framed as a consequence of heterosexual oedipal disappointment and as an act of adolescent obstreperousness with which the girl "remained" homosexual, but it is also implied in the above passage that homosexuality should and could only have been a stage from which the girl might have emerged into "a normal state of mind." Indeed, in a way she almost did, because her homosexual attachment remained only because it was a heterosexual one *as well*. Just as she had to *become* a man in order to love a woman, so her object of desire now has to *be* partly a man for the whole oedipal drama to come to a neat resolution. Paradoxically, object choice approximates her further to a heterosexual, for if the woman she loves reminds her of a man (her brother) and is a tool to rouse the emotions of a man (her father), then we have restored the patient to bisexuality, which according to Freud's earlier reflections is the only route "to a normal state of mind":

> It is only where the homosexual fixation has not yet become strong enough, or where there are considerable rudiments and vestiges of a heterosexual choice of object, i.e., in a still oscillating or in a definitely bisexual organization, that one may make a more favorable prognosis for psychoanalytic therapy. (375f.)

We have come full circle. It seems that in Freud's investigation into the young woman's homosexual disposition, we were bound to find the little girl who really loves only her father. Whoever she adores at the moment is a version ("in rudiments" or "vestiges") of that father and therefore she is always *at least* bisexual and *never wholly* homosexual. We have been on a rather dizzying journey from uncomplaining homosexuality to twisted heterosexuality, but not even Freud seems quite convinced of his argument. He concludes this case history, like the section on the sexual aberrations in the *Three Essays* added in the same year,[7] with extensive references to Steinach's *surgical* conversion efforts. This does not sit well with his earlier refusal to entertain hopes of a heterosexual "cure": "In general, to undertake to convert a fully developed homosexual into a heterosexual does not offer much more prospect of success than the reverse, except that for good practical reasons the latter is never attempted" (375f.). Yet he does not refuse to *contemplate* all possibilities by which this "returning her to a normal state of mind" (for which he is paid) could be achieved. His rhetorics demonstrate his inability to accept the female homosexual within his clinical experience *and* his theoretical framework as real. As long as inversion is a rather ungendered, abstract phenomenon in the *Three Essays*, we find a great deal of sympathy. The signification of lesbian desire must be altered as soon as it becomes more manifest in the form of an obstreperous young woman who suffers from "the problem of homosexuality" (homophobia and heteronormative teleologies) without caring about its mystery, as soon as it demands to be acknowledged as authentic, as a sign of the real. Freud may not be able to turn her into a heterosexual woman (as her biographers Ines Rieder and Diana Voigt argue, she remained attracted to women all her life),[8] but conceptually he has heterosexualized lesbian desire through the straight story of the revived oedipal complex.

We may have our doubts about Freud's reconstruction of the "chain of events" in this case, but so has he. Aware of his rhetorical contortions, and possibly aware also of his readers' reluctance to follow him all the way, Freud halts the argument's flow several times for further explanations about the practicalities of therapy, the function of resistance, the difficulties of linear presentation, and the discussion of sexological concepts. Toward the end of his analysis he offers us a remarkable insight into his methodological doubts:

> So long as we trace the development from its final outcome backwards, the chain of events appears continuous, and we feel we have gained an insight which is completely satisfactory or even exhaustive. But if we proceed the reverse way, if we start from the premises inferred from the analysis and try to follow these up to the final result, then we no longer get the impression of an inevitable sequence of events which could not have been otherwise determined. We notice at once that there might have been another result, and that we might have been just as well able to understand and explain the latter. The synthesis is thus not so satisfactory as the analysis; in other words, from a knowledge of the premises we could not have foretold the nature of the result. (395)

What Freud is saying here is that not every girl who experiences this girl's oedipal constellations during puberty becomes a lesbian. We remember indeed that at decisive moments "a number of things could have happened. What actually happened was the most extreme case." There are problems here with premises and results, with logic and order. Does it not question the entire Oedipus complex as an implicit heterosexual norm if there is no such thing as "an inevitable sequence of events"? Instead, this passage seems to hint at a much more complex pattern for human development, possibly even at a plethora of alternatives that may or may not be oedipally motivated. Does not Freud's doubt here implicitly suggest that homosexuality and heterosexuality might be more on a developmental par, bifurcations rather than hierarchically ranked stages? Both "inversion" and "arrested development" graft homosexual desire and identity onto a heterosexual matrix: an inversion of the norm, a stage within a normative sexual teleology. Consequently these concepts imply that the homosexual is always *incrementally* heterosexual, either as an other (the reverse) or as a part. If, however, we use Freud's doubt productively and "proceed the reverse way" we could also deduce that by the same logic every heterosexual is incrementally homosexual (as Freud indeed suggested in the *Three Essays*). In the psychogenesis of this case, a number of things could have happened. What actually happened was that Freud struggled to meaningfully distinguish between homosexuality and heterosexuality within his oedipal master narrative: "normal sexuality too depends upon a restriction in the choice of object" (375f.). It is in these moments of doubt that Freud returns to the radical moments of progressive tolerance in the *Three Essays*.

Freud's difficulties in coming to terms with lesbian desire are a corollary to his problems in understanding female sexuality, but they have wider methodological and conceptual implications as well. Underneath his reflections on conversion and his doubts about methodology he is beginning to grasp that lesbian desire might be part of female sexuality (as opposed to an early stage or an oedipal blockage), and this shadowy inkling will lead him on to his essays on female sexuality in the 1930s.[9] More importantly, it will also prompt him to revise his oedipal matrix during the 1920s. It is perhaps no coincidence that "Psychogenesis" is Freud's last major case history. His rhetorical failure to tell the young homosexual woman's story straight and his reluctance to conceive of sexual vicissitudes beyond the oedipal theater, is indicative of the problematics of the case history as the most empirical of Freud's writings from which concepts evolve but in which they are also rigorously tested. Significantly, it is incontrovertible and incommensurate lesbian desire that points to the shortcomings of the oedipal master narrative for human sexuality.

A few months after Freud published "Psychogenesis" Virginia Woolf dismissed a now forgotten novel by J. D. Beresford as "Freudian fiction." In her review she criticized not only Beresford's tendency to reduce characters to cases, plots to oedipal constellations, and readers to amateur psychologists, but she also reflected critically on the limitations of a *universal* concept such as the Oedipus complex: "We must protest that we do not wish to debar Mr. Beresford from making use of any key that seems to him to fit the human mind. Our complaint is rather that in [his novel] the new key is a patent key that opens every door. It simplifies rather than complicates, detracts rather than enriches."[10] We could easily substitute Freud for Beresford here, and apply this statement to "Psychogenesis": if the master plot actually converts (and thereby eradicates) the variety of human experience to the same old straight story, it does not really do what Freud set out to achieve—understand female homosexuality.

The Hotel: A Case of Heterosexuality in a Woman

If it is possible for Freud to deal with lesbian desire only within a heterosexual teleology (or oedipal archaeology) of conversion, Elizabeth Bowen's novel too struggles with it for very similar reasons. *The Hotel* is a halfhearted conversion narrative, which is, from the start, very much concerned with alternatives to the heterosexual teleology demanded by traditional realist forms such as romance and the *Bildungsroman*. As we shall see, the effort to represent lesbian desire is again linked to the modernist project of reflecting reality more appropriately. When in 1952 Bowen looked back on her beginnings as a novelist, she admitted: "It was a mistake to think of The Novel in the abstract, to be daunted by its 'musts' and its 'oughts', to imagine being constricted by its rules."[11] This is a familiar modernist quandary between the demands of form and the requirements of mimesis. The Novel—by which Bowen arguably means the realist novel—produces an *ideal* reality that is constructed as much through social ideals and moral imperatives (what people ought to do) as through formal ramifications (what the novel must do). Like Virginia Woolf's *The Voyage Out* (1915), Bowen's first novel situates itself somewhere in between attempting to play by the rules of realism and discarding them as useless for the kind of story she is trying to tell. Rather than a stream-of-consciousness narrative we encounter a bricollage of realist set-pieces (such as the Austenesque picnic, the Jamesian balcony scene, or the Forsterian Italian backdrop) that are meant to evoke a conventional realist teleology for its characters but paradoxically function to make this trajectory profoundly unreal on the level of the story. The novel begins with a sapphic disruption: the quarrel between two spinsters, Miss Fitzgerald and Miss Pym. The torment of their separation ("worse than a sense of destruction" [8]) combined with the relief of their making up at the very end of the narrative indicates the intensity of their companionship and mutual dependence. From the start, the novel's sapphic frame does not just envelope and curb but actually forecloses heterosexual development as narrative teleology.

The heroine of *The Hotel*, Sydney Warren, is a recognizable "modern" girl with vocational rather than amatory aspirations, although her characterization is sparse.[12] "A probable twenty-two," she has been studying at university, passed too many exams and is allegedly on the verge of a nervous breakdown. Packing her off to the Italian Riviera to win tennis tournaments and get engaged seems to her relatives "an inspired solution to the Sydney problem" (17) for which they no doubt have "good practical reasons." Sydney's "modernity" is often a subtle shorthand for unorthodox ideas and transgressive desire: we remember that Freud used the same strategy for classifying the homosexual patient as a "feminist" (modernity stands for deviance). Repeatedly throughout the novel, the heroine and her actions are described by other characters and by the narrator as "queer," "unnatural," "sinister," "unhealthy," "morbid," or "not popular"[13]—the very terms with which British critics dismissed French representations of sexual transgressions in the nineteenth century.[14] But for Sydney Warren, who has fallen in love with an older hotel guest, the divorcée Mrs. Kerr, reality is circumscribed by her lesbian desire; indeed living this desire seems the only reality imaginable:

> Maybe if she did not exist for Mrs Kerr as a tennis player, in this most ordinary, popular of her aspects, had she reason to feel she existed at all? It became

> no longer a question of—What did Mrs Kerr think of her?—but rather—Did Mrs Kerr ever think of her? The possibility of not being kept in mind seemed to Sydney at that moment a kind of extinction. (14)

Andrew Bennett and Nicholas Royle have argued that characters in *The Hotel* exist by virtue of being part of and affecting another's consciousness.[15] While this certainly identifies Bowen's modernist agenda, it neglects the centrality of lesbian desire as the link between modernist modes of representation and a rejection of realist conventions. The reason why the heroine in *The Hotel* so consistently feels out of place, unreal, or subjected to forces beyond her control—automatisms that determine her life for her—is not just because this is a modernist book concerned with alienation (after all, the setting is abroad), but because the heroine steers toward a sexual identity that is unrepresentable ("not being kept in mind," "a kind of extinction") within the realist trajectory of the rest of the book.[16]

When Sydney is rejected by Mrs. Kerr, who devotes her attention to her son Rodney, Sydney turns to the kind but bland Reverend James Milton, who proposes to her twice and to whom she finally becomes engaged. This conversion to heterosexuality is necessarily accompanied by a return to realist plotlines. Yet just as Freud's conversion effort via the universal oedipal matrix causes the strange leaps and turns of his rhetoric that dismantle the logic of his case history, so does the realist teleology of *The Hotel* further the disintegration of the narrative because the main lesbian character literally remains outside its moral framework. Finding it "odder than ever . . . that men and women should be expected to pair off for life" (18), Sydney cannot imagine herself within the terms of heterosexual romance. Even before her engagement, she finds heterosexual rituals strangely unconvincing. Here she observes a young woman's flirtation with a young war veteran during a hillside picnic:

> To her, looking down unawares, the couple gesticulating soundlessly below her in the sunshine appeared as in some perfect piece of cinema-acting, emotion represented without emotion. Then she wondered by what roads now unknown to her she might arrive at this: to be seen swinging back against a man's shoulder in that abandon of Veronica's. She wondered whether at such a moment she would be cut off from herself, as by her other emotions. She watched the miniature unreal Veronica toss back her hair and walk away. At Victor she forgot to look again; she had not thought of him. (42)

It is heterosexual romance here that is repeatedly commented on as implausible, unimaginable, and unconvincing for Sydney—a sign without a signifier. Heterosexuality becomes a ritual, in the sense that its meaning lies in its performability ("cinema-acting") and in its representability, which in turn does not need to be lived or verified by experience but serves as a foil against which experience is measured. This passage reminds us of Freud's dramatic presentation of the underlying oedipal passions that allegedly determined his lesbian patient's desire for women. The analyst invests so passionately in the oedipal choreography that, to him, its artificiality is no longer calculable or perceptible. Yet just as the patient in "Psychogenesis" remains "completely indifferent" (390) to Freud's heterosexual explanations of her desire, the heroine in *The Hotel* remains unconvinced by this display of "emotion represented without emotion." The conventions of romance here are interpreted as a technique of verisimilitude, rather than as empiricism or authenticity. Subsequently the conversion plot demonstrates to us how the "roads now unknown," which might lead to Sydney being "cut off from herself," will take us to one of the key scenes of romance, the proposal scene:

> Their conspicuous if isolated situation, the matter-of-fact sunshine and the sense that with all said and done they were English Visitors, he and she, sitting appropriately on a bench before a view designed for their admiration, had up to now kept her purely impersonal. So objective did she feel that she imagined a delightful Commune gazing down at the two of them: "English Visitors." In the expansion of the free air she had laughed and felt that neither of them were realer than the scenery. Now, at some tone in his voice she was surprised by a feeling that some new mood, not of her own, was coming down over them like a bell-glass. (83f.)

This scene parodies a convention and is strongly reminiscent of earlier investigations of expatriate vicissitudes in Europe by Henry James or Edith Wharton, of the Italian sections of E. M. Forster's novels, or Woolf's parodies in *Jacob's Room*. The gloss comes from the heroine who feels like a trope in a *locus communis* that eventually turns into a trap or a "bell-glass": the proposal, entirely unmotivated by the plot, seems prompted by the scenery, which suggests itself as a romantic opportunity. For the heroine, the scene is unreal because it is recognisable as a cliché that suggests "emotion represented without emotion" and therefore prompts again an "objective" response. What Bowen effectively does in subjecting her heroine to a conversion narrative is to unmask this heterosexual teleology as a series of tropes and conventions that function like cues and have become a kind of automatism. The hackneyed techniques of realism no longer mirror reality through mimesis, but fictionalize it. As in "Psychogenesis" it is the underlying heteronormative pattern (the Oedipus complex, the romance strand) that actually renders the desire that it is supposed to evoke or explain utterly implausible. For Bowen's heroine, there literally is no way "into" heterosexual master plots: "She could see her life very plainly, but there seemed no way into it; the whole thing might have been painted on canvas with a clever enough but unconvincing appearance of reality" (118). Here again we have a very clear indication that realism does not permit experiences that it deems inadmissible and that as a mode of representation it is therefore not just incomplete and limited but downright "unconvincing."

The heroine is increasingly bewildered by romance as "a wide but horribly purposeful groping about" (p. 99). When she breaks off her engagement to Reverend Milton she recognizes that it is only a "haze of possibilities with a very faint nucleus" (148):

> *Now* I understand—but it seems as if I ought to tell you what I didn't understand. I think we have been asleep here; you know in a dream how quickly and lightly shapes move, they have no weight, nothing offers them any resistance. They are governed by some funny law of convenience that seems to us perfectly rational, they clash together without any noise and come apart without injury. (160)

This returns us to the earlier proposal scene with its feeling of "objectivity" and alienation during which the heroine was cut off from her emotions as if in a bell-glass. The metaphor used here for romance is that of a dream governed by its own secondary processes. Conversion at this point has actually excluded romance as a viable option because it has been dismissed as "some funny law of convenience" and appears as unreal as a dream. The novel ends with Sydney's return to her studies: we have come some way from the radical solution Woolf offered in *The Voyage Out*, where her refusal to go through with the conventional marriage plot led to the feverish death of Rachel Vinrace. In *The Hotel*, the heroine simply walks away from conversion and leaves the plot that never quite materialized anyway. Very like the utterly disinterested patient in "Psychogenesis," Sydney refuses to be defined by terms that deny her identity and reality.

Beyond Oedipus

The Hotel might stand at the end of conversion rhetorics, as if the heroine's departure from romance pointed the way for new representational possibilities and challenges. The year following its publication, Radclyffe Hall made a much less subtle effort at representing lesbian desire in *The Well of Loneliness*, which despite widespread sympathy among most reviewers still outraged the righteous few.[17] In September 1928 E. M. Forster and Virginia Woolf wrote a letter to the editor of *Nation and Athenæum* in response to the Home Secretary's efforts to ban the novel:

> The subject matter of [*The Well of Loneliness*] exists as a fact among the many other facts of life. It is recognized by science and recognizable in history. It

> forms, of course, an extremely small fraction of the sum-total of human emotions, it enters personally into very few lives, and is uninteresting or repellent to the majority; nevertheless it exists, and novelists in England have now been forbidden to mention it by Sir W. Joynson-Hicks. May they mention it incidentally? Although it is forbidden as a main theme, may it be alluded to, or ascribed to subsidiary characters? Perhaps the Home Secretary will issue further orders on this point. And is it the only taboo, or are there others? What of the other subjects known to be more or less unpopular in Whitehall, such as birth-control, suicide, and pacifism? May we mention these? We await our instructions![18]

What is at stake for Woolf and Forster is discursive freedom in art: literature must not be gagged by the moral values of those in political power. While they refer to "science" as a verifying discipline, they actually also contest its supremacy: why should only sexologists and psychoanalysts be allowed to discuss human sexuality freely? And our analysis of Freud's straight rhetorics in "Psychogenesis" should have taken Woolf and Forster's point one step further. Scientific discourses are by no means objective, nor do they exist in a moral vacuum, nor are they devoid of conceptual or ideological blind spots. In their mocking question about representational alternatives to the taboo subject of homosexuality as a main theme—allusion, subsidiary characters—Woolf and Forster tie this issue to one of the key concerns of modernist esthetics, how to represent life with both its "myriad impressions"[19] and equally "its small fraction of the sum-total of human emotions" in a more plausible and appropriate mode than the Edwardians or the Victorians had done. The point with which Forster and Woolf begin their argument, that the mere existence of a phenomenon vouchsafes its representability (rather than necessitates its subjection to a censorious filter of moral imperatives and social values), rejects the limited scope of the English realist novel. That this filter can no longer "convert" other forms of love and desire into traditional plotlines of (oedipal) romance has become evident in Freud's implausible rhetorics and Bowen's romantic impasse in *The Hotel*: patients resist and characters simply walk away. The rhetorics of Woolf and Forster's letter, I would argue, forge an explicit link between English modernism and the representation of homosexuality. It is perhaps ironic that the novel that came to epitomize this link, *The Well of Loneliness*, actually follows the codes of realist representation because, as Woolf and Forster argue, it is "restrained and perfectly decent."[20] But it certainly no longer entertains conversion.

Notes

I would like to thank Marina Mackay and Deborah Shaw for generous and helpful comments in the preparation of this essay.

1. See Katherine Mansfield, "Bliss" in D. M. Davin, ed., *Selected Stories* (Oxford: Oxford University Press, 1981), pp. 111–25; Virginia Woolf, *Mrs Dalloway* (1925), Claire Tomalin, ed. (Oxford: Oxford University Press, 1992), p. 41; Rosamond Lehmann, *Dusty Answer* (London: Flamingo, 1996).
2. On the notion of "turning" in Freud's case history see Diana Fuss, "Fallen Woman," in Ronnie C. Lesser and Erica Schoenberg, eds., *That Obscure Subject of Desire: Freud's Female Homosexual Revisisted* (London: Routledge, 1999), pp. 54–76.
3. "Psychogenesis of a Case of Homosexuality in a Woman" (1920) in Angela Richards, ed., *Case Histories II*, trans. James Strachey (Penguin Freud Library, vol. 9), (Harmondsworth: Penguin, 1987), pp. 367–401. All quotations refer to this edition. All references to the German original are taken from Sigmund Freud, *Schriften zur Krankheitslehre der Psychoanalyse* (Frankfurt am Main: Fischer Verlag, 1991), pp. 221–51.
4. Sigmund Freud, "Fragment of an Analysis of a Case of Hysteria" in Angela Richards, ed., *Case Histories I*, trans. Alix and James Strachey (Penguin Freud Library, vol. 8), (Harmondsworth: Penguin, 1980), pp. 131–67 especially, p. 162 FN1.
5. *Three Essays on the Theory of Sexuality* (1905) in Angela Richards, ed., *On Sexuality*, trans. James Strachey (Freud Penguin Library, vol. 7), (Harmondsworth: Penguin, 1991), pp. 133–171. In the same essay Freud also asserted that "inversion [. . .] answers fully to the sexual inclinations of no small number of people," p. 153.
6. Lesser and Schoenberg's collection reprints essays by Mandy Merck, Diana Fuss and Teresa de Lauretis; see also Luce Irigaray, *This Sex Which Is Not One*, trans. Catherine Porter with Carolyn Burke (Ithaca: Cornell University Press, 1985); Judith Roof, *A Lure of Knowledge: Lesbian Sexuality and Theory* (New York: Columbia University Press, 1991); Mary Jacobus, *First Things: The Maternal Imaginary in Literature, Art and Psychoanalysis* (London: Routledge, 1995).
7. *Three Essays*, p. 58.
8. See *Heimliches Begehren: Die Geschichte der Sidonie C.* (Vienna: Deuticke, 2000).
9. For Jacqueline Rose, Freud acknowledges "the homosexual factor in all feminine sexuality" in this case study. This acknowledgment, if we can call it that, expresses itself at most in rhetorical manoeuvres of methodological and conceptual uncertainty. See "Dora: Fragment of an Analysis" in Charles Bernheimer and Claire Kahane, eds., *In Dora's Case: Freud—Hysteria—Feminism* (London: Virago, 1985), pp. 128–49, especially p. 135.
10. "Freudian Fiction" (1920), repr. in Rachel Bowlby, ed., *A Woman's Essays* (Harmondsworth: Penguin, 1991), pp. 21–23, especially p. 23.
11. Preface (1952) to *The Last September* repr. in Elizabeth Bowen, *The Mulberry Tree*, Hermione Lee, ed. (London: Vintage, 1999), pp. 122–26, especially p. 123.
12. Elizabeth Bowen, *The Hotel* (1927) (Harmondsworth: Penguin, 1956), p. 99. All subsequent quotations are cited parenthetically in the text.
13. See Bowen, *The Hotel*, pp. 12, 13, 53, 93, 114, 137, and 172.

14. See Sharon Marcus, "Comparative Sapphism," in Margaret Cohen and Carolyn Dever, eds., *The Literary Channel: The Inter-National Invention of the Novel* (Princeton: Princeton University Press, 2002), pp. 251–86.
15. *Elizabeth Bowen and the Dissolution of the Novel* (London: Palgrave, 1995), p. 10.
16. For an astute analysis of Bowen's reticence about her own sexual ambivalence see Patricia Coughlan, "Women and Desire in the Work of Elizabeth Bowen," in Eibhéar Walshe, ed., *Sex, Nation and Dissent in Irish Writing* (New York: St. Martin's Press, 1997), pp. 101–34, especially 107ff.
17. See Laura Doan, *Fashioning Sapphism: The Origins of a Modern English Lesbian Culture* (New York: Columbia University Press, 2001).
18. "The New Censorship," *Nation and Athenæum* 43, no. 28 (September 1928): 726.
19. Woolf, "Modern Fiction" (1919), *Collected Essays*, vol. 2 (London: Hogarth Press, 1966), p. 106.
20. "The New Censorship," p. 726.

Chapter 13

Mary Butts's "Fanatical Pédérastie": Queer Urban Life in 1920s London and Paris

Jane Garrity

Writing in the *Voice Literary Supplement* in 1994, Bruce Hainley refers to the remarkable English modernist Mary Butts (1890–1937) as a "fag-hag," characterizing her posthumously published 1937 autobiography, *The Crystal Cabinet*, as "the tale of how a little fag-hag grows up."[1] Although readers may object to Hainley's phrasing, or his occasional lack of evidence (e.g., his account of "Mary Butts going down on . . . Jane Heap" is provocative, but this imagined moment of modernist cunnilingus between Butts and the lesbian coeditor of *The Little Review* has never been documented), his evocative observations nonetheless speak to a central and ongoing preoccupation in Mary Butts's life and work: the relationship between women—whether straight, bisexual, or lesbian—and gay men. Hainley refers to the bisexual Butts as "an ecologist of the queer," maintaining that her writing is an "elegant proof that the disappearance—in memory or body or word—of the queer is an environmental crisis" (11–22). The constellation that Hainley posits between the individual, the environment, and homosexuality, reminds us of Butts's portrayal of a World War I gay veteran suffering from shell shock in her 1928 novel, *Armed with Madness*, but here in this highly experimental text "the disappearance . . . of the queer" is far from being "an environmental crisis" (12). On the contrary, it is precisely the displacement of homosexuality, and the subsequent embrace of heterosexually conceived notions of spiritual renewal and purity, that allows the sacred geography of rural England to flourish and survive. In both *Armed with Madness* and its sequel, *Death of Felicity Taverner* (1932), Butts bemoans the cultural and economic dispossession of life in postwar Europe, anathematizing the city as a space of depravity because it is aligned with technology, rationalism, hypermasculinity, and mechanization—all elements that she opposes to the rural, supernatural, feminized order of authentic Englishness, with its rhetoric of bloodlines and racial purity. In this equation, homosexuality must be either displaced or, in the case of *Felicity Taverner*, put in the service of a heterosexual imperative by facilitating the procreative process.[2] Interestingly, however, despite Butts's antipathy for the contemporary urban wasteland and her celebration of heterosexuality, she simultaneously published several short works that capture the pleasures of what she calls "every perversion of sentiment" in the city, demonstrating her particular fascination with gay male culture in 1920s London and Paris.[3] Butts's obsession with the environmental concerns of rural England are mixed up with her sympathetic, if idiosyncratic, portrayal of urban homosexuality. As she herself puts it: "I have a weakness for Queer Street, and people who have that are soon past being astonished at anything."[4]

Butts's frequent depictions of gay men is a topic that has to date received virtually no critical attention beyond biographical anecdotes that note what novelist and gossip Douglas Goldring called her "flair for everything queer in art and life . . . a tremendous . . . delight in all the more exotic forms of naughtiness."[5] Nathalie Blondel, Butts's biographer, documents the author's interest in male homosexuality but provides no framework through which to understand this phenomenon, either in relation to Butts's own psychology, how it influenced her artistic vision, or in terms of the larger cultural prohibitions against homosexuality during this period. Throughout the 1920s Butts was repeatedly exposed to gay male culture as she moved between France and England. As far as biographical details go, we have evidence that in 1927 Butts had an intense relationship with Virgil Thompson, the gay American music critic and composer.[6] Quentin Bell refers to Butts's second husband, Gabriel Aitken, as "the toast of . . . British Sodom," and Butts devotes a separate notebook to documenting Aitkin's multiple affairs with men. We know that Butts was intimately involved with Jean Cocteau, the gay avant-garde artist who illustrated her 1928 novella, *Imaginary Letters*, (the first time that Cocteau illustrated the work of another writer).[7] Butts's estranged younger brother, Tony, was the long-term lover of William Plomer, a South African writer, and some argue that Butts's attraction to gay men can be traced to her desire to care for Tony, who was said to be tortured by his homosexuality.[8] Butts also befriended the gay American writer and critic Glenway Wescott, one of the first writers of her generation to recognize her extraordinary talent. During the mid-1920s

Butts fell in love with a gay Russian émigré, Sergey Maslenikof, an often broke but charming and talented designer whom Butts supported both emotionally and financially, Butts referred to her gay friends as her "Achilles set"—an epithet that exposes her attraction to classical models of male beauty, for, like her contemporaries H. D. and Bryher, Butts was a modernist who consistently filtered her homoerotic preoccupations through a classical lens.[9]

Blondel's argument that Butts holds a "nonjudgmental attitude toward . . . homosexuality" is well-intentioned but naive, for while the author certainly "treats [her homosexual characters] with a sympathy and openness astonishing for the England of her time,"[10] she simultaneously harbors several stereotypical assumptions about gay men (in particular) that complicate this reading. A preoccupation with the city as a queer space in which predatory sex, cruising, and one-night stands transpire permeates several of Butts's short stories that are either set in or evoke 1920s Paris, such as "Speed the Plough" and "The House-Party" (which was dedicated to Cocteau), as well as her 1928 novella, *Imaginary Letters*, an epistolary work in which the English female narrator addresses a series of letters to the Russian mother of her gay would-be lover, Boris. In these works, Paris is by turns a "filthy" and "glorified" space in which casual sex between sailors and expatriate aristocrats is commonplace, but the city is not altogether devoid of the ideas of spiritual mysticism and renewal that pervade *The Taverner Novels*.[11] Instead, the city is reimagined as a profane yet sacred space of naughty pleasures and exotic delights, to borrow Goldring's language. In general, Paris is "both a sink of iniquity and a fountain of life," a city whose "secret map"—its seedy underside and clandestine spaces of sexual availability—is accessible only to those who know how to read its latent cartography: that "on the other side of the shadows there is another country" of covert desire.[12] Butts's fiction captures the excitement and titillation of navigating this "secret map" of sexual possibility between men, even as she conveys a certain distaste for what she calls "fanatical pédérastie" (*IL*, 239).[13]

This essay seeks to track Butts's fascination with male homosexuality by situating it within the larger cultural context of early twentieth-century same-sex passion in London and Paris. It attempts, moreover, to show how Butts's linkage of the urban with spiritual deprivation, which is so pervasive throughout her 1930s novels and pamphlets, is interestingly absent in "Speed the Plough" and *Imaginary Letters*. Whereas elsewhere Butts pits the contemporary urban wasteland against the presence of a rural and feminized supernatural order, in the works I examine here Butts yokes mystical experience with homosexuality and claims the city as queer domain. In these works Butts portrays the city as a space that offers regenerative escape and spiritual renewal for the gay man, a connection that is only made possible through the critical influence and interventions of femininity.

Butts's claim that she could "magically" grasp the city and "its psychic auras," and her contention that Paris in particular is one of the "great feminine places" on the earth, are illustrated in the two works I consider here, each of which demonstrates Butts's view that Paris holds the key to spiritual renewal because its architectural and geographical layers can be exfoliated to reveal the density and complexity of queer history.[14] In these texts Butts explores the Englishwoman's response to male homosexuality, in particular, the "magical relation" between gay men and the city, toward an elucidation of modernity and of the creative genealogy of the woman artist.[15] In this equation gay men function variously as signs of degeneracy, embodiments of feminine artifice and excess, symptoms of national distress, sources of poetic inspiration, and divine conduits for primitive ritual.

Embracing Effeminacy: "Speed the Plough"

Butts in effect condones "unnatural" practices by allowing such vices to circulate freely throughout her fiction; her thematic preoccupations included not only homosexuality, but sexual violence, sadomasochism, blackmail, extortion, addiction, environmental disease, black magic, and the horrors of the nuclear family. It is thus not difficult to see why critics contemporary with Butts condemned her work on the grounds that it deviated—without censure—from sexual norms: her stories are dismissed as "promiscuous reading," they are called abnormal, queer, perverse, are said to "smell of blood and filth" and leave a "nasty" and "sticky" taste in the mouth.[16] By equating the reading of Butts's fiction with pornographic practice, certain reviewers effectively lumped the author alongside other controversial modernists (such as Lawrence, Joyce, and Hall) whose work had been suppressed for obscenity. To be sure, Butts was writing and publishing at a time when homosexuality could not be discussed openly in English books or in the English press. Although, in general, most of the early reviews are favorable, several critics concur that Butts's work is bewildering in its eccentricities; her authorial pen is at one point referred to as a "surgical instrument," ruthless, callous, and devoid of "normality."[17] This phallic metaphor is consistent with the assessment of several reviewers who find her objectionable on the grounds that she does not conform to a feminine standard; one critic refers to her as a "woman writer with maleness" in her approach, a characterization that helps to explain the vehement critique of her alleged vileness.[18] Butts's short-story collection, *Speed the Plough* (1923), was banned from public libraries on the basis of "indecency" and "the absence of normality and health" because it contained an irreverent fictionalization of the annunciation story, in which angels are represented as homosexual figures, as well as a deviant depiction of a young soldier who fantasizes about the trappings of female artifice.[19]

Such stories enable us to begin to evaluate Bruce Hainley's claim that "[f]ag-hag is a style of writing."[20] Formally, Butts's difficult experimental prose style reflects the technical discipline of her early engagement with poetry; both her novels and short stories are elliptical, disjointed, peppered with lacunae, and saturated with laconic snippets of seemingly irrelevant information. Her sentences are characterized by an exactitude that we might call mannered terseness. Often, disconnected scenes saturated with visual imagery are sutured into a single narrative by unfamiliar syntax and jarring juxtapositions. The reader marvels at her dazzling, clipped sentences, but cannot always track their erratic movement. Are these then the stylistic features of fag-hag writing, and is Butts one of the first innovators of this tradition? However intriguing, such a proposition, I would argue, is specious, for this would not be the first time that experimental writing has been reductively linked with repressed materials and put in the service of a political agenda (e.g., the linkage between *écriture feminine* and female liberation). Butts's experimentalism in itself contains nothing that is inherently fag-haggish, to use Hainley's locution, just as so-called feminine writing is not more authentically liberatory than realism. Much more productive than embracing essentialist understandings of queer inscription would be to consider how Butts's stylistic eccentricities are thematically inseparable from what early critics denounced as her decidedly vulgar, neurotic, lurid, and perverse topics. Here, I am interested in examining how Butts spatializes these topics by linking homosexuality with urban space, specifically Paris, where even the "lamp-posts and bicycles were over-sexed."[21] In general, Butts crafts a stylish idiom calculated to capture the geography of sexual practices, showing through her jumpy prose's hallucinatory and surreal qualities how the circuit of queer desire reflects disjunction and self-reflexiveness. Butts's experimentalism portrays the friction of gay life, for "our language was not invented to express these experiences, words will have to be found."[22] As Butts moves increasingly toward fissures, pastiche, disjointed abstractions, and collisions between genres, she succeeds in showing how queer networks in the city enable social and affective ties between men, even if gay desire contains the threat of sexual depravity and gender deviance.

A case in point is "Speed the Plough" (1923), an experimental story that focuses upon a shell shocked, homosexually coded veteran of World War I who reads the popular English society and fashion magazine, *The Sketch*, in a London hospital and is preoccupied with the memory and representation of women's dress fabrics—"crepe velours, crepe de Chine, organdie, aerophane, georgette" (10)—and insists upon the French words for women's undergarments: "Coquetterie, mannequin, lingerie" (9). When this unnamed protagonist sees a young nurse with a freshly scrubbed face it irritates him and gives rise to a fantasy of "women whose skins were lustrous with powder, and whose eyes were shadowed with violet from an ivory box" (11). This preoccupation with cosmetics can be read as a proxy for queerness, reminding us of Quentin Crisp's observation that the adoption of certain performative gender conventions—such as dress, cosmetics, and an effeminate posture—contribute to the "set of stylisations . . . known as camp."[23] The English soldier in "Speed the Plough" is not overtly campy, but his attraction to fashionable femininity and his engagement with consumer culture are constituent components of his homosexuality. He spends his days "finger[ing]" (9) his beloved *Sketch*, a magazine that often featured the "Kirchner album" (10), colorful sketches of young women by the Austrian illustrator, Raphael Kirchner (1876–1917), whose eroticized drawings proved popular during World War I not only among his compatriots but also among British and French servicemen. With the "Kirchner album" in mind, the soldier performs what is in effect a queer "ritual and a litany": he repeatedly unwraps his bandaged arms and mentally dresses and undresses a series of imagined Kirchner girls—"Suzanne, and Verveine, Ambre and Desti"—in "immaculate fabrics," remembering his prior life as a dressmaker and fearing that his wounded body would "soil its loveliness" (10) if he were to return. Butts here suggests that homosexuality must "look outside Britain, to another sensibility, another language" in order to locate its desire, for, as with the earlier references to French fabrics, these women's artificial names mark the soldier's desire as noticeably unEnglish.[24] Matters of dress and familiarity with women's toilette are the domain of homosexuality in this story, for the soldier's preoccupation with the Kirchner girls stems from identification, not desire, and has to do with a longing for artifice—what Mary Hamer has called "shamelessly unnatural versions of femininity"—that confirm his rejection of "the heterosexual order."[25] The story never dwells on the soldier's desire for women; rather, it shows us how the gay man's identification with women functions as a salvific tool, shoring up his belief that contact with such "unstable delicate things" might be the route through "which he might be cured" (10). Before the trials of Oscar Wilde, while effeminacy and homosexuality did not correlate in the same way they did subsequently, Butts seems clearly to be working off of the associations between homosexuality, consumption, and the formation of a fashionable identity that Wilde's effete image had established in the public domain.[26] The young soldier is drawn to patently artificial representations of femininity, which work to confirm his fluid sense of gender identity and sexual expression.

Butts codes the soldier as queer too through other markers of his effeminacy expressed through the body: he is "lame," cries, daydreams, and is full of "nerves" that "project loathsome images" (9), a characterization that invokes both the horrors of war and the discourse of inversion. When he is exiled to the country in a therapeutic attempt to restore his shell-shocked mind to sanity, he is assigned the job of cow milking. The soldier briefly reimagines the cowshed as a famous London dress-shop, but this imaginary foray into his past life as a dressmaker evaporates almost instantly when he is confronted with the rankness of the animal corral. The scene invokes both queer and heterosexual imagery, demonstrating the young man's attraction and repulsion for milk, whose beauty both "please[s]" and "nauseate[s]" (12) him. Butts utilizes masturbatory imagery to convey the young man's fascination with the "hot milk," the "amazing substance, pure, and thick with bubbles" whose spurting and "winking, pearling flow" (12) suggests semen. Butts winks at the reader when her narrator contrasts the "difference in nature" between the "pearling flow" and the "decency" of a cup of English tea (12), and she injects gay humor into the scene when the farmer for whom the veteran works calls him a "born milkman" (13), homoerotically observing that "[he] could milk a bull if [he] were so inclined" (13). Yet, while the young man adores his milky substance, he loathes the heterosexually coded context in which he is forced to observe the white liquid come into contact with the "huge buttocks" of twenty "female animals" (12). Moreover, the milk reminds him of maternity, provoking him to reflect upon reproduction, the primal moment "where most of life started" (12). This realization threatens the soldier's psychological stability, which rests upon the foundation stones of feminine artifice, performance, spectacle, and commodification. Worried that the highly artificial version of femininity that he adores and identifies with is undermined by his contact with nature, the soldier wonders: "Rosalba and all the Kirchner tribe . . . was Polaire only a cow . . . or Delysia?" (13). Yet this invocation of the Kirschner girls functions as a talismanic antidote to the threat of heterosexual contamination. Instantly, "the light had now the full measure of day" (13), suggesting that the masquerade of femininity function as a salvific and liberatory balm for the homosexual esthete, reminding him of his allegiance to the city, not nature.

Thus "sickened" and made "nause[ous]" (12) by the milking experience, the soldier determines that his farm job makes him feel "dirty, yes dirty" (13) and longs again for the artifice of the metropolis, where he remembers with "rapture" a London stage production in which the spectacular image of a woman in a music-hall, "plumed and violent, wrapped in leopard skin and cloth-of-gold" (13), dominates the scene. Here, as elsewhere, it is an affinity for the esthetics of performance and the mysterious erotic power of the city, peopled with deviants, performers, and "exotics" (10), that is a refuge for the gay man. The story's climax, a scene in which the soldier stands before a country pub and sees a feminized image of "the fine delicate life" (14) he had left behind in London, underscores Butts's sense that the emergence of the modern homosexual as a recognizable type is dependent upon certain visual signifiers that have to do with consumption, masquerade, and performance. In certain ways "Speed the Plough" appears to anticipate Joan Riviere's classic argument that the masquerade of womanliness is constituted through a hyperbolization of the trappings of femininity, but, in contrast to Riviere, Butts explores how the display and appropriation of femininity works to consolidate the homosexual man's (rather than the intellectual woman's) sense of self. In the story's epiphanic moment, the young soldier sees an affluent London actress—swathed in white furs and wearing stylish boots and rich gloves that are "thick, like moulded ivory" (14)—approach her chauffeur driven car. As he gazes intently upon the woman and her car, both emblems of modernity, the soldier feels himself "ravished" by the scene, a word that conveys that he has been imaginatively seized and transported by this escapist "dream" of London, "the quintessence of cities, the perfection of the world" (14). Although Butts offers no single material template for homosexuality in this story, she repeatedly yokes her protagonist's desires to "unnatural" (14) and contrived images of fashionable femininity and leaves no doubt that the city—that idealized, quintessential space of imaginative possibility—is the true domain of the "invert."

In casting the countryside as "dirty" and "unnatural" (14), Butts appropriates the language that is conventionally used to demonize the homosexual, casting nature instead as inassimilable. In doing so, she suggests that the young soldier's "essential difference" (15) from the villagers—his love of French undergarments, feminine artifice, and urban spectacles—necessitates an alternate context. In this story, "London [is] civilized" (13) because it is the only space in which a gay man can fondle expensive rolls of fabric without censure. The story ends with the war veteran reinstated into his former life as a dress-shop employee, a job associated with the long history of locating homosexual desire in fashion, design, and decoration.[27] The reader sees him as a caricature of effeminate mannerisms, wearing a bow tie and, "on his knees" in a fitting room, fingering a roll of peach and silver "Lyons brocade," which he massages pleasurably "between his fingers as the teats of a cow" (16) as he pins up a woman's dress. By conflating French fabric and the teats of a cow, Butts successfully ascribes a new meaning to deeply etched cultural categories; the simple utilitarian act of milking is transformed into a fashionable gesture, enabling the soldier to repossess, symbolically and in fact, the queer part of himself that his exile to the farm had attempted to eradicate. It is this provocative, and arguably masochistic, image of a soldier kneeling and submissively pinning a petulant woman's dress that provoked some of the early reviewers of this story to dismiss it as "queer," "blasphemous," and lacking in "restraint and morality."[28] The soldier's acquiescent and deferential posture here, repeatedly apologizing on bended knee to the spoiled society woman who is unhappy with her dress design, parallels the earlier scene in the hospital where, as an invalid, he had happily dressed and undressed his Kirschner women while "his mouth would be barred with pins" and "he could not speak to them" (10). In both instances, the soldier occupies a submissive posture and is silenced by the spectacle of femininity, a speechlessness that appears to fill him with considerable gratification. Perhaps it is precisely the possibility of masochistic pleasure, Butts suggests, that can subvert conventional notions of the relationship between masculinity, sexuality, and desire. In this story the soldier rejects both heterosexuality and the nostalgic propaganda of rural England that dominated popular culture and Butts's novels during the interwar period, effectively transforming the meaning of both the "natural" and masculine subjectivity. "Speed the Plough" inverts the rural/urban hierarchy that is upheld elsewhere in Butts's work, suggesting that the city is the only natural place for gay men in postwar England. In doing so, the story seeks to denaturalize heterosexuality and call into question the assumption that homosexuality is "unnatural."

Queering "Things in other Categories": *Imaginary Letters*

In "Speed the Plough" the cityscapes of London and Paris play a crucial role in the mapping of male desire, but it is in *Imaginary Letters* (composed in 1924 but not published until 1928) that Butts fully imagines the material and spatial embeddedness of metropolitan homosexual identity. In this epistolary fiction Butts regards the urban as not only the physical embodiment of homosexual desire, but also as a mystical space of poetic inspiration for the Englishwoman, a figure who, as we shall see, occupies a deeply ambivalent position with respect to male homosexuality. In *Imaginary Letters* Butts represents male inversion as both a threat to established gender norms and as a constitutive component of the cultural and social formation of modernity. The way she does this, I argue, is through her representation of the city—in particular, Paris—as a space that is integral to the historical constitution of queer subjectivity. Butts's selection of Paris is not a surprise. As one critic observes, "Paris between the wars enjoyed an international reputation as a tolerant, wide-open city . . . a homosexual paradise compared to 'that enormous, puritanical and joyless city' of London."[29] This dour view of London ignores the fact that queer networks, such as "Lady Austin's Camp Boys," circulated there during the interwar period, but it does speak to the repressiveness of such legislation as the Labouchere amendment, which criminalized male homosexuality in England in 1885 (by contrast, the French penal code of 1791 dropped all references to sodomy).[30] Butts privileges Paris as a liberatory space in which dissident sexualities flourish. This celebration of homosexual geography, however, is tempered by the fact that "Paris's basketful of boys" is a source of confusion and pain for the Englishwoman.[31] Butts tracks the ways in which gay men owe their emergence to the modern metropolis and simultaneously demonstrates the positive as well as ill effects of "this pédérastie that depends on women, which asks everything and gives nothing in return" (254). To understand precisely how for Butts male homosexuality is dependent upon women, we need to see how she establishes Boris as an erratic character in manifest need of continuous caretaking.

Imaginary Letters is an epistolary fiction that is structured as a series of eight letters, written in Paris, from an unnamed Englishwoman to the Russian mother of her gay, would-be lover, Boris. These lyrical and disjointed letters—which combine autobiographical allusions, snippets of idiosyncratic French, and several stanzas of poetry—are never intended to be mailed and instead function as a kind of experiential diary through which the narrator attempts to come to terms with what it means to love an unattainable gay man. Butts's depiction of the protagonist of *Imaginary Letters*, Boris Polteratsky, is based upon her troubled relationship with the gay Russian émigré Sergey Maslenikof, and one sees reflected in the fictional account her private conviction that Sergey is incapable of love. Writing in her journal in 1928, Butts laments: "Blaze of love, Sergey and I for each other . . . [but] it is odd how paederasts only think about paederasty; never about love."[32] The journal is filled with such accounts of the conceptual and physical limits of "paederasty." Butts resorts to heavy-handed metaphors to describe this impasse, which she ultimately blames on Sergey's obstinacy: "And it is like a thirsty man refusing a drink of water because he has never seen water before, has been brought up to think that he can't drink water. Stays thirsty, or with only the wrong drinks . . . it is this which separates us."[33] It is precisely this problematic idea of the gay man's refusal to "drink" the gift of heterosexual love that informs *Imaginary Letters*, whose most fundamental subject is the failed relationship between the narrator (whose sexuality is never disclosed but is assumed to be heterosexual) and Boris, whom she regards as both a "high-bred, honorable boy" and a capricious "monster of vanity and pride" who is "[l]echerous" as well as "chaste" (235). Such irreconcilable extremes characterize Boris, who can be read as an embodiment of modernity to the extent that he is fragmented, slippery, nationally divided (as an expatriated Russian), perpetually in motion, and—for both the narrator and reader—difficult to fully grasp. Like a modernist montage, he is "a picture cut in bits; the parts slide up and down each; shoot, crawl round, dart and chase each other" (237). His facility for "playing with a conversation; developing, never resolving it" (255) further marks him as a figure for modernist unintelligibility, forever resisting closure, resolution, and stasis. These markers, as we shall see, are ultimately what link him to writing; as the narrator puts it: " 'Boris is poetry' " (235).

Boris also operates as a modernist symbol of exilic displacement. While several Euro-American modernist literary critics have viewed physical displacement as conducive to groundbreaking experimentalism, in *Imaginary Letters* it is not the dilettante painter Boris himself who produces this connection. Rather, it is the narrator who dwells on Boris's estrangement, incessant mobility, and irreparable separation from his homeland and family, appropriating the now clichéd idea of the "artist in exile" who is never "at home" as an imaginary construct through which to pursue her own artistic practice—letter writing. The narrator's conviction that Boris is "the cause of art in others" (235) stems from several factors, preeminent among which is his status as a refugee from nationalist conflicts in Russia. Characterized by hybridity to the extent that he is a diasporic émigré who confounds national and territorial distinctions between east and west, Boris "seem[s] to carry two continents in [his] shell of a body, from the pale Baltic to China, in whom the east and west play pitch and toss" (257). Boris's racial pluralism marks him as a transnational subject—the narrator uses orientalist tropes to describe his frightening "chalk-white mask and chinese-pitched cheekbones" (250)—but he is simultaneously upheld as the quintessential Russian: "As one person stands for the West of Scotland, *black rock and skerry*, another for the green wood, another for ragged vines and split soil; one for the Hotel Foyot, and another for the British Museum, so he is Russia to us" (235). As is true for his gay counterpart, Boris Polteratsky, in *Armed with Madness* and *Death of Felicity Taverner*, the orientalized references to Russia—what Butts elsewhere calls "the eastern-slav tincture in his blood"—are evidence both of Boris's sexual otherness and his aristocratic virtue (a status accorded to him without reference to income).[34] Indeed, throughout *Imaginary Letters*, Boris is represented as a financially impoverished Russian who never works and depends entirely upon the hospitality of his English host, who financially scrimps so they can both survive. Russian qualities are as signs of creativity, intuition, mysticism, and displacement found throughout Butts's oeuvre, and in this text in particular Boris's nationality signals a kind of mystical tourism that emphasizes both a link with national and cultural origins and the formation of a new imagined community. He is in this way less a man than a unifying consciousness, "a state of the imagination whose reality is only found *east of the sun, west of the moon*" (241).

For the narrator, there is something tremendously alluring—and distinctively modern—about the revolutionary nationalist struggles of Boris's "race history," a sweeping historical category that for her includes "the Tsardom and the Third International, the westward drive of the east, trek of the Tartars and the Chosen people, and the emptying out [into Paris] of [Russia's] disinherited" (258). The narrator's privileging of exile and her nostalgia for the past together foster her identification with Boris who, like Butts herself, was severed from his ancestral home. Just as Boris is "[t]horoughly refreshed by contacts with his race" (240) when he frolics with his gay boys in the " 'boites de nuit' " (254), so too is the narrator "balanced again by contact with [her] race" (248) upon her return from a trip to England. Here we see evidence of Butts's belief in the mutually reinforcing discourses of race and nationality, a connection that was prevalent throughout the interwar period. What's novel about Butts's use of these categories here is the semantic confusion over the word "race" in relation to Boris. Does the narrator here mean "Russian" when she says "race," or does she mean "homosexual"? This question is never resolved, but the conflation does illustrate the impossibility of treating race (or nation) and sexuality as discrete and autonomous constructs. *Imaginary Letters* consistently discusses sexuality with reference to nation, suggesting that one can only understand Boris's homosexuality by situating it within the larger social and cultural context of early twentieth-century England and France, in which knowledge of "Wilde's tragic, tiresome martyrdom" is pervasive and "the choicest men of our time are turned that way, and the women like them" (255). The narrator's erotic investment in Boris is irreducibly tied up in the discourses of both sexuality and nation. When the narrator meticulously lists the familiar things that have been lost from Boris's Russian past, she conflates this with her own "English sentimentality" (251) and homesickness for a way of life that no longer exists: "No more smooth furs smelling of scented beasts. No more soundless carpets and quiet servants to receive us home. No more mothers, the lovely mothers our imaginations construct out of the surprising realities, as I have constructed you" (264). The narrator here mourns not only an exclusionary class structure that is no longer imaginatively accessible to her (or to Boris), but also the loss of a mother tongue—"lovely mothers our imaginations construct"—that represents nostalgia for the notion that one's separation from home, be it Russia or England, can never be assuaged.

The quest for home and family are preoccupying concepts throughout *Imaginary Letters*, and speak directly to the topic of homosexuality and its corollary, triangulated desire. We see Butts's obsession with triangulated structures of desire represented through textual references to Boris and his Russian parents; to Boris, the narrator, and Boris's mother; and to Boris, the narrator, and Boris's male lovers. Butts seems to make use of Freud's argument in *Three Essays on the Theory of Sexuality* that the finding of an object of desire is always a refinding of an object previously lost, for Boris represents the narrator's desire for both a lover and a son, a constellation that speaks to her primal longing for the absent family.[35] Of course, the family structure she recreates is a queer and idiosyncratic version of the Freudian oedipal narrative in which psychic mechanisms determine sexual object choice. When the narrator enigmatically characterizes Boris as "[t]he ray, the shadow, the memory, and mirror in which I have looked, seen and understood, imperfectly, many things" (265), we read this as evidence of her use of him as a kind of projection screen for her own chaotic desires which remain unquenched. As she laments of their odd romantic courtship, "he is a lover . . . [but] he is not mine" (239). The narrator's passionate focus on Boris as the lost object may seem preposterous, but it makes sense within the context of her identification with his exilic state, his familial estrangement, and his queerness. When he comes home from a long night of Parisian carousing with his "little fancy-boys" (254), Boris wraps the narrator up in his arms and says: " 'Comme nons sommes deus orphelins, n'est-ce-pas, ma cherie?' " (240). Here, the mother–child dyad is manifestly queered, for the narrator is comforted by the man whom she both desires and nurtures. In writing to Boris's mother the narrator self-consciously assumes the position of "English mother" (240) rather than that of a lover, often referring to Boris as "our child" (244) and insisting, "[w]e mothers must hang together" (253) in the face of their son's self-destructiveness and instability. In one letter the narrator refers to Boris as "your fleshly and my ghostly son" (265), an allusion to the fact that he is sexually unavailable to her. One way the narrator lashes out against Boris's unavailability is by infantilizing him and suggesting that his homosexuality is a kind of atavism, the result of his refusal to grow up. At several intervals Boris is described as having the "[e]yes of a wicked baby" (244); he is "childish" (247), irresponsible, egotistical, sleeps incessantly, and sprawls on the bed "practically sucking his thumb" (241). Cumulatively, such references allude to the argument that is implicit in Freud's work, that homosexuality is a regressive phenomenon—or as the narrator puts it, a form of " 'arrested development' " (236). The narrator invokes Freud by name when she ominously claims that behind Boris's homosexuality lurks "the shadow of Freud" (261), even though Freud himself claimed that a homosexual object choice was neither abnormal nor inferior. And yet, Freud did tend to cast homosexuality as an inhibition of so-called normal psychosexual development, a fact that the narrator registers when she remarks that Boris's "[p]ederasty [is] born out of aversion to his father, and devotion to [the mother]" (265). The undisclosed crimes of the father are singled out for particular ridicule—the "father is the key to this business" (261)—but ultimately it is homosexuality itself that is denounced as the reason why Boris "[n]either loves nor is loved as he should be" (261).

According to the narrator, male homosexuality is attributable not only to the abuses of the father and an overcathection to the mother but, importantly, to the gay man's simple refusal to accept the love of a good woman. The narrator refers to Boris's homosexuality as "a lie" (249) and angrily denounces their asexual relationship as too "cerebral" (249), describing them as a young couple "beaux and bien nés et bien faits" who enjoy "every link but the link of bodies" (249). Why, she demands, must every quarrel and every pleasure be intellectualized "against . . . our romantic interests" (263)? The narrator frustratedly claims that she makes the "sacrifices of an adored mistress" (254) without any of the sexual rewards, and she exasperatedly scolds Boris for staying out too late, seeking sex with anonymous men, and coming to her for "money for an orgy" (242). In this dispiriting story Boris repeatedly responds to her caretaking with betrayals and dishonesty, yet the narrator still finds him tremendously alluring, imagining the two of them as lovers, "the prince and princess walking in the wood" (248)—a description that directly echoes her own fantasy of life with Gabriel. What is interesting about the narrator's account of their relationship is both her denial of reality and her capacity for enlightened false consciousness. She appears on the one hand to neglect the evidence she presents throughout *Imaginary Letters*, that Boris's homosexuality is "congenital" and therefore not susceptible to the therapeutic interventions of a woman. On the other hand, she clearly recognizes that the heterosexual fairytale she spins about the prince and princess is pure fantasy: "My invention" (248). Nonetheless, she even goes so far as to suggest that Boris's true heterosexuality is merely closeted, and concludes that he is like a "creature in a dream" who, while sleeping, makes explicit "an instinct" (243)—namely, his desire for her—which he consciously denies. This is intriguing not only because it sheds light on Butts's own weird psychology, but because it fictively documents a modernist fag-hag relationship that is certain to make readers uncomfortable. The Boris who rejects the narrator is a campy composite of queer stereotypes: he is an effeminate man, "as elusive as any female minx" (254), "a naughty boy" (258) who is "capable of every perversion" (236) and lives by the motto: "queens survive" (239). The reader has no problem mistaking Boris for a straight or even bi-man, so it is bewildering to watch the narrator's psychological convolutions.

The "friendship bargain" (243) that the narrator cuts and meticulously documents is ultimately a devastating exposé of her own sexual humiliations at the hands of a debauched and "intolerable" (251) gay man. To this extent *Imaginary Letters* reveals as much about female masochism—the denial of one woman's erotic "appetites" (239)—as it does about the "fashionable snobbery of our age, the romantic and sensual passions of men for men" (239). The most glaringly autobiographical aspect of this novella is the narrator's treatment of Boris as, in effect, "psychically sick" due to his homosexuality, reminding us of Butts's homophobic portrayal of Sergey Maslenikof in her journal. In *Imaginary Letters* the narrator denounces "this pederasty nonsense" (249) as a kind of annoying aberration that induces Boris to circulate throughout the gay nightclubs of Paris doing "something disagreeable" (248) while she sits home alone awaiting his return. She wonders, once his "boy's beauty" hardens, will he—like the majority of gay men of his generation—eventually marry and plague other "women with the sentimental rape of the next generations' boys" (255)? Despite the fact that Boris's capacity for love is allegedly "aborted and wasted" (255) because it has no heterosexual outlet, the emotional and psychological intimacy that he engenders does have some real compensations for the narrator.

Like Butts, who thrived on caring for her "sick" (264) lovers, the narrator takes great satisfaction in having rescued Boris from his road to ruin and nursed him back to health: "[I] have a certain pleasure because I have been of use to him" (237). It is precisely this compelling idea of eroticized caretaking that motivates the narrator to remain involved with Boris in the face of so much heartache. For her, his neediness is a masochistic turn-on that perpetuates their "cycle of miseries" (245) yet enables her to claim a "spiritual victory" (252) over him—namely, the fact that without her "he would do worse things and mind them less" (242). There is, crucially, a tremendous sense of power that the narrator enjoys and wields in witnessing his dependence upon her. As she confesses, nothing is more compelling than seeing "him restored and taking life. Life at my hands" (264). This, in essence, is the crux of their relationship. The narrator's ministrations provide a salvational balm that works both locally and—symbolically—at the global level. Because Boris operates in two registers, as both man and figure for modernity, he is the embodiment and microcosm of a troubled and nationally fragmented world in search of healing. Through Boris, the exemplary cosmopolitan subject, Butts estheticizes homelessness and also mythologizes the concept of homecoming. In a perpetual state of motion, displacement, and upheaval, he represents for the narrator the dream of coming "home to be cured" (251) to a mythic, metaphysical space that can only be found "when you have made a map out of it" (265) and have learned to "*think things in other categories*" (258).

To fully register Boris's meaning one must consider the narrator's interest in the "inexplicable fourth dimensio[n]" (241), a mysterious, transhistorical, cross-cultural sphere that is associated with clairvoyance, psychic phenomena, and—surprisingly—the profound "miracle" (251) of male homosexuality. While this seems counterintuitive, given the novella's excoriation of homosexuality, it speaks to the narrator's simultaneous embrace of queerness and her avid interest in the "fashionable excitement" (242) of gay sexuality. Through gay men, the narrator vicariously lives out certain kinds of sexual freedoms that are otherwise unavailable to the middle-class Englishwoman. Boris functions primarily as an identificatory conduit that fosters the myth of the modernist exile and enables the narrator to safely incorporate and identify with the sexual exploits of the gay man in the cosmopolitan modernist city of Paris. At the same time, his status as an intermediary between worlds speaks to her intuitive sense that Boris is a double for some divine power, "one of the unknown categories" (260). To the extent that Butts identifies a positive relationship between homosexuality and spiritual development, she is arguably borrowing from the sexological theories of Havelock Ellis and Edward Carpenter, both of whom pointed to the special "fitness or adaptation of the invert for priestly or divinatory functions."[36] Carpenter in particular, in *Intermediate Types among Primitive Folk* (1914), argued that "there really is an organic connection between the homosexual temperament and unusual or psychic or divinatory powers."[37] As the narrator gazes at Boris across the table, she has a sense of "stars jumping about . . . [of] electrons dancing round their atom" and concludes that he is "a constellation sweeping past my system to alter it course" (243). Through Boris, we see evidence of Carpenter's analysis that homosexuality, far from being a sign of degeneration, is in fact an evolutionary step forward to "a higher form of consciousness."[38] Boris, then, is a conflation of the historical and the mythic, the conduit through which the narrator stages the importance of ritual to modernity and demonstrates the necessity of incorporating purgative acts into daily life.

The most salient example of this occurs during the "brother-in-blood" (257) ritual, the moment in the text that is most indebted to Butts's engagement with the anthropological discoveries of Jane Ellen Harrison on primitive ritual—particularly the belief that femininity carries a residue of the mystical and the prelogical. When the narrator looks at the effeminate Boris and perceives that "a series of events were coming together to make a new arrangement . . . like a work of art" (256), we are reminded of Harrison's argument that art, like ritual, arises out of an inchoate emotional impulse that is able to facilitate a ritual reenactment for the collective. In *Imaginary Letters* the narrator announces "[i]t's time for magic," (256), then she breaks a piece of bread, sprinkles it with salt, dips it in wine, and gives it to Boris and herself; what we witness here is a private Eucharistic moment—the '*saint sacrement*' " (257)—which, when read within the context of Harrison's theory, has implications for the collective rather than private emotions of the individual.[39] The "princely spirit" (254) of Boris and the actions of the narrator together constitute a cathartic attempt to heal the fragmentation and disorder of the modern world. In paying homage to the narrator, a maternal figure, and being receptive to her female influence, Boris demonstrates his devotion to the power of the mother. When read through Harrison's interpretive lens, this devotion aligns him with a belief in matriarchal origins and the presumption that femininity carries a residue of the mystical and the prelogical. This figuring of the sacred through ritual is the central tenet of Harrison's theory, a fact that the narrator seems to register when she observes that their communal gesture is a "[s]ign that we can bear it, that we'll see things through" (257). Boris plays a critical role in the narrator's domestic and cosmic drama, enabling her to draw connections between homosexuality and the sacred: "I know that these notes . . . on the 'sexual life of our time' are ways of looking at something else, a partially understood category" (258). Through Boris, the queer "graceful savage" (244), Butts links sexuality with spirituality and arguably draws from Harrison's conviction that affiliations exist between the mystical savage and the sensibility of the artist. In *Imaginary Letters* Boris is a "good painter" (260), but it is the narrator herself who, as an artist in life, enacts the ritual that Boris helps to bring about: "To create through him. To create him. In his own image" (243).

The gender identification at work in the sacramental scene is fascinating because, having "*taken the oath of brother-in-blood*" (256) with Boris, the narrator self-consciously aligns herself with both masculinity and queerness. What does it mean that the gay man is the source of creative inspiration, and what does it mean that the narrator here identifies as a gay man? How, moreover, are we to reconcile the text's simultaneous denunciation and celebration of homosexuality? There is, I would argue, no easy resolution to Butts's conflicted portrayal of homosexuality in her fiction, but her *Journal* does provide some insight into the peculiarity of her divided loyalties. Writing in 1929, she recalls giving her husband Gabriel a bath, marveling at the beauty of his "slender, archaic Apollo" body and reimagining her desire for him through the eyes of a male lover: "I don't wonder that all Maynard Keynes could cry was: Get those clothes off. Strip! Strip!"[40] This projected fantasy suggests that Butts is either turned on by her husband's queerness, or that at times she imagines her desire from the perspective of a gay man. We see this dynamic reiterated when she remarks of Gabriel, "Apollo is the god he is most like, & my Kouros," an association that speaks to Butts's identification with the idealization of male love. Does Butts suffer from an "anal-erotic complex,"[41] as Clive Bell once suggested, or is her investment in male homosexuality merely the expression of her libidinous cross-identification?

Either way, such moments reveal the power of male identification for the bisexual woman writer, helping us to understand why, in *Imaginary Letters*, the gay man is excoriated for his perversions even as he is simultaneously celebrated for being a remarkable source of poetic inspiration. Ultimately, Butts invests male homosexuality with a kind of mystical power that is tied to authorship; while literal sex may face an impasse, Butts suggests, gay men can function as an invaluable source of "spiritual fertilization" (255) that is able to inspire writing.

Notes

1. Bruce Hainley, "Quite Contrary: Mary Butts's Wild Queendom," *Voice Literary Supplement* (May 1994), pp. 21–22.
2. See Jane Garrity, *Step-daughters of England: British Women Modernists and the National Imaginary* (Manchester and NY: Manchester University Press, 2003), chapter 4.
3. Mary Butts, "Imaginary Letters," in *Ashe of Rings and Other Writings*, (NY: McPherson and Company, 1998), p. 236; hereafter cited in the text and abbreviated *IL*.
4. Mary Butts, "Mappa Mundi," in *From Altar to Chimney-Piece: Selected Stories of Mary Butts* (Kingston, NY: McPherson and Co., 1992), p. 221.
5. Douglas Goldring, as cited by Robin Blazer in her Afterward to *Imaginary Letters* (Vancouver: Talonbooks, 1979), p. 64.
6. Nathalie Blondel, *Mary Butts: Scenes from the Life* (Kingston, NY: McPherson and Company, 1998), p. 177.
7. Quentin Bell, *Bloomsbury Recalled* (New York: Columbia University Press, 1995), p. 197.
8. Harcourt Wesson Bull, "Truth Is the Heart's Desire," in *Christopher Wagstaff*, ed., *A Sacred Quest: The Life and Writings of Mary Butts* (Kingston, NY: McPherson and Company, 1995), pp. 56, 61.
9. *The Journals of Mary Butts*, Nathalie Blondel, ed. (New Haven: Yale University Press, 2002), p. 28.
10. John Ashbery, "Preface," *From Altar to Chimney-Piece*, p. xii.
11. Butts, "Mappa Mundi," pp. 229, 222.
12. Ibid., pp. 218, 229, 233.
13. Ibid., p. 229.
14. Blondel, *Mary Butts*, p. 218. Butts, "Mappa Mundi," p. 218.
15. Blondel, *Mary Butts*, p. 218.
16. See Marguerite Steen, "The Glory that Was Greece," *The Macedonian, Everyman* March 1933; Frank Vernon, "Books We'd Like to Burn," *John Bull*, April 25, 1923; "Literary Surgery," *Liverpool Post*, April 11, 1923.
17. "Literary Surgery."
18. Review of *Several Occasions, Yorkshire Post*, March 16, 1932.

19. "Literary Surgery."
20. Hainley, "Quite Contrary," p. 21.
21. Butts, "The House-Party," in *From Altar to Chimney-Piece*, p. 34.
22. Blondel, *Journals*, p. 332.
23. Quentin Crisp, *The Naked Civil Servant*, (London: Jonathan Cape, 1968), p. 28.
24. Mary Hamer "Mary Butts, Mothers, and War," in Suzanne Raitt and Trudi Tate, eds., *Women's Fiction and the Great War* (Oxford: Clarendon Press, 1997), p. 226.
25. Hamer, "Mary Butts," pp. 226–27.
26. Alan Sinfield discusses the links between Wilde's effeminacy, dandyism, and estheticism in *The Wilde Century: Effeminacy, Oscar Wilde and the Queer Moment* (New York: Columbia University Press, 1994). For a discussion of the relationship between masculinity, consumption, fashion, and dress, see Christopher Breward, *The Hidden Consumer: Masculinities, Fashion and City Life: 1860–1914* (Manchester and New York: Manchester University Press, 1999).
27. Hamer, "Mary Butts," p. 227.
28. K. K., "Blood in a Spoon," *Evening Standard*, December 4, 1923. Vernon, "Books We'd Like to Burn."
29. Michael D. Sibalis, "Homophobia, Vichy France, and the 'Crime of Homosexuality,' " *GLQ* 8, no. 3: 306–7.
30. Matt Houlbrook, " 'Lady Austin's Camp Boys': Constituting the Queer Subject in 1930s London," *Gender and History* 14, no. 1 (April 2002): 31–61. For a discussion of London as the site of a profound revolution in gender relations and sexual behavior after 1700, see Randolph Trumbach, "London," *Queer Sites: Gay Urban Histories since 1600* (London and New York: Routledge, 1999), pp. 89–111. Sibalis, "Homophobia,": 302–4.
31. Marry Butts, *The Taverner Novels* (Kingston, NY: McPherson and Company, 1992), p. 107.
32. Butts, journal entry for March 4, 1928; at the Beinecke Rare Book and Manuscript Library, Yale University.
33. Ibid., May 2, 1928.
34. *The Taverner Novels*, Butts, p. 198.
35. Sigmund Freud, *Three Essays on the Theory of Sexuality* (New York: Basic Books, 1962), p. 88.
36. Edward Carpenter, *Intermediate Types among Primitive Folk: A Study in Social Evolution* (London: George Allen, 1914), p. 56.
37. Havelock Ellis, "Intermediate Types among Primitive Folk: A Review," *Occult Review* 20 (1914): 30–32.
38. Carpenter, *Intermediate Types*, p. 62.
39. Jane Harrison, *Ancient Art and Ritual* (New York: Henry Holt; London: Williams and Norgate, 1913).
40. Butts, journal entry for December 6, 1929; at the Beinecke Rare Book and Manuscript Library, Yale University.
41. Butts, typescript of "Bloomsbury" (1936); at the Beinecke Rare Book and Manuscript Library, Yale University.

Notes on Contributors

Georgine Clarsen is Lecturer in the School of History and Politics in the Faculty of Arts at the University of Wollongong. She is currently completing a book for the, John Hopkins University Press entitled *Auto-evotics: Early Women Motorists' Love of Cars*. She is a qualified motor mechanic and was for many years the technical director for the Australian performing company Circus Oz.

Laura Doan is Professor of Cultural History and Sexuality Studies and Codirector of the Centre for the Study of Sexuality and Culture at the University of Manchester, with research interests in lesbian cultural history and English modernity. She is author of *Fashioning Sapphism: The Origins of a Modern English Lesbian Culture* (Columbia University Press 2001), and coeditor, with Jay Prosser, of *Palatable Poison: Critical Perspectives on The Well of Loneliness* (Columbia University Press 2001).

Bridget Elliott is Professor of Visual Arts at the University of Western Ontario where she teaches in the areas of art history, film studies, and visual culture. She has published widely on the subject of women artists including *Women Artists and Writers* (Routledge 1994) coauthored with Jo-Ann Wallace and *Women Artists and the Decorative Arts in the Early Modernist Era, 1895–1935* (Ashgate 2002) coedited with Janice Helland. She is currently completing a book on the migration of art deco from Europe to North America.

Jane Garrity is Associate Professor of English and a Senior Scholar in Women and Gender Studies at the University of Colorado, at Boulder; her research interests include British modernism and empire, colonial/postcolonial studies, and lesbian/queer theory. She is author of *Step-Daughters of England: British Women Modernists and the National Imaginary* (Manchester University Press 2003), and has published articles on Virginia Woolf, the Bloomsbury Group, Sylvia Townsend Warner, Anna Kavan, and contemporary lesbian film. She is currently working on a project on modernism and fashion.

Colleen Lamos teaches at Rice University. She is author of *Deviant Modernism: Sexual and Textual Errancy in T.S. Eliot, James Joyce and Marcel Proust* (Cambridge University Press 1999).

Tirza True Latimer earned her Ph.D. in art history at Stanford University. Her book, *Women Together/Women Apart: Portraits of Lesbian Paris* (Rutgers University

Press 2005), investigates problems of feminine and lesbian self-representation within a historical context in which the independence of women (their political, professional, economic, domestic, and sexual autonomy) had yet to be acknowledged by the law. Latimer lectures in art history, feminist studies, and gender studies at institutions in the San Francisco Bay Area.

Heather Love is Assistant Professor of English at the University of Pennsylvania. She has published articles on modernism and gender studies in *GLQ, Transition, New Literary History*, and *Feminist Theory*, and is the coeditor of a special issue of New Literary History entitled *Is There Life After Identity Politics*? (2000). She is at work on a book entitled *Feeling Backward: Affect, Politics, and the Making of Queer History.*

Jodie Medd is Assistant Professor in the Department of English at Carleton University in Ottawa, Canada. Her recent publications have appeared in *Modernism/Modernity* and *Palatable Poison: Critical Perspectives on The Well of Loneliness* (Columbia University Press 2001). She is finishing a book on lesbian scandal in the early twentieth century and researching a new project on modernist patronage relations.

Alison Oram is Reader in Women's Studies at University College Northampton. She is coauthor of *The Lesbian History Sourcebook: Love and Sex between Women in Britain from 1780 to 1970* (Routledge 2001) and is currently writing a book about changing representations of cross-dressing women in the twentieth-century British popular press.

Petra Rau is Lecturer in English Literature at the School of Social, Historical, and Literary Studies at the University of Portsmouth. She has published articles on modernist women writers, and on nineteenth-century German writers and the Bildungsroman. Her research interests are mainly psychoanalytic criticism and modernist writing. She is currently working on a monograph on Anglo-German literary relations from the late Victorian period to the immediate post–World War II years.

Penny Tinkler is Senior Lecturer at the University of Manchester. She is currently writing a book for Berg on the feminization of smoking, 1880–1980 entitled *Smoke Signals: Women, Smoking and Visual Culture in Britain* (forthcoming). She has also written extensively on aspects of English girlhood, including *Constructing Girlhood: Popular Magazines for Girls Growing up in England, 1920–1950* (Taylor and Francis 1995).

Jo-Ann Wallace is Professor in the Department of English and Film Studies at the University of Alberta. The coauthor with Bridget Elliott of *Women Artists and Writers: Modernist (Im)Positionings* (Routledge 1994), she has also published articles or chapters on women's literary history, feminist theories of the body, late nineteenth-century feminism and advocacy, and children's literature and postcolonial theory. Her current research is a cultural biography of Edith (Mrs. Havelock) Ellis. She is Editor of *ESC: English Studies in Canada.*

Joanne Winning teaches in the School of English and Humanities, Birkbeck College. Recent publications include *The Pilgrimage of Dorothy Richardson* (University of Wisconsin Press 2000) and *Bryher: Two Novels, Development and Two Selves* (University of Wisconsin Press 2000). She is currently working on two books: *The Shape of Lesbian Modernism*, which maps the cultural production and influence of the Anglo-American lesbian modernists and a book on Edwin Morgan, the new Scots Makar.

Index

Printed and bound by CPI Group (UK) Ltd, Croydon, CR0 4YY